The Poetic Craft
of
Bella Akhmadulina

The Poetic Craft
of
Bella Akhmadulina

Sonia I. Ketchian

The Pennsylvania State University Press
University Park, Pennsylvania

Library of Congress Cataloging-in-Publication Data

Ketchian, Sonia.
    The poetic craft of Bella Akhmadulina / Sonia I. Ketchian.

       p.   cm.
    Includes bibliographical references and index.
    ISBN 0-271-00916-0 (alk. paper)
    1. Akhmadulina, Bella, 1937–   —Criticism and interpretation.
  I. Title.
  PG3478.K45Z75   1993
  891.71'44—dc20   92-30850
                                                       CIP

Published by The Pennsylvania State University Press,
Barbara Building, Suite C, University Park, PA 16802-1003

It is the policy of The Pennsylvania State University Press to use acid-free paper for the
first printing of all clothbound books. Publications on uncoated stock satisfy the mini-
mum requirements of American National Standard for Information Sciences—
Permanence of Paper for Printed Library Materials, ANSI Z39.48–1984.

Contents

To the luminous memory of my parents,
Bertha Nakshian Ketchian and Tzolag "Harry" Ketchian

Preface

It has been both a privilege and a daunting responsibility to write on the challenging verse of a contemporary poet. Meeting Bella Akhmadulina has been one of the highlights in my life and scholarly career. I saw in her warmth and graciousness a compensation for never having met Anna Akhmatova and all the other beloved poets whose poetry constitutes the crux of my research.

This book owes its very existence to two circumstances. First of all, to the foresight of my colleague Maria Nemcova Banerjee of Smith College, who suggested that I teach a course "Major Russian Women Writers of the Twentieth Century" in 1980 and again in 1981. The fringe benefit of the course was an article that was an earlier version of Chapter 2: "Poetic Creation in Bella Akhmadulina," *Slavic and East European Journal* 28, no. 1 (1984). Then, in 1983, during a three-month research sojourn under the sponsorship of the International Research and Exchanges Board (IREX), I met Bella Akhmadulina and presented her with the typescript of the accepted article. Second, at our first meeting Bella presented me with an advance copy of her new book, *The Secret* (*Taina*), in which she wrote corrections. It was so captivating that I wrote a second article, "The Wonder of Nature and Art: Bella Akhmadulina's *Secret*," which appeared in *Studies Presented to Bayara Aroutunova*, ed. A. L. Crone and Catherine V. Chvany (Columbus, Oh.: Slavica, 1987), and is an early version of Chapter 3. The fascination remained, and the research continued even after the publication of Akhmadulina's next collection, *The Garden* (*Sad*), which immediately enlarged my investigation. Final refining touches were added to the completed manuscript and additional insights were gained while teaching a reading course on Russian women writers at Harvard University in the spring of 1992.

It is my hope that this first book in any language on the poetry of Bella Akhmadulina will do it justice and spur related studies. Unlike my previous book, *The Poetry of Anna Akhmatova: A Conquest of Time and Space*, which was predicated on a long tradition of Akhmatova scholarship, including the books of Sam Driver and Amanda Haight, and could be directed toward the specialist already well versed in the subject, this book on the poetry of Bella Akhmadulina is intended for a wide audience of scholars and literature enthusiasts.

It is my pleasure to acknowledge two Mellon grants from the Russian Research Center, Harvard University, in 1986–87 (honorary) and in 1987–88, as well as my longtime affiliation with the Center's intellectually stimulating and congenial atmosphere. Research for this book was supported in part by grants in 1983 and in 1990 from the International Research and Exchanges Board (IREX), with funds provided by the National Endowment for the Humanities, the United States Information Agency, and the U.S. Department of State, under the provisions of the Soviet and East European Training Act of 1983 (Title VIII). My gratitude is profound toward all the wonderful people at the Russian Research Center, who helped me in innumerable ways. Special thanks are due to my colleagues Alexander Nekrich, the late Alexander Gershkovich, Felix Roziner, and Musya Glants, whose opinions helped me pinpoint the intricacies of the sophisticated verse. The comments of the discerning audiences of the Literary Seminars at the Russian Research Center and at various conferences helped me refine my thoughts. My friends, the remarkable staff at Widener Library, helped me immeasurably in locating materials and in calling my attention to new imprints. I would especially like to thank my friend of long standing, Enith Vardamann, as well as Anna Arthur, Minna Kisler, and Janet Crane Vitkevich. Furthermore, I acknowledge with pleasure my indebtedness to former ambassador Arthur A. Hartman, a good friend of Bella Akhmadulina, for his interest in my work both in Moscow in 1983 and more recently, and to William Mills Todd III for invaluable advice. Finally, I would like to express my gratitude to the scholars whose thoughtful comments on early versions of this work have enhanced it considerably: Vahan D. Barooshian, Anna Lisa Crone, Sam Driver, and F. D. Reeve.

Introduction

The poetry of earth is ceasing never.
—John Keats

От странной лирики, где каждый шаг—секрет.
—Anna Akhmatova

Bella Akhmadulina is Russia's premier contemporary woman poet. In her poetry the Russian language attains a sophisticated symbiosis of meaning, dazzling imagery, rhythm, and sound in articulation that conveys to advantage the artist's unique evolution and service to Russian letters.[1] This new peak for the Russian poetic language, reached in her collection *The Secret* (*Taina*, 1983)[2] and continued in the collection *The Garden*

1. Comparatively little has been written on Akhmadulina and her verse and little has been translated into English. On the poetry of her early years, see Evgenii Evtushenko's introduction to Bella Akhmadulina, *Fever and Other New Poems*, trans. G. Dutton and Igor Mizhakoff-Koriakin (New York: Morrow, 1969). For revealing statements, see Chad Heap and Matt Steinglass, "An Interview with Bella Akhmadulina," *The Harvard Advocate*, May 1988. Sam Driver has translated *Oznob* as *The Chills* in *ARDIS: Anthology of Recent Russian Literature*, ed. Carl Proffer and Ellendea Proffer (Ann Arbor: Ardis, 1975). See the introduction by F. D. Reeve in his selected translations of poems and prose, including the autobiographical piece "Grandmother" ("Babushka") in Bella Akhmadulina, *The Garden: New and Selected Poetry and Prose*, edited, translated, and introduced by F. D. Reeve (New York: Henry Holt, 1990). Also see Christine Rydel, "The Metapoetical World of Bella Akhmadulina," *Russian Literature Triquarterly*, no. 1 (1971). Of further interest is Nancy Condee, "Axmadulina's *Poemy:* Poems of Transformations and Origins," *Slavic and East European Journal* 29, no. 2 (1985). For an exhaustive list of Akhmadulina's publications prior to 1978, see *Russkie sovetskie pisateli. Poety. Bibliograficheskii ukazatel'*, 15 vols. (Moscow: Kniga, 1978), 2:118–32. Unless otherwise indicated, all translations are mine.
   At the first mention of a poem's title in English, the transliterated version of the Russian is furnished in parentheses for easy identification. To distinguish in English between actual titles of poems and first lines used as titles, I capitalize all meaningful words in the former but capitalize the first word only in the latter.
2. I translate "taina" as "secret" because that is the meaning contained in the collection's opening poem. The other meaning of the word, "mystery," which is favored by Bella Akhmadulina

(*Sad*, 1987),[3] firmly places her in the great pantheon of classic Russian poets.

Izabella Akhatovna Akhmadulina was born on 10 April 1937, in Moscow to a Tartar father and a mother of Russian-Italian ancestry. An only child, she was raised by a doting maternal grandmother. She spent the war years in evacuation in the Urals. Upon graduating from high school in Moscow in 1954, Akhmadulina worked for the newspaper *Metrostroevets*. Her first poem was published in 1955. Study at the Gorky Institute of Literature in Moscow (1955–60) was interrupted by expulsion for her overtly apolitical verse. She was reinstated at the institute through the efforts of the writer Pavel Antokol'skii (1896–1978), who had initially launched the career of this promising poet.

Akhmadulina entered the poetic arena with other poets of the Thaw (1953–63), a relatively benevolent period in the history of the Soviet Union following the death of Stalin in 1953. It was a time when many people craved bold new voices untainted by the lies of the past. The most famous poets in this group, often called the "New Wave," were the Moscow poets— Bella Akhmadulina, Evgenii Evtushenko, Bulat Okudzhava, Robert Rozhdestvenskii, and Andrei Voznesenskii.[4] Receptive audiences, eager for more freely expressed ideas and for young artists not connected with the personality cult of Stalin, filled the concert halls and stadiums to hear the young poets' declamatory verse and the sung ballads of Okudzhava. The West hailed the fresh voices as well. Akhmadulina commenced with a combination of the declamatory and lyric principles, but she soon adopted a self-reflective stance that frequently addressed the process of creating verse, hence her poems of a metapoetic bent.

Fame came to Bella Akhmadulina in 1962 with the appearance of her first book *The String* (*Struna*, 1962). Certain critics, however, accused her of

---

and which, coincidentally, aligns it with Keats, figures less prominently in the collection. See Bella Akhmadulina, *Taina. Novye stikhi* (Moscow: Sovetskii pisatel', 1983).

3. Bella Akhmadulina, *Sad. Novye stikhi* (Moscow: Sovetskii pisatel', 1987).

4. Evgenii Evtushenko (b. 1933) is well known for the exclamatory style of his poetry on topical issues and for his flamboyant readings. Recently his interests have turned to prose and film. Bulat Okudzhava (b. 1924), a bard famous for his contemplative verse and his singing of it, has more recently turned to prose. Robert Rozhdestvenskii (b. 1932) writes in the tradition of declamatory poetry on a wide variety of themes that balance love and civic topics with travel in the broadest sense. Andrei Voznesenskii (b. 1933) crafts declamatory poetry that explores numerous striking devices and themes. For excellent entries on Russian literature, see Victor Terras, ed., *Handbook of Russian Literature* (New Haven: Yale University Press, 1985).

imitating the brilliant lyric poet Anna Akhmatova (1889–1966) whom the authorities had persecuted repeatedly.[5] What the commentators failed to perceive was the possibility that in evincing overt influence, Akhmadulina was probably following the lead of her idol, the superb poet Marina Tsvetaeva (1892–1941), in whose early work Akhmatova—a peer—was treated as her Muse.[6] The cognoscenti, on the other hand, applauded Akhmadulina's classically flowing, often humorous verse, which, coupled with her inspired dramatic public readings and famed beauty, made her a trendsetter for the young. Other books followed: *Chills: Selected Works* (*Oznob. Izbrannye proizvedeniia*, 1968), *Music Lessons* (*Uroki muzyki*, 1969), *Poems* (*Stikhi*, 1975), *Candle* (*Svecha*, 1977), *Snowstorm* (*Metel'*, 1977), *Dreams of Georgia* (*Sny o Gruzii*, 1977), *The Secret. New Poems* (*Taina. Novye stikhi*, 1983), *The Garden. New Poems* (*Sad. Novye stikhi*, 1987), *Poems* (*Stikhotvoreniia*, 1988), and *Selected Works. Poems* (*Izbrannoe. Stikhi*, 1988).

Marriage to Evgenii Evtushenko did not last, nor did her subsequent marriage to the lyrical prose writer Iurii Nagibin (b. 1920), nor to the writer Gennadii Mamlin. For many years now Bella Akhmadulina, the mother of two daughters, Elizaveta and Anna, has been married to the artist and stage designer Boris Messerer. She defended the physicist and dissident Dr. Andrei Sakharov and the monumental dissident writer Aleksandr Solzhenitsyn (b. 1918). In 1977 Akhmadulina was elected to the American Academy of Arts and Literature. For her audacity in participating with a prose work, "Many Dogs and the Dog" ("Mnogo sobak i sobaka"), in the unofficial literary almanac featuring twenty-three writers, *Metropol* (*Metropol'*, 1979),

5. Bella Akhmadulina, *Struna. Stikhi* (Moscow: Sovetskii pisatel', 1962). Anna Akhmatova was an outstanding circumspect lyric poet of filigreed short pieces with hidden and dramatic depths on unhappy love, the search for solace in religious observance, and on poetry and poetic craft, among other themes. Long persecuted by Soviet officials—her husband, the poet Nikolai Gumilev (1886–1921), was shot, her son, Lev Gumilev (1912–92), spent fourteen years in Soviet hard labor prison camps, and she was not published for many years—Akhmatova continues to be a predominant and growing influence in Russian letters. See Sam Driver, *Anna Akhmatova* (New York: Twayne, 1972), 16–37.

6. Comprising with Akhmatova the duo of great Russian women poets, Marina Tsvetaeva was a poet innovative in content and form whose verse rings with intensity. Her emotionally charged, brilliant elliptical verse is offset by her equally arresting prose. Born in Moscow in 1892, she emigrated to Germany in 1922, then lived in Czechoslovakia and France where she endured much hardship. She returned with her son to the Soviet Union in 1939 in the wake of her husband Sergei Efron and daughter Ariadna, but their reunion was brief. Sergei was executed, and Ariadna was interned in a hard labor prison camp. Evacuated from Moscow to the town of Elabuga during the war, she committed suicide. For many years Tsvetaeva's work was suppressed in the Soviet Union. See Jane A. Taubman, *A Life through Poetry: Marina Tsvetaeva's Lyric Diary* (Columbus, Oh.: Slavica, 1989), 262.

which was sponsored by the popular prose writer Vasilii Aksenov (b. 1932) as an attempt to promote young writers never published by the official press, Akhmadulina suffered a tacit ban on her works until 1983. Forced to leave the country, Aksenov settled in the United States. Meanwhile Akhmadulina used the time of enforced silence to crystallize and hone her verse-writing skills until the poems of a certain period culminated in that rare cohesion and harmony between independent pieces when they seemingly effortlessly coalesce into a unified collection of verse more like a book of the sort the magnificent cerebral poet Osip Mandel'shtam (1891–1938) sought and the lyricist Boris Pasternak (1890–1960) achieved in his *My Sister—Life* (*Sestra moia—zhizn'*).[7] In 1989, following the publication of the seminal collections, *The Secret* and *The Garden*, Akhmadulina was awarded the Soviet Union's highest prize—the State Prize in Literature.

Thus it is the compelling quality of the refined poetry in the collection of 1983, *The Secret*, with its leitmotif of poetic creation, which Akhmadulina's lyric persona pursues to its fullest degree, that comprises the main focus of this study—namely, the idea, the attempt, and the act in the past and the present. While the specifics of poetic creation—the metapoetic theme and even stance—assume lyric form in the early verse preceding *The Secret* as explored in Chapter 2, their scope and profundity are realized in greater scope in this second, mature or "garden" period. Nor does the leitmotif of poetic creation conclude within the covers of *The Secret;* instead, powerful echoes migrate to the collection *The Garden* and to the separately published later poems. Her metapoetry, like Pasternak's, in this period concentrates on the verse-creating process.

In *The Secret*, the succession of major themes establishes sequences of

7. Osip Mandel'shtam (1891–1938) is a giant of Russian literature whose ideationally and referentially compressed poetry finds some elaboration in his luminous autobigraphical and other prose. His free, uncompromising spirit and peripatetic lifestyle incurred official disfavor, but it was for his anti-Stalin poems that he was imprisoned and sent to a Siberian hard labor prison camp where he died. A good deal of his later poetry was preserved only in the memory of his valiant wife, Nadezhda Mandel'shtam (1899–1980). Boris Pasternak (1890–1960) is one of Russia's finest lyric poets. Upon conferral of the Nobel Prize in Literature on his novel *Dr. Zhivago* he was officially disowned. One could easily replace the title *My Sister—Life* in this quotation below with *The Secret* and every word would be applicable to Akhmadulina's *The Secret:* "Rather than being a sampling of poems collected under one cover, *MSL* [*My Sister—Life*] is indeed an idiosyncratic and highly conscious poetic narrative which recalls the formal structure of a novel at the same time that it celebrates the linguistic freedom and the metaphorical inventiveness of lyric prose." See Katherine Tiernan O'Connor, *Boris Pasternak's "My Sister—Life": The Illusion of Narrative* (Ann Arbor: Ardis, 1988), 11. On Pasternak, see Christopher Barnes, *Boris Pasternak: A Literary Biography*, vol. 1, *1890–1928* (Cambridge: Cambridge University Press, 1989).

poems that, in turn, are grouped consecutively without formal unification into cycles.[8] Indeed, only one formal cycle of six poems figures in the collection—the cycle "Tarusa." The fact of its uniqueness obviously underscores its significance and aligns it to the sole epigraph in the collection, taken from Marina Tsvetaeva. In the absence of formal cycles, the major themes in *The Secret* originate fleetingly as motifs until the time that each has its moment "on stage" as a theme before being superseded in primacy by its successor. Yet the ebbing themes linger on for some time before each one phases out at its own pace, often migrating into *The Garden*. These intricately orchestrated themes demonstrate the creation of verse in the midst of nature by a lyrical speaker privy to nature's most intimate secrets. And the poems enable the reader to participate in the stages of gradual disclosure.

Akhmadulina's treatment of poetic creation is a means for her poetic persona to perceive her immediate world of nature and of selected people, as well as of certain depths of art and of history before crafting her own verse through the medium of this same nature and the rhythm of man's accomplishments in art, culture, history, and life. Toward this end, to comprehend and to interpret the concentrated, seemingly all-inclusive poems through the prism of poetic creation, I investigate the collection *The Secret* in detail in Chapters 3 through 9 with references to the early poetry, to *The Garden*, and to the recent independent poems. Whereas Chapter 2 charts the variegated directions to which the poems lead and singles out and defines Akhmadulina's approach to poetic creation in the early period, Chapter 3 focuses on the opening poem in *The Secret*—"I have the secret of wondrous blooming" ("Est' taina u menia ot chudnogo tsveten'ia")—as the inclusive programmatic piece conveying in capsule form the message, concepts, and ideas that are to be developed. Chapter 4 treats Akhmadulina's approach to the moon as the direct inspirer of verse, a veritable surrogate Muse in whose presence the verse should ideally self-create, leaving only the final honing and form to the ardently observing poetic speaker. Eventually, as seen in Chapter 5, the moon as creator of verse yields to the notion of day as deity, a notion, which, by utilizing ancient mythology as a touchstone, draws on the Russian literary tradition to augment the poet's own imagination and ingenuity. Soon day's position as helpmate in creating verse is usurped by intrusive space, as examined in Chapter 6, and, subsequently, by

---

8. I use the word "cycle" in the Russian way to mean a group of related poems formally united by the poet through a title and numbering. In English this is called a sequence. I use "sequence" to denote a succession of thematically related poems in a collection that are not united formally by the author.

the fragrant bird cherry as investigated in Chapter 7. Homage to writers past and present, who represent a vital source for Akhmadulina's approach to poetic creation, permeates the collection and is addressed throughout the discussion where relevant, but it is articulated at length in Chapters 8 and 9. Each of these themes, concentrated in a few sequential poems, recedes gradually as the next sequential cluster of poems comes into its ascendency.

This analysis of Akhmadulina's poetic craft centers, above all, on a chiefly poem-by-poem analysis of pieces in *The Secret* touching on the wondrous secret, of which each consecutive cluster of poems uncovers an additional aspect and fills in the next piece of the mosaic for the final magnificent picture. In the process of plumbing the secrets of poetic creation, all of the poet's work comes into view through references and comparisons, and numerous literary parallels serve as a steady backdrop to the recent poetry. This poetry is firmly grounded in the rich literary and linguistic tradition of the past.

As a leading artistic creator for her postmodernist generation, Bella Akhmadulina combines Russian cultural and literary points of view with their Georgian and world counterparts. The "exotic" Georgian element, so prevalent in her early work, ostensibly draws on a tradition well established in Russian literature by the nineteenth-century writers—Aleksandr Pushkin (1799–1837), Mikhail Lermontov (1814–41), and the great Russian writer and thinker Lev Tolstoi (1828–1910)—as well as the twentieth-century writers Boris Pasternak and Osip Mandel'shtam. History and a sense of religion intertwine in the recent work. Akhmadulina couches her poetic vision and ideas in an idiom that does justice to the subtle nuances and the multiple possibilities inherent in the Russian language. Indeed, the rich literary devices and tradition of Russian literature masterfully enhance her poems. All the while, Akhmadulina's poetry observes continuity with the wealth of nineteenth-century Russian literature as represented by such luminaries as the fountainhead of modern Russian literature, Aleksandr Pushkin, the Romantic poet who introduced the psychological novella to Russian letters, Mikhail Lermontov, and the contemplative, philosophically charged miniaturist Fedor Tiutchev (1803–73), and draws on her immediate modernist predecessors, in particular on Tsvetaeva, Pasternak, Akhmatova, and Mandel'shtam.

It will be seen that although Akhmadulina's poetry has been lauded for forcefulness of expression and masterful execution of form, in its finesse and sentient approach to her subject and its underlying surroundings, the product of Bella Akhmadulina's pen bears the unmistakable signature of a woman. What is more, she grounds its tradition, particularly in *The Secret*, in the oeuvre and biography of the two great women poets of Russia—the ebullient Marina Tsvetaeva, known for her staccato, unusual rhythms and her elliptical imagery,[9] and the deceptively quiet, private Anna Akhmatova. This analysis will strive to unveil many of the connections.

At this writing Bella Akhmadulina stands out among a constellation of fine women peers. Chief among them are the Moscow-born dissident poet Natal'ia Gorbanevskaia (b. 1936), who currently resides in Paris, and whose themes of love and pain find expression in poems on prison and on urban topics; Rimma Kazakova (b. 1932, Sebastopol), whose topics center on nature, love of her country, and the role of women in love and in mother-hood; the engaging miniaturist Inna Lisnianskaia (b. 1924, Baku), whose aphoristic and sententious pieces with unexpected turns include poems of parting and love gone sour, of homelessness and hopelessness as well as poems on biblical and religious themes; Novella Matveeva (b. 1934), whose symbolism embraces childhood, memories, and Russian nature and is often set to music which she sings; and the lyric poet Iunna Morits (b. Kiev, 1937), whose poetry has been compared to Pasternak's.[10]

Ultimately, to find the key to the secret of Akhmadulina's poetic craft, so attuned to the Russian literary heritage and that of the world, is to follow her poetic speaker through the successive poems in the collection *The Secret* as she examines events and phenomena in nature. For greater fidelity to Akhmadulina's artistic vision the treatment of themes in Chapters 4 through 9 observes their succession in the collection. The reader of this book will follow the speaker's scrutiny of and interaction with nature as she deliber-ates with the intention of composing verse in the town of Tarusa in the Kaluga Region and then moves to Moscow, Leningrad, Riga, and back again to Moscow and on to the writers' colony of Peredelkino, all the while savoring the beauty of the imagery, language, form, and sound that inform this remarkable poetry while delighting in the revelations made alongside the secretive speaker.

9. See *Three Russian Women Poets: Anna Akhmatova, Marina Tsvetayeva, Bella Akhmadulina*, trans. Mary Maddock (New York: Crossing Press, 1983), 42.

10. For a broad discussion of women in Russian literature, both as heroines and authors, see Barbara Heldt, *Terrible Perfection: Women and Russian Literature* (Bloomington: Indiana University Press, 1987). Of further interest is *Women Writers in Russian Modernism: An Anthology*, ed. and trans. Temira Pachmuss (Urbana: University of Illinois Press, 1978).

1

The Spiritual Essence
of the Poetic Speaker

Scenery is fine, but human nature is finer.
—John Keats

Before embarking on an examination of Bella Akhmadulina's early verse (1955–74) in Chapter 2 and the mature, "garden" period (1975–85) in the remaining seven chapters on the basis of the collection *The Secret* with seminal references to *The Garden* and to poems of the current philosophically spiritual period, it is of interest to determine the specifics of the lyric voice or voices that speak out in the poems. For the voices range from the lyrical, to the witty, the rhetorical, and the disputative. The voices are referred to in this book either as the (lyric) persona or the (poetic) speaker. First, there will be an examination of the "physical" demarcation or embodiment of Akhmadulina's poetic speaker; second, there will be an overview of the speaker's manner of presenting the creative process through dialog with nature and her own garnering; third, to underscore in practice Akhmadulina's artistic ties with the West, some influence of the English poet John Keats (1795–1821) will be sought out here as well as throughout the investigation.

In the early period Akhmadulina has obviously multiple, or pluralistic, personas that vary to accommodate the lyrical voices that present the numerous topics, such as the cynical speaker in the *Chills* (*Oznob*); they are close to Akhmadulina the poet and, presumably, to the private person. They are often poets, speaking of her real friends, such as the American Slavist Dean Worth in "Letter to Bulat from California" ("Pis'mo Bulatu iz Kalifornii").[1]

---

1. Bella Akhmadulina, *Sny o Gruzii* (Tbilisi: Merani, 1979), 210. All quotations in Chapters 1 and 2 are from this collection, unless otherwise specified. The pages will be marked at the first

Her persona seems more like herself, Akhmadulina, an observer and describer less reliant on personal emotions to create poetry than Akhmatova and in particular Tsvetaeva seem to be.[2] In contrast to Akhmatova, her display of overt humor in verse, as in *Chills,* allows for comparison with Marina Tsvetaeva and Evgenii Evtushenko. She is also like Evtushenko in her choice of fantastic elements, albeit her ballad "The Rider Garden" ("Sad-vsadnik"; *The Secret,* 79)[3] evokes Akhmatova's often more literary, Hoffmannesque elements in *Poem without a Hero* (*Poema bez geroia*)[4] and the hints at Gothic features in some poems. Through her wide variety of topics and tones, Akhmadulina has developed a resplendent style with vivid imagery. While her love poems are often bitter, if hauntingly beautiful ("I thought you were my enemy"—"Ia dumala, chto ty moi vrag," 45; "Your House"—"Tvoi dom," 50; "Do not spare me much time"—"Ne udeliai mne mnogo vremeni," 58), still Akhmadulina has crafted one of the truly superb love lyrics in Russian poetry with "Passerby, Kid" ("Prokhozhii, mal'chik"; 177). The poem's obliqueness of morphological expression evokes Pushkin's lyric "I remember a wondrous moment" ("Ia pomniu chudnoe mgnoven'e"),[5] although in contrast to his speaker's unrequited selfless love and devotion, it treats radiant reciprocated love for the heroine, but not for the youth: "He is loved by me, by whom I am loved!"

Some early personas are noticeably similar to the later type of persona, particularly the ones dealing with the theme of poetic creation—metapoetry. They carry over many qualities and similarities into the later works. Given Akhmadulina's lack of reference to the classic Muse in her verse, she displays, instead, a greater preoccupation with her surroundings and draws from them the source and substance of her art. Early on, she makes clear that the speaker in metapoetic poems merely represents the instrument for conveying art, as in *Chills.* Furthermore, it is noteworthy that in a departure

---

appearance of a title or rarely at the end of the quoted texts. All quotations in Chapters 3–9 are from *The Secret,* unless otherwise marked.

2. On Akhmatova's variety in personas, see Sam Driver, "Directions in Axmatova's Poetry since the Early Period," *Russian Language Journal* (*Supplementary Issue: Toward a Definition of Acmeism,* ed. Denis Mickiewicz, Spring 1975): 85.

3. Bella Akhmadulina, *Taina. Novye stikhi* (Moscow: Sovetskii pisatel', 1983), 79.

4. Anna Akhmatova, *Poema bez geroia,* in *Stikhotvoreniia i poemy,* compiled by V. M. Zhirmunskii (Leningrad: Sovetskii pisatel', 1976), 356–69. Hereafter references to Akhmatova's poems from this edition will list the poem's number, or less frequently, its page in the text.

5. A. S. Pushkin, *Polnoe sobranie sochinenii v desiati tomakh,* ed. B. V. Tomashevskii (Moscow: AN SSSR, 1962–1966), 2:267.

from Russian classic poetry Akhmadulina, like fellow poets of the Thaw, Evtushenko, Okudzhava, and Voznesenskii, capitalizes the initial word in a line of verse only if it also begins the sentence:

> Beat me as a tambourine, don't spare me,
> chills, I am all yours! We can't live apart!
> I am the ballerina to your music!

> Ударь в меня, как в бубен, не жалей,
> озноб, я вся твоя! Не жить нам розно!
> Я — балерина музыки твоей!
>
> (227)

This is one kind of consistently appearing persona who serves as instrument to outside forces. Here, in a somewhat fantastic and humorous piece on a seminal theme for this poet, the speaker is addressed as "Bella":

> Could I be sick, for the third day I've been trembling
> like a horse awaiting the race.
> My arrogant neighbor on the floor,
> even he cried out:
> "How you are shivering, Bella!

> But come to your senses! Your strange illness
> shakes the walls and blows a draft everywhere.
> It inflames my children's spirit
> And at night it rings in my dishes.

> Хвораю, что ли,—третий день дрожу,
> как лошадь, ожидающая бега.
> Надменный мой сосед по этажу
> и тот вскричал:
> —Как вы дрожите, Белла!

> Но образумьтесь! Странный ваш недуг
> колеблет стены и сквозит повсюду.
> Моих детей он воспаляет дух
> И по ночам звонит в мою посуду.
>
> (223–24)

Positively a rebel and a dissident in art, the speaker somehow conveys her attitude to the very young and affects them over the objections of their parents. In the early verse the argumentative speaker acquires an addressee-opponent in such pieces as "Altercation with the Crimea" ("Prerekanie s Krymom"; 117), as noted by Pavel Antokol'skii on her poem "Adventures in an Antique Store" ("Prikliucheniia v antikvarnom magazine"; 227), which draws on "world Romanticism," on Balzac, Dickens, and more immediately, on Pushkin's poem "Conversation of a Book-Seller with the Poet" ("Razgovor knigoprodavtsa s poetom"; 2:191–97), and part 2 of Akhmatova's masterwork, *Poem without a Hero* (*Poema bez geroia*).[6] The addressee in the early poetry can be a friend, the reader ("A Summerhouse Romance"—"Dachnyi roman"; 155), a place ("Altercation with the Crimea"), or the "strange guest" of the poem "Winter Seclusion" ("Zimniaia zamknutost' "; 108). This would-be interlocutor is often a petty person concerned only with the comforts of life over the lofty objectives of art—a neighbor or a distant ancestor representing the philosophy of kitsch. In the later poetry the addressee can be would-be learned persons, as in the opening poem "I have the secret of wondrous blooming," or a "dear friend" in the poem "A deep gentle garden sloping to the Oka" ("Glubokii nezhnyi sad, vpadaiushchii v Oku"; *The Secret*, 9), with whom she can drop in on the young Lermontov and his aristocratic grandmother, or part of nature, such as the Oka River in "Squabblings and Reconciliations" ("Prepiratel'stva i primireniia"; *The Secret*, 23–26), or even a poem that refuses to be created, as in "February Full Moon" ("Fevral'skoe polnolunie"; *The Secret*, 33–35). Moreover, the addressee can be a writer, such as Tsvetaeva in the poem "Sea-thing—so go to your seas" ("Morskaia—tak idi v svoi moria"; "Tarusa," III, 12). Admittedly, the speaker is aware that excursions into the past are not a substitute for her role in the contemporary world and its art: "And no matter how you recede into the centuries and gardens, / your soul cannot find in them oblivion or bliss" ("I, kak ni otstupai v stolet'ia i sady, / dusha ne syshchet v nikh zabven'ia i blazhenstva"; *The Secret*, 10).

Next there is the youthful beauty superficially "loved" by a score of young boys in the poem "Fifteen Boys" ("Piatnadtsat' mal'chikov"; *Collected Works—Izbrannoe* (1988), 9) who from the wisdom of her early maturity comprehends the rite of passage reflected in the boys' avowed love for her until each of them finds his true and lasting love. She advances from gentle

6. See Pavel Antokol'skii's foreword in Bella Akhmadulina, *Stikhi* (Moscow: Khudozhestvennaia literatura, 1975), 5.

irony and concentration on herself to a remarkably philosophic disinterestedness that evokes Keats's ideal.[7] Hers is a judicious and "seasoned" speaker who feels that her life has been full, that all her objectives will be realized, as in the poem "I know, everything will happen: archives, tables"—"Ia znaiu, vse budet: arkhivy, tablitsy"; 194), and she merely lacks old age, as in the poem "Sluggishness" ("Medlitel'nost' "; 145): "Only old age is lacking, / everything else has happened" ("Tol'ko starosti nedostaet, / ostal'noe uzhe sovershilos' "), later reverberated in "Return to Tarusa" ("Vozvrashchenie v Tarusu"; *The Secret*, 83):

> I would say that life has turned out well,
> Everything has been realized, and it's not in the least
>   painful.

> Я б сказала, что жизнь—удалась,
> все сбылось, и нисколько не больно.

The dialog with Lermontov's famous poem of meditation and the road "I come out alone onto the road" ("Vykhozu odin ia na dorogu") is patent here.[8]

Third, there is the haunting introspection and anguish of the youthful compassionate speaker perceiving as a human being the German enemy pilot bombing Moscow in the poem "Small Planes" ("Malen'kie samolety"; 76). She ends by saying:

> But where you have been lifted to,
> in the multitude of call signal melodies,
> let my kind, strange dream
> protect you, o little airplane!

> Но там, куда ты вознесен,
> во тьме всех позывных мелодий,
> пускай мой добрый, странный сон
> хранит тебя, о самолетик!

In reality, the plane was shot down, as Akhmadulina told her audience at Harvard University in March of 1987.

7. Walter Jackson Bate, *John Keats* (Cambridge: Harvard University Press, 1964), 227–28.
8. Mikhail Lermontov, *Sobranie sochinenii v chetyrekh tomakh* (Moscow: AN SSSR, 1958–59), 1:543.

The mature, or "garden" period (from about 1975 to 1985) has produced the collections *The Secret: New Poems* (1983) and *The Garden: New Poems* (1987) and can be further separated from the present, philosophically spiritual period (after 1985), which, at this writing, has yet to culminate in a named collection. There have been, however, generic volumes: *Selected Works. Poems,* 1988, the largest compilation of poetry to date, and *Poems,* 1988.[9]

The poetic speaker of the middle period—the mature, garden period— has shed a good deal of her plurality as various distinct voices. She appears to have united the voices within one speaker or as variations within one speaker. The fantastic element is retained as a device in some poems, such as "The Rider Garden." Nowhere, however, does she merge wholly with Bella Akhmadulina the public poet and the private person, with the exception of rare moments that crystallize from the poem's context. Such are the poetic speaker's principal forms and the main incarnations of her lyrical voice.

It will be seen that in these various incarnations of lyrical voice the early speaker goes forth to garner artistic material in late spring, summer, and early fall until in winter she is able to ensconce herself in a snowbound pristine house with possibly a cricket for company. In these ideal circumstances she composes rigorously until her stores of artistic impressions are exhausted and muteness sets in.

In the second, "garden" stage's collection *The Secret* the speaker again removes herself from family and friends, this time to the rural town of Tarusa—the place where the young Marina Tsvetaeva summered with her family. Tsvetaeva's half-sister Valeriia Tsvetaeva recalls: "One and a half versts [approximately one mile] from Tarusa on the bank of the Oka stood a small delapidated country estate with a winter house, an old garden, and outbuildings. This estate belonged to the town and was rented as a summer dacha. Our family lived there for about twenty years on a long-term lease."[10] The dacha was called "Pesochnoe."

---

9. What is unusual and valuable about Bella Akhmadulina's *Izbrannoe. Stikhi* (Moscow: Sovetskii pisatel', 1988) is that, unlike in her other books, all the poems are dated. Although her next book, *Stikhotvoreniia* (Moscow: Khudozhestvennaia literatura, 1988), does not date the poems in it, it does indicate which collections the poems are taken from and which are new poems outside any collections.

10. Tarusa is a town on the left bank of the Oka River, a tributary of the Volga. It is located in the Kaluga region to the south of Moscow. An ancient town, it was first mentioned in the chronicles in 1246. *Kratkaia geograficheskaia entsiklopediia,* ed. A. A. Grigor'ev, 5 vols. (Moscow: Sovetskaia entsiklopediia, 1960), 4:82. Valeriia Tsvetaeva's "Notes" are quoted from Marina Tsvetaeva, *Sochineniia v dvukh tomakh,* compiled by Anna Saakiants (Moscow: Khudozhestvennaia literatura, 1980), 2:491. See also Marina Tsvetaeva's "The Birth of a Museum" ("Rozhdenie muzeia"), 2:8.

Because in Russian literature this place is stamped with the mark of Tsvetaeva, it is to be expected that she serves as an artistic model and presence in these poems on Tarusa. In this locus the speaker craves isolation from family and friends to reflect and to create verse. Isolation and retreat to write is also a requisite of Bella Akhmadulina's creative biography. In fact, in an interview with the Russian journal *Ogonek*, Akhmadulina explains how her poetry is created:

> Verse . . . is not written; it materializes. And an important factor is your state. Not so long ago I had a holiday at a place where Alexander Kushner was.[11] He said, "I look at the sea and a poem is born." I have always admired Kushner and his poetry. But for me, it is not enough to see something in order to write something. I need solitude. I must go away from Moscow, to a place where life is different. I wrote a lot in Tarusa, Karelia, and the Vologda region. But what matters is not any definite place, but probably a change of daily routine and the environment. After I have lived in some faraway place for about ten days, I suddenly hear a sound and . . . the necessary word is found. And then I write and write and write. I can write for twenty-four hours a day without a break, until the guiding sound has faded away.[12]

For metapoetic topics the speaker looks beyond herself, taking walks to writers' haunts and often gazing out the window at the growing world and communing at night with the universe. Her speaker still remains the instrument, or barometer, for the translation of the world into art, most frequently through the medium of other natural objects or phenomena as surrogate muses, such as the moon or day, and the shades of revered writers at a given venue. Yet through personification there is some interchange between the speaker as instrument and nature as dictator and guide, as in the sternness of space to be explored in Chapter 6, and even in man-made surroundings, such as the city. It is of interest to compare here the line: "But the city whispers to me, 'Silence!' " ("No gorod mne shepchet: molchi!") from the poem "It is exactly midnight but the night remains a maverick" ("Rovno polnoch', a noch' prebyvaet v izgoiakh"; *Poems*, 1988, 313). In the poem

---

11. Aleksandr Kushner (b. 1935), a Leningrad poet who writes refined, classic lyrics.
12. One is reminded here of Pushkin writing at the estate of Boldino and Keats's writing trips to Margate, Scotland, and the Isle of Wright.

"It's Me" ("Eto ia"; 139) the personified city of Ufa in the Urals stands watch over her during wartime evacuation:

> It's from the war that I am dying
> under the sullen care of Ufa.
>
> Это я от войны погибаю
> под угрюмым присмотром Уфы.

To be sure, it is interesting to observe that the critic Zinovii Papernyi notes in a review of *The Secret*, "Under the Surveillence of Nature" that, unlike in the nineteenth century and in the verse of Pushkin, in which there would be at best the poet's monolog to nature, for Akhmadulina nature comprises the topic of her poetry in the dialog mode.[13] For the metapoetic verse of Boris Pasternak, on the other hand, the topic of nature assumes the observant, often personified and metonymic mode. What should be added to this observation is that for Akhmadulina's speaker nature creates, synthesizes, and dictates, as it were, poetry to its vessel and instrument in the form of the speaker whose only function is to record the art in comprehensible, acceptable Russian verse form following different types of observation and vigil in and of nature. Paraphrasing the words of Akhmadulina from an earlier interview, Papernyi states: "The poet is reticent with the reader where she is open with nature" ("Poet nedogovarivaet chitateliu to, o chem nachistotu govorit s prirodoi"). Even her feelings are merely a medium. Akhmatova, on the other hand, employs the outer world, and nature specifically, as well as other people, namely, the male addressee (often a former beloved) or holy men to explain, comprehend, and universalize through the medium of the Muse the thoughts (at times the anguish) and inner feelings of her persona. To be sure, Akhmatova's concept of one poetry and of the poet as one with all past and future poets, that is a unified body of poetry throughout the ages and in all literatures, could be an attempt for her speaker to merge with the universe. It could also be a visual "folk" reinterpretation of the morphological parts in the word "universe" to mean *uni* (one) and *verse* (poetry) as in the word "*uniform*" (one form). Also relevant in connection with the concept of the poet harboring in herself the verse of many poets and retaining for herself the secret of creating poetry are Tsvetaeva's words:

---

13. Zinovii Papernyi, "Pod nadzorom prirody," *Oktiabr'*, no. 10 (1984), 205.

I am many poets, and how this resounded in me
    —that's my secret.

Я—много поэтов, а как это во мне
    спелось—это уже моя тайна.[14]

In stage three of Akhmadulina's poetry, currently in full swing, the spiritual and philosophical period, the observation of nature and art by the window eventuates fleetingly in the concept of "zaokonnost' " (beyond the window, "transfenesterism") in the poem "I am merely a volume inhabited by something" ("Ia lish' ob"em, gde obitaet chto-to"). Two sources spring to mind for this concept. The first is Tsvetaeva's concept of that which is beyond the eyes or sight. Translated as a linguistic calque it would be "transocularity":

Transocularity is a greater reality,
Which lies beyond the eyes.

Заочность: за оком
Лежащая, вящая явь.
("Transocularity"—"Zaochnost'," 1:257)

The poem's play on words and morphemes is similar to what Akhmadulina will develop in her mature period. This concept of beyond the normal is, moreover, obliquely reminiscent of Akhmatova's "zazerkal'e" (beyond the looking glass, or transmirror), which comes from Lewis Carroll's *Through the Looking Glass* (translated in 1924 as *V zazerkal'e*), for a place outside ordinary life, comparable to her later use of music and dreams. Moreover, *zaokonnost'* in Akhmadulina could in part stem from the notion of "beyond the Oka River" ("za Okoi") as in the line from the poem "Ladyzhino" (*Poems*, 1988, 289) on the two sisters, Ol'ga Ivanovna and Mar'ia Ivanovna, who were custodians of the rest home *Dom arkhitektora* in Tarusa during Akhmadulina's sojourn and who now lie buried there. The classic concept of the dead crossing the river Lethe into Hades comes to mind here:

14. For the concept of one poetry and the poet as one with all poets, see my article, "A Source for Anna Akhmatova's 'A String of Quatrains': Hovannes Tumanian's *Quatrains*," *Slavic and East European Journal* 31, no. 44 (1987): 523.

> You are beyond the Oka, over there, beyond the dark
>   pine forest.
>
> And your tears in the night saw
> me in Tarusa, which is one and the same.
>
> Вы—*за Окой*, *вон* там, за *темным* бором.
>
> И ваши слезы видели в ночи
> меня в Тарусе, что одно и то же.

My italics above are intended to point out the sounds evoking the hidden subliminal as it were, presence of "transfenesterism" ("zaokonnost' "). The poet's oblique literary devices are augmented through the metonymy in the locution "your tears saw." In recalling their times together on this later return to the area where most of the poems in *The Secret* were originally composed, the speaker apparently has qualms about certain words that were said or even left unsaid (if this is not merely a topos):

> O Aunt Mania, have pity, forgive
> me for everything, for the word and the non-word.
>
> О тетя Маня, смилуйся, прости
> меня за все, за слово и неслово.

Akhmadulina's personal fundamental humility permeates her speaker's words here. This could be, moreover, a refraction of Keats's profound remarks on the poetic imagination—its humility and its absorption in what is outside. One senses here in Akhmadulina the English poet's notion of disinterestedness and striving toward it:

> I am merely a volume inhabited by something
> for which earthly names are inadequate.
> A construction of bones and sweat—
> are its possessions and not my flesh.
>
> I don't know it. Sense the stranger
> having settled in another's (dog)house—
> (wants to) chase out the owners, spring into
>   transfenesterism,
> (and) not to look back were I to die.

Я лишь объем, где обитает что-то,
чему малы земные имена.
Сооруженье из костей и пота—
его угодья, а не плоть моя.

Его не знаю я: смысл-незнакомец,
вселившийся в чужую конуру—
хозяев выжить, прянуть в заоконность,
не оглянуться, если я умру.

(Poems, 1988, 304)

There is, then, in Akhmadulina the supreme reign of the word (in the sense of poetry and/or possibly religion) which for this poet equals nature and is carefully spelled out in the poem "I have the secret of wondrous blooming" to be discussed in Chapter 3. It alone bridges the gap with immortality:

Only the word bridges delirium and chaos
and speaks to mortals of immortality.

Лишь слово попирает бред и хаос
и смертным о бессмертье говорит.

But nature and the word equal adulation and adoration in the religious sense, such as in the poem "I have the secret of wondrous blooming," which legitimizes, as it were, Akhmadulina's advancement toward nature and through this interlinking demonstrates that the entire process was pre-planned, premeditated, and well mapped out.

The persona may be merely an instrument in the hands of nature and the universe, but putting down the art of nature into acceptable Russian verse does require many conditions, one of them being the freshness and purity of topics. Topics exhausted at the end of winter result in either muteness or its sophisticated equivalent—mechanical, overly ornate verse, as in the early poem "Something Else" ("Drugoe"; 84).

In the middle, garden period, poems crafted by the mind alone as opposed to those resulting from genuine talent are again deplored. But at this stage the speaker refuses to compromise. She simply will not write the poem. An inability to craft the desired poem, for which the speaker has arranged the proper ambience and has kept the requisite vigil, becomes the subject of that poem such as in the piece "Line of Work" ("Rod zaniatii";

The Secret, 36). The preceding poem "February Full Moon" shows that she has not slept for three nights in an attempt to secure the poem:

> You're being obstinant. You don't want to be. Farewell,
> my poem about the tenth day of February. The
>   fifteenth day
> of February has been conceived.

> Упорствуешь. Не хочешь быть. Прощай,
> мое стихотворенье о десятом
> дне февраля. Пятнадцатый почат
> день февраля.

(36)

Akhmadulina is indeed addressing an uncomposed poem, but the negative, or minus, state is nothing new to the speaker who in the early period spoke, urged, and dreamed in a pre-conception state in her narrative poem *My Genealogy* ("Moia rodoslovnaia"). Thus although the desired poem eludes the speaker's pen, it becomes the ersatz subject of the given poem by Bella Akhmadulina. In this respect Akhmadulina's predecessor seems to be John Keats, whose verse epistle "To My Brother George" is a frank confession of the despair caused by the fear that nothing "could e'er be caught" from his new surroundings in Margate, the resort by the sea that he visited in the summer of 1816 with the intention of writing poetry:

> Full many a dreary hour have I past,
> My brain bewilder'd, and my mind o'ercast
> With heaviness.[15]

Keats fears he will "never hear Apollo's song." Akhmadulina furnishes her own version of Keats's breakthrough in poetry—writing on the inability to compose—for as W. J. Bate writes in *John Keats:* "With all his frank misgivings, and with virtually no other subject than how it feels to lack subjects, Keats still manages to make a breakthrough of sorts" (73).

In her third, spiritual and philosophical, period Akhmadulina no longer fights forms or degrees of muteness or ornateness, instead her objective now becomes to ridicule seekers of sense in her poems. She has in some

---

15. John Keats, *The Complete Poems*, ed. John Barnard, 3d ed. (London: Penguin, 1988), 64.

poems nearly reached the practice of art for art's sake, of contemplation for contemplation's sake, and even of sound for sound's sake. In the poem "Christmas Tree in a Hospital Corridor" ("Elka v bol'nichnom koridore"; *The Garden*, 63)[16] the speaker says:

> Long have I been reproached that my works are empty.
> Creator of emptiness, I look in the corridor at my
>   compatriots.

> Мне пеняли давно, что мои сочиненья пусты.
> Сочинитель пустот, в коридоре смотрю на
>   сограждан.

Her humor of the early period has obviously not abated, it has merely become honed. The same poem is remarkable for its religious imagery given the time of initial publication: "kanun Rozhdestva" ("Christmas Eve"), "Devo" (the vocative for the Virgin Mary), "Mladenets" (the infant Christ), "Mater' bozhiia" ("Mother of God"), "Zvezda Vifleema" ("The Star of Bethlehem"). Indeed, beginning with the middle period the speaker seems to be acknowledging a supreme higher being close to, if not, God himself.[17] True, passing allusion to God in connection with creating can be found in the early poem "Altercation with the Crimea": "He knows who in seven days created the sevenhue of the white [wide] world ("semitsvetie belogo sveta"). Religious notes continue in this later period as the speaker addresses Christ in the poem of the third period "Saturday in Tarusa" ("Subbota v Taruse"; *Poems*, 1988, 308):

> send me, oh Thou Who Was Crucified,
> the hope of the imminence of Easter Week.

> пошли мне, о Ты, на кресте убиенный,
> надежду на близость пасхальной недели.[18]

Thus Akhmadulina, unlike her contemporaries or recent predecessors, has moved from poetic imagination immersed in the very Russian pursuit of

16. Bella Akhmadulina, *Sad. Novye stikhi* (Moscow: Sovetskii pisatel', 1987), 61–63.
17. When in 1988 I questioned Akhmadulina on this, she seemed to acknowledge the presence of a supreme being in her verse.
18. Because the word "nedelia" in Old Church Slavonic denotes both "week" and "Sunday," Akhmadulina may be playing on this ambivalence, although here she probably means "week."

nature to arrive at something akin to religion. In the poem "So be it. Leave me" ("Byt' po semu. Ostav'te mne"; *Selected Works*, 362) the religious imagery and the desire to reach out to the universe become patent:

> Is it not because on the Oka
> there are other valuations of being,
> that we are all versed in the recipe:
> how, whiling away the time [literally, "an age"] at the
>   regional center,[19]
> to be on friendly terms with eternity.
>
> We are alone among people.
> Haughty is our impoverishment.
> You are in this time (period), we are farther away.
> We long ago drowned in the universe,
> before Noah's ark.

> Не потому ли на Оке
> иные бытия расценки,
> что все мы сведущи в рецепте:
> как, коротая век в райцентре,
> быть с вечностью накоротке.
>
> Мы одиноки меж людьми.
> Надменно наше захуданье.
> Вы—в этом времени, мы—дале.
> Мы утонули в мирозданье
> давно, до Ноевой ладьи.

In the third period the speaker's religious yearnings culminate in a striving to merge with the universe, for which this time she uses another Russian synonym:

> I spread out. I become the universe,
> We are in concert with it, we are one with it.

---

19. This is the district Soviet Center (of People's Deputies), but it could evoke "rai" (paradise) and "tsentr" (center). The accepted idiom for "whiling away the time" is "korotat' vremia." Akhmadulina lengthens the time spent through her change to "age." Note also her play on the root *korot* in "korotaia" and "nakorotke," as well as on "vek" and "*vech*nost'."

Я растекаюсь, становлюсь вселенной,
Мы с нею заодно, мы с ней—одно.
(*Poems,* 1988, 304)

In this way, Akhmadulina's poetic voice transforms with each period, from multiple speakers engrossed in the contemporary world and in nature, to the sensitive seeker of the garden period looking toward the universe for the poetic word, to the philosophic and spiritual speaker who merges with the universe and is comfortable with religious concepts. With this overview of the poetic speaker's principal incarnations and spiritual essence, the subsequent chapters will examine in detail the very poetry that she strives to compose.

Fig. 1. Bella Akhmadulina following her reading in Cambridge, on November 4, 1990, with Sonia Ketchian. (Photo: Philip P. Ketchian)

Fig. 2. Bella Akhmadulina at the Ketchian residence in Belmont, Massachusetts, March 1987. (Photo: Philip P. Ketchian)

Fig. 3. Bella Akhmadulina at home in Peredelkino with her daughters, Anna and Elizaveta, and husband, Boris Messerer, November 13, 1983.

Fig. 4. Bella Akhmadulina with the American poets F. D. Reeve and Diana Der Hovanessian at the latter's home in Cambridge, November 4, 1990. (Photo: Philip P. Ketchian)

Лишь грамота и вы — других не видно Родин.
Коли выгонян лук — и вам не сдобровать
стрелок садовод. Стрелок, огородник.
что ль, потяпаи и я возделаю
Тетради.

* * *

Есть тайна у меня от чудного цветенья,
здесь было б: чуднАГО — уместней написать.
Не зная новостей, на старый лад желтея,
цветок себе всегда выпрашивает «ять».

Где для него возьму услад правописанья,
хоть первороден он, как речи приворот?
Что — речь, краса полей и ты, краса лесная,
как не ответный труд вобравших вас аорт?

Я этою весной все встретила растенья.
Из-под земли их ждал мой повивальный взор.
Есть тайна у меня от чудного цветенья.
И как же ей не быть? Все, что не тайна,— вздор.

Отраден первоцвет для зренья и для слуха.
— Эй, ключики! — скажи — он будет тут как тут.
Не взыщет, коль дразнить: баранчики! желтуха!
А грамотеи — чтут и буквицей зовут.

Ах, буквица моя, все твой букварь читаю.
Как азбука проста, которой невдомек,
что даже от тебя я охраняю тайну,
твой ключик золотой ее не отомкнет.

Фиалки прожила и проводила в старость
уменье медуниц изображать закат.
Черемухе моей — и той не проболталась,
под пыткой божества и под его диктант.

Уж вишня расцвела, а яблоня на завтра
оставила расцвесть... и тут же, вопреки
пустым словам, в окне, так близко и внезапно
прозрел ее цветок в конце моей строки.

Стих падает пчелой на стебли и на ветви,
чтобы цветочный мед названий целовать.
Уже не знаю я: где слово, где соцветье?
Но весь цветник земной — не гуще, чем словарь.

В отместку мне — пчела в мою строку влетела.
В чужую сласть впилась ошибка жадных уст.
Есть тайна у меня от чудного цветенья.
Но ландыш расцветет — и я проговорюсь.

Fig. 5. The opening poem in *The Secret* with the deleted third stanza written in by Bella Akhmadulina, November 13, 1993.
(Photo: Rick Stafford)

Fig. 6.   Title page and frontispiece of *The Secret* with dedication: "To dear Sonia with love and gratitude, in memory of the severe snow (the first this year), of Peredelkino, of Bella Akhmadulina, November 13, 1983." (Photo: Rick Stafford)

Fig. 7. Feline "Peter Allen" promotes international goodwill while renewing friendship with Bella Akhmadulina, April 1988. Boris Messerer and F. D. Reeve join in. (Photo: Philip P. Ketchian)

Fig. 8. Bella Akhmadulina reciting her new poetry at Harvard, March 1987. (Photo: Philip P. Ketchian)

Fig. 9. Bella Akhmadulina at Middlebury College, summer 1991. (Photo: Erik Borg)

Fig. 10. Relaxing with friends at her dacha in Peredelkino, summer 1983. *Right to left:* Ambassador Arthur Hartman, Bella, and friends. (Photo: Courtesy of Arthur Hartman)

Fig. 11. Poets Bella Akhmadulina and Andrei Voznesenskii at Peredelkino, summer 1983. (Photo: Courtesy of Arthur Hartman)

Fig. 12. Bella Akhmadulina toasting her friends at Peredelkino, summer 1983. (Photo: Courtesy of Arthur Hartman)

2

The Poetry of the Early Years

You are molecules in flux
My work is to write you.
—Diana Der Hovanessian

A cicada
     scrapes a lost tune.
          —F. D. Reeve

In her early verse Bella Akhmadulina, unlike the relative self-limitation of the early Anna Akhmatova on themes of love and despair leading to poetry, practices thematic variety. Accordingly, Akhmadulina's early persona discusses friends ("My Friends"—"Moi druz'ia"; 73), the wonders of the modern age—a vending machine ("Carbonated Water"—"Gazirovannaia voda"; 67), praises labor ("Another's Craft"—"Chuzhoe remeslo"; 18), notes Moscow topography, metro stations, and squares.[1] Georgian themes lend exotica and internationalism and also recall Pushkin and Lermontov, who romanticized the Caucasus. Akhmadulina's verse is frequently addressed to a general reader or a vituperative adversary, whereas Akhmatova addresses her work to a beloved with whom her speaker often duels emotionally in most poems of the early period. Akhmadulina's Georgian themes become less pronounced in *The Secret* and the later collection *The Garden*. Included in her homage to the Russian classics are Pasternak, Mandel'shtam, Akhmatova, and Tsvetaeva. Of her coevals, Bulat Okudzhava and Andrei Voznesenkii receive particular attention.

Preoccupied with poetic creation in her verse, Akhmadulina works out unusual configurations within the basic scheme. There is no Muse in her early poetry, unless it is the rare male superior being shown in the person of a

---

1. All poems are from *Dreams of Georgia* unless otherwise noted.

conductor who dictates to artists in the piece "Wonderful theater of the poem" ("Stikhotvoreniia chudnyi teatr"; 189). Instead, the role of inspiration, usually attributed to the Muse by other poets, is relegated to nature and life, which Akhmadulina describes in some detail, where Akhmatova would have caught the essence in a few strokes. For Akhmadulina, nature in spring and summer represents physical freedom, movement, development, change, and a backdrop for garnering impressions, experiences, and inspiration. Trips in late spring to Georgia in the South serve an identical purpose—getting closer to the sources of growing life. In fact, poems treating the months and seasons form an important yet unspecified cycle. Several pieces bear the titles: "August" ("Avgust"; 52), "April" ("Aprel' "; 52), "September" ("Sentiabr' "; 59), "December" ("Dekabr' "; 64), and "Autumn" ("Osen' "; 93). In the poem "Muteness" ("Nemota"; 83) the first month of spring, March, incurs in her a loss of artistic voice—the onset of muteness—which afflicts her verse through heaviness of style, as in the poem "Wretched Spring" ("Plokhaia vesna"; 128), i.e., when she has written herself out. It is time to head for Georgia—a paradise of eternal summer and hospitality—and to begin the long succession of months for rejuvenating oneself and gathering impressions. For the persona, summer is always an airline flight away from Moscow, if one prefers not to wait the six months between the cold and warm months in the temperate zone: "and in our time from winter until summer / it is half a year of life, two hours' flight" ("To Simon Chikovani"—"Simonu Chikovani"; 105). During the joyous summer months everyday living takes precedence over writing for "August needs no glory" ("The garden has not yet shed its leaves"—"Sad eshche ne obletal"; 183). In the poem "August" she and the addressee made music together, an act that reverberates the persona's winter duets with the cricket (52).

Rainfall in summer and early autumn symbolizes the freedom of untamed, unrestricted water which the Russian critic Benedikt Sarnov terms "living life"—inspiration—in connection with the poem *A Tale of Rain* (*Skazka o dozhde*).[2] Indeed, in "A Tale of Rain," Rain repeatedly dictates to the speaker: "My tongue was inflamed by nonsense, / O, that was Rain repeating its dictation to me" (219). In the five-piece cycle "September" dedicated to the writer Iurii Nagibin, September embodies a time for love

2. See the review article by Benedikt Sarnov, " 'Privychka stavit' slovo posle slova . . .' " Bella Akhmadulina. Uroki muzyki," *Novyi mir* 12 (1970), 260. It must be noted that rain, the seasons, the garden, and illness are also important themes in the poetry of Pasternak. See Katherine T. O'Connor, *Boris Pasternak's "My Sister—Life": The Illusion of Narrative* (Ann Arbor: Ardis, 1988), 30–31, 41, 65, and *passim*.

and intense living: "and in January I live, as in September, / urgently and frantically" (59).

Insofar as September is a month in which the speaker lives her personal life fully, she tries to expand it; sometimes "twelve times a year: I am in September" (63). It is a time when voices originate almost independently of her in her throat, "parched for new sounds" (61). Connected here is the color orange, symbolizing love, reverie, and joy found only at that time of year: "In the midst of winter and summer, / in other months—we will never / experience the color orange" (63). The color orange is visualized through the ripening of the orange-red berry of the mountain ash as well as the changing gold of the leaves and the drying out of the grass in the slanted rays of autumn sunlight when even the sun shines with a weaker, orange color in contrast to brilliant white and yellow tones of summer. In October begins the persona's occasional spiritual independence from the demands of friends and daily obligations through illness, which actually clears her mind and may well lubricate her throat for easier formation of poetic sounds:

> Simple is the path to freedom, to clarity of mind—
> suffice it to chill one's feet.
> Autumnal walks along the road
> dispose very much toward this. . . .
>
> You are still bored and healthy and rough,
> but here for you with a good-natured smile
> a cold blows its kiss
> and slowly it reaches your lips.
>
> Прост путь к свободе, к ясности ума—
> достаточно, чтобы озябли ноги.
> Осенние прогулки вдоль дороги
> располагают к этому весьма.
>
> Еще ты скучен, и здоров, и груб,
> но вот тебе с улыбкой добродушной
> простуда шлет свой поцелуй воздушный,
> и медленно он достигает губ.
> ("Introduction to a Cold"—"Vstuplenie v prostudu";
>   84–85)

Here autumn represents a languid time to synthesize impressions for the eventual ripening and sifting through of thoughts, garnered in spring and summer through the medium of orange September light and abstracted in October during rain and chills.

Ultimately, nature and the speaker's germinating ideas acquire substance and molded form in December with the onset of frost and snow. Formless water and rain become decorative white snow and sculpted hoarfrost. Branches of rustling trees are immobilized in snow and ice. Akhmadulina describes this situation metaphorically in the poem "December" as curing form of amorphousness: "you sculpt well / and cure form of formlessness" (64). In other words, the winter synthesizing of summer fluids and of developing impressions corresponds to the solidifying of nature through white snowstorms and the freezing of liquids, covering life with a white mantle. Mobile summer lightness and frolic are frozen—captured within an area for contemplation and description in poetry. Conversely, in summer and especially in the South with its seemingly endless summer, a heightening of the senses permits the persona to absorb enough impressions and ideas for sifting into art later. The concept of the cocoon is shown in the poem "Winter Seclusion" ("Zimniaia zamknutost' "; 108) in which winter forms a cocoon where the speaker creates works as expressed through the similes:

> The snow covered my roof already in January,
> leaving me to the privacy of thoughts and actions.
> I lived locked up like fire in a lantern
> or like an insect that in amber
> has settled in the spaciousness of ideal tightness.

> Снег занес мою крышу еще в январе,
> предоставив мне замкнутость дум и деяний.
> Я жила взаперти, как огонь в фонаре
> или как насекомое, что в янтаре
> уместилось в простор тесноты идеальной.

Similarly, in the poem "Snapshot" ("Snimok"; 137) which portrays a photograph of Akhmatova capturing an impression for all times, a simile cements the fossilizing attributes of amber:

> Through "iat' " having merged into one
> with (that) damp and gentle April,
> as in petrified amber,
> she will remain unharmed.

С тем—через «ять»—сырым и нежным
апрелем слившись воедино,
как в янтаре окаменевшем,
она пребудет невредима.

(138)

In the poem "Winter in the South" ("Zima na iuge"; 91) Akhmadulina
demonstrates that summer's growth, change, and ripening are akin to youth
with its bustle: "It is too youthful to give itself up to snow" (91).

Winter, in keeping with traditional literary symbolism, resembles staid old
age in its immobility and whiteness. Given such similarity, this season fos-
ters meditative poetry. To create good verse, the persona needs the wisdom
of old age. She opines in the poem "Sluggishness" that her full life lacks
only old age (146). The winter beating down of snow and the dripping of
water remind the persona of eternal dictation, possibly like nature dictating
poetry to her:

> December hardens.
> It's fun during a snowfall
> to hear how eternal dictation
> suddenly reaches the notebook . . .
>
> Затвердевает декабрь.
> Весело при снегопаде
> слышать, как вечный диктант
> вдруг достигает тетради . . .
> ("The garden has not yet shed its leaves"—"Sad
>   eshche ne obletal," 184)

Similarly, in the poem "Snowfall" ("Snegopad") the snowfall marks the
period between the germination of sound and its fulfillment in poetic words:

> is merely a motive for versification,
> for momentary success of the mind.
>
> But while in the strict snowfalling
> intellect is clear and will is fresh,
> in the interval between sound and word
> rashly lingers the soul.

> лишь причина для стихосложенья,
> для мгновенной удачи ума.
>
> Но, пока в снегопаданье строгом
> ясен разум и воля свежа,
> в промежутке меж звуком и словом
> опрометчиво медлит душа.
>
> (103)

Apparently, winter's pristine cleanliness impels the persona to work by producing the actual ambience for the composition of poems. The white of winter and of paper attracts her like a magnet:

> and the winter day is like a white sheet (of paper),
> not yet filled with a design.
>
> Emptiness awaits to be filled, . . .
>
> O, winter day, why do you order (me)
> to work so, to the point of stupor?
>
> и зимний день—как белый лист,
> еще не занятый рисунком.
>
> Ждет заполненья пустота,
>
> О зимний день, зачем велишь
> работать так, до одуренья?
>
> ("Winter Day"—"Zimnii den' "; 36–37)

Importantly, in nature and in the poet's imagination, white, encompassing all colors, is broken down to the essence of its components—the seven basic colors. Hence, in viewing the wintry scene and the inner, presumably white, wall of the house, the persona-poet conjures up through the color its components and, accordingly, the fossilized impressions of a vibrant summer. Coldness, snow, snowbanks, ice, and hoarfrost encase the persona and all the requisite objects, colors, and sounds to provide an ambience that freezes the impressions, making possible their study. The poems are then dictated effortlessly into the notebook. Significantly, Akhmadulina named a collection *Snowstorm*.[3] The whiteness of snow in itself induces creation: "and in

---

3. Bella Akhmadulina, *Metel'. Stikhi* (Moscow: Sovetskii pisatel', 1977).

this whitest bliss / will join the notebook and the hand" (181). The persona needs a notebook or white paper to jot down her compositions, the writing down being an important primary part of giving life to the poems, unlike Akhmatova, who often commits poems to paper after they assume the form of a song with lyrics. In other words, while Akhmadulina's poem is created in and through the presence of paper or a notebook, Akhmatova's is put down on paper after it is ready for preservation.[4] For Akhmadulina the notebook also serves as metonymy for creating; a poem is composed in the presence of paper and quickly recorded in writing: "And where is my notebook to consolidate my melancholy in word?" ("Drawing"—"Risunok"; 114). Later in *The Secret* the creative process focuses on the difficulties of composition. Whiteness of notebook and paper recurs in contexts of creation through the epithet "belyi," as in the poem "The Night before a Performance" ("Noch' pered vystupleniem"): "Without a single blot of deceit / incorruptibly glares white the paper" (*Snowstorm*, 21). In this image Akhmadulina seems to have taken off on Akhmatova's poem that begins: "The evening hours at a table, / An irreparably white page."[5] To be sure, the Russian adjective for "white" in both its long and short forms is associated phonetically with the name Bella, its short form differing in the position of the stress: bélyi, belá. In making artistic use of her name Akhmadulina follows Tsvetaeva and Akhmatova and a host of other, less immediate, predecessors in the Russian literary tradition.[6]

Through similes inviting whiteness, Akhmadulina transforms the notebook into a container for the poems; they are brought to life only in it, as in the poem "New Notebook" ("Novaia tetrad' "; 29). The speaker approaches writing with awe as in entering a shrine, her simile a remote echo of Akhmatova's creative process:

> I am embarrassed and shy before the sheet
> of clean paper.
> So stands a pilgrim

4. This is pro forma only for in 1983 Nina Ol'shevskaia told me that Akhmatova used to compose poems as she sat on the couch in the living room of the former's apartment. She would mutter the lines and sway a little to the rhythm of the poem. No one would disturb her during these times.

5. Anna Akhmatova, *Stikhotvoreniia i poemy*, compiled by V. M. Zhirmunskii (Leningrad: Sovetskii pisatel', 1976), no. 97.

6. On Akhmatova's artistic use of her name in her verse, see my *Poetry of Anna Akhmatova: A Conquest of Time and Space.* Verse Translation by F. D. Reeve, Slavistische Beiträge, 196 (Munich: Otto Sagner, 1986), 39–55. Mention of Tsvetaeva's use of her own name and that of Akhmatova's and the Symbolist poet Aleksandr Blok's is made in Chapter 3.

by the entrance to a temple.
Before a maiden's face
so lowers his eyes the experienced admirer. . . .

So into the depth of the notebook, as into a thicket of
    woods,
I foolhardily and forever sink.

Смущаюсь и робею пред листом
бумаги чистой.
Так стоит паломник
у входа в храм.
Пред девичьим лицом
так опытный потупится поклонник.

Так в глубь тетради, словно в глубь лесов.
я безрассудно и навечно кану.

(29)

At times whiteness can indicate problems caused by the persona's inability to create, ostensibly, due to stilted language and to having exhausted summer impressions: in the poem "It is my last day in the strange house" ("Poslednii den' zhivu ia v strannom dome") the silent soul suffers from the inability to create (113). Yet writing can be done only at the proper time. The piece "Do not Write about the Thunderstorm" ("Ne pisat' o groze"; 114) shows that writing on a phenomenon in progress—a thunderstorm—constricts it and demeans its grandeur unless it is a motionless winter phenomenon. Similarly, Pushkin and Akhmatova often write following an experience. Indeed, Pushkin notes in his narrative poem *Eugene Onegin* (*Evgenii Onegin*), "Love passed, my Muse appeared."

Furthermore, Akhmadulina utilizes the antonym to white implied in her name—black—in an unusual way. In the narrative poem *My Genealogy* bearing an identical title with Pushkin's poem on his predecessors, she treats the urgency of her persona's desire to be born. In it figures the antithesis of the live Bella, the yet unborn Bella; her absence suggests a distinct possibility of being born:

. . . And I slept all the past ages
lightly and quietly in the depth of nature.
In the damp earth, blacker than a rough notebook,
only the shoots of my soul were marked.

... И я спала все прошлые века
светло и тихо в глубине природы.
В сырой земле, черней черновика,
души моей лишь намечались всходы.

(261)

So that which is yet unrealized, be it an unconceived or unborn child or a poem in draft form (in Russian "*chern*ovik"—a draft—contains "black" in its root), is construed as being black—the total absence of anything, particularly of light and color. The idea is promoted through the simile quoted above: "chernei chernovika."

White, the antonym of black, conversely, incorporates within itself all seven basic colors and through them, every possible color combination. Just as her first name evokes thoughts of white, so too the poet harbors within herself the ability to engender many varieties of verse. Correspondingly, the single white color of frozen winter thaws out in spring to free the imprisoned colors through its own destruction.[7] The poem "We part—and simultaneously" ("My rasstaemsia—i odnovremenno") demonstrates the breakdown of white into its components: "and the color white does not exist— / its seven colored orphans remain" (65). With the defrosting of winter's white comes the liberation of all colors of the rainbow as well as myriad possible combinations. The poem "Altercation with the Crimea" articulates ideas on white being a unified color of creation: "who in seven days created the sevenhue of the color white" (118). Obviously, Akhmadulina had in mind the Russian folk idiom "belyi svet" (the wide world), which in her poetic world view encompassed all seven colors, corresponding obliquely with the creation of the whole world and universe in seven days according to the Bible and the Babylonian epic *Enuma Elish*. The seven colors through juxtaposition with the seven days of creation, i.e., as parts of the whole, acquire grouping into the color white and the wide world to denote the unity of the completed universe. Similarly, Bella the persona-poet, with her name reminiscent of white, combines all experiences of colorful late spring and summer within herself during the synthesized white season of winter to select the essence of life and experience, which will be crystallized into

---

7. It brings to mind the cyclicity of the seasons in the Adonis myth with six months of death and remaining underground versus resurrection for Persephone. See *Mifologicheskii slovar'*, ed M. N. Botvinnik et al., 2d ed. (Leningrad: Gosudarstvennoe uchebnopedagogicheskoe izdatel'stvo, 1961), 7. In the later poem "Sorrows and Jokes: The Room" ("Pechali i shutochki: komnata"), Akhmadulina brings out the conflation of the endearing form for her first name as Belka with a squirrel. See Akhmadulina, *Stikhotvoreniia* (Moscow: Khudozhestvennaia literatura, 1988), 295.

verse. Ostensibly, in spring the winter frozen condensation of colors into white breaks down into their component seven colors, which will remain separate to develop independently until the first white in nature. Moreover, the disintegration of the inclusive color white into its components signals an end to the period most fruitful for writing in the early period—until the following winter. The subdivision of white into seven colors evolves into imagery evoking Snow White (Belosnezhka) and the Seven Dwarfs:

> my sleeping princess—the crystal.
>
> That spectrum, aflush with seven blushes,
> In the glass coffin, dead and lovely.

> мою царевну спящую—хрусталь.
>
> Тот, в семь румянцев розовевший спектр,
> в гробу стеклянном, мертвый и прелестный.
>
> (217)

In turn the fairy-tale imagery brings to mind a poem by Afanasii Fet (1820–92), the impressionistic miniature lyricist, on the spring awakening of nature and of man, "The depth of the heavens is again clear" ("Glub' nebes opiat' iasna").[8] In the poem "April" people congregate, rivers are freed from shackles of ice, trees bud, flowers bloom; and color is in motion everywhere.[9] Conversely, in winter, through the monotony of black and white and frozen isolation, the entire ambience is conducive to creation based on accumulated experience. Moreover, winter has a purifying influence through its frost and pristine whiteness that Akhmadulina equates with medical science in the piece "Winter" ("Zima"): "there is something in winter of gentle medicine" (95).[10]

The concept of isolation from outside influences is amplified through imagery advanced by similes, such as fire contained in a lamp or a prehis-

---

8. See A. A. Fet, *Sochineniia v dvukh tomakh*, compiled by A. E. Tarkhov (Moscow: Khudozhestvennaia literatura, 1982), 1:91–92.

9. In Annenskii's poem "The Ice Prison" from "Icy Trefoil" ("Ledianaia tiur'ma"; "Trilistnik ledianoi"), which treats the theme of freedom from the icy shackles of winter, the ice is "dark-blue captivity" ("sinii plen"). See Innokentii Annenskii, *Stikhotvoreniia i tragedii*, compiled by A. V. Fedorov, Biblioteka poeta, Bol'shaia seriia, 3d ed. (Leningrad: Sovetskii pisatel', 1990), 114.

10. Interestingly, cold stimulates the imagination in Wallace Stevens, "A Quiet Normal Life." See *The Collected Poems of Wallace Stevens* (New York: Vintage, 1982), 523.

toric insect in amber. Catching cold, mostly in autumn, likewise allows the persona's seclusion from doting friends. The poem "Illness" ("Bolezn' "; 93) shows how illness in the fall allows her to ruminate in languor, an important step in marshaling her thoughts in preparation for winter. When later at a certain stage in life she leads a carefree existence, probably in happy marriage, she does no creative thinking nor writing: "I became healthy like grass" ("It so happened that at age twenty-seven"—"Sluchilos' tak, chto dvadtsati semi"; 126). Health, then, brings experiences without the needed contemplative processing, whereas a cold with a runny nose and watery eyes, evocative of a rainy day, promotes the reworking of impressions. As mentioned above, rain—unfettered water—is construed as "living life" and obviously draws on Pasternak's prevalent usage of rain in his collection *My Sister—Life*. The converse of philistine life and of kitsch, it is appreciated only by the simple and the naive, such as children. Indeed, in *Chills* parents complain to the persona of the rain: "it inflames my children's minds" (224). Furthermore, the chills make people act differently, more spontaneously, often in an uninhibited way. With rain, the chills are not far away. In *Chills*, the speaker's vibrating shivering chills appear to be the result of her sensitivity to life and art as well as a prelude to her own creation of poetry.[11] Taking control of her, the chills free her from convention: "my body having overthrown my authority." The vibrations here are the result of the extreme tension of a mind preparing for processing material for creation: "vibrations from an incredible effort of the mind and creation" (225). She becomes an interpreter of the chills and their embodiment—a tambourine or a ballerina dancing to their tune.

In Akhmadulina, then, cold and dampness stimulate her creative resources into making artistic use of summer and current impressions: *oznob* (chills) equals, or induces, inspiration and creative work but it is a cold, quivering state (even with a temperature) distinct from feverish heat that moves Akhmatova's persona to compose. Due to the chills, Akhmadulina's body turns into a receptive instrument for artistic creation during which it vibrates like a resounding violin string, hence *The String* as the title of an early poem and collection.[12]

Thus, in autumn, the coldness of rain and the flu bring on feverish chills and demand an ambience for composing in winter, snugly ensconced in a

---

11. Bella Akhmadulina, *Oznob: izbrannye proizvedeniia* (Frankfurt: Posev, 1968). The significance of the poem is revealed through the title to the entire collection.

12. Bella Akhmadulina, *Struna: Stikhi* (Moscow: Sovetskii pisatel', 1962).

snow-covered house. However, the speaker at times recreates cold in the warmth by taking ice in her mouth. It refreshes and cools her vocal apparatus and possibly improves the articulation of verse in writing poems:

> And I, so young,
> with a sweet (piece of) ice in my mouth,
> slipping, courtseying,
> go along in the white snow.

> И я, такая молодая,
> со сладкой льдинкою во рту,
> оскальзываясь, приседая,
> по снегу белому иду.
>
> ("Landscape"—"Peizazh"; 95)

In the poem "Music Lessons," dedicated to Tsvetaeva, the persona makes further references to ice: "I do not speak with a frozen throat. . . . / with an effort of my neck as if I am swallowing ice" (99). Indeed, during composition, the coldness of the ice induces a pleasurable sensation and probably leads to the formation of poetic words as well as to the retention of their shape on her lips for correct utterance: "And the gentle taste of native speech / so purely cools the lips" ("Candle"—"Svecha"; 102). Coincidentally, an icicle in the mouth is visually comparable for the eyes to a candle in form and white color. Ice is also useful to the persona for whitening or activating the black gap of memory during illness in *My Genealogy:* "To cool the black gap of my memory— / give, give me some white ice" (269). A black gap denotes nothingness—as in a deep abyss; it is akin to the usage in common parlance of white denoting a lack of something as evidenced by the root of the Russian word "pro*bel*" (gap)—white—in the meaning of "clean, devoid of."[13]

Summing up what has been examined so far, we see that following autumn rain and shivering illness, Akhmadulina's poetry takes shape in winter during snowstorms or when the house is encased in snow, ice, and frost. Like most poets, she writes at night while sitting over a notebook of white paper. Ice in her mouth, or the memory of it, shapes or retains the words.

13. Compare the "black hole" in Tsvetaeva's *Poem of the Mountain* (*Poema gory*): "Neither today nor tomorrow / Will I plug the black hole" ("Chernoi ni dnes', ni vpred' / Ne zatknu dyry"). Marina Tsvetaeva, *Sochineniia v dvukh tomakh,* compiled by Anna Saakiants (Moscow: Khudozhestvennaia literatura, 1980), 1:366.

Akhmadulina's speaker writes not under a modern lamp but by a candle—a remnant of a bygone age, connected with her love for the old language and her idols, Pushkin and Lermontov. In "Candle," the candle becomes associated with memories of flowery obsolete language, with Pushkin and his concise idiom, with the time of creation—night—and with the native tongue, which is distinct from artificial stiltedness and artistic insincerity:

> All you need is a candle,
> a simple wax candle,
> and venerable old-fashionedness
> will become so fresh in (your) memory.

> Всего-то—чтоб была свеча,
> свеча простая, восковая,
> и старомодность вековая
> так станет в памяти свежа.
>
> (102)

It is to the notebook and the candle that the persona directs her entreaties for help in creating genuine poetry in the poem "The precious pre-dawn hour" ("Predutrennii chas dragotsennyi"; 153). The symbolism of the candle develops in "Music Lessons," in which a candle's ability to light is connected with Tsvetaeva's talent for musical poetry and her dislike of music lessons. When at one point Akhmadulina's persona could no longer create and believed herself to be dying, poetically at least, she snuffed out the candles in the poem "Once swaying on the brink" ("Odnazhdy, pokachnuvshis' na kraiu"):

> No one knew, only the white notebook
> noticed that I blew out the candles
> that had been lit for creating speech . . .

> Никто не знал, лишь белая тетрадь
> заметила, что я задула свечи,
> зажженные для сотворенья речи,
>
> (81)

Interestingly, the poem reverberates with a certain reversal of the first quatrain of Akhmatova's diptych "Death" ("Smert' "; 220). The difference between the two poets is that whereas Akhmatova sings of grief eulogizing it, as it were, Akhmadulina converts everything, even suffering, into bliss. Writing for the early Akhmadulina is usually perceived as relaxation, a reward for torment, for the preceding throes of creation: "Bearing my exultant punishment" ("New Notebook"; 29). The early Akhmadulina, then, suffers only while creating, and not often at that; Akhmatova, on the other hand, grieves before and during creation. For Akhmadulina "earthly torment" constitutes all that she has not yet sung; it is a craving, a yearning to produce verse and to reflect more and more. Akhmatova says, "still much, probably, wants to be sung with my voice," but the unsung situation *per se* is not sorrow for her (206). In Akhmatova, the objects and phenomena beg to be interpreted and immortalized by her in art. In her "Northern Elegies. The Third" ("Severnye elegii. Tret'ia") Akhmatova laments the unwritten poems that swarm about her. She even feels that they can possibly choke her:

> And how many poems I have not written,
> And their secret chorus wanders about me.
> And perhaps it still can sometime
> Strangle me . . .

> И сколько я стихов не написала,
> И тайный хор их бродит вкруг меня,
> И, может быть, еще когда-нибудь
> Меня задушит . . .

> (331)

The fear of not composing all the verse that is welling up in the poet's imagination evokes Keats's sonnet that begins:

> When I have fears that I may cease to be
> Before my pen has glean'd my teeming brain.[14]

Singularly, in the act of poetic creation, the candle can metamorphose into Akhmadulina's speaker, as if the artistic torch of Pushkin and Lermontov were being relayed to her: "a candle burning in the night / knows how to transform into me" ("Recollection"—"Vospominanie"; 178). It would appear that here she has to be explicit to avert incomprehension in the reader. Curiously, the aureole of the burning candle is equated visually to an eye's

14. John Keats, *The Complete Poems*, ed. John Barnard, 3d ed. (London: Penguin, 1988), 94.

pupil and attributed powers of seeing. Possibly the converse holds true also—
the persona turns into the candle and sees beyond the night into the past:

> God forbid that a candle gawks
> into your pupils with its pupil.
> And what's more: kill the cricket!
> I have had the occasion to be a cricket.

> Не дай, чтоб пялилась свеча
> в твои зрачки своим зрачком.
> Вот что еще: убей сверчка!
> Мне доводилось быть сверчком.

(178–79)

So not only does a burning candle transmute into the persona, but she had
occasion to be a cricket.[15] Enigmatically, the cricket has to be killed; otherwise, in December, one's home will be transformed into dawn ("zaria"), for
a cricket's chirping is likened to that of birds by Keats in the poem "On the
Grasshopper and Cricket" (94), and birds chirp only in the light. It seems as
if Akhmadulina's speaker wants no part of her former self to remain behind
should she die.

In the theme of poetic creation, the cricket figures with some consistency.
Of course, "sverchok" was Pushkin's appellation in the anti-Slavophile literary group Arzamas.[16] This in itself is reason for its appearance during poetic
creation. The connection in "Wretched Spring" ("Plokhaia vesna") of the
old-fashioned poetic quill—*pero—svecha—sverchok*—with literary heredity
through Pushkin is unmistakable (128–31). Even the sounds of both words
are mutually binding: *svechá / sverchók* plus stress on the second syllable. In
the poem "Yearning for Lermontov" ("Toska po Lermontovu") the speaker
living in *chuzhoi dom* (a strange home) could be referring to Georgia or to
the environment of a classic poet, like Lermontov, i.e., within his legacy or
work. She is comfortable there: "in this house, in the bathroom a cricket
lived, / (it) would squeak, (it) rendered me a favor" (69). She and the cricket
used to compose songs without contradicting each other; they even performed duets:

---

15. These hints at metempsychosis are reminiscent of Akhmatova. See Ketchian, *The Poetry
of . . .* , 75–118.

16. *Kratkaia literaturnaia entsiklopediia*, 9 vols., ed. A. A. Surkov (Moscow: Sovetskaia entsiklopediia, 1962–78), 1:293.

> . . . without refuting each other,
> two trifles of nature—it and I—
> live quietly, composing songs.
>
> Thus—I am here. We do not sleep at night,
> I begin to sing—it is able to answer.

> друг друга не опровергая,
> два пустяка природы—он и я—
> живут тихонько, песенки слагая.
>
> Итак—я здесь. Мы по ночам не спим,
> я запою—он отвечать умеет.

(69)

The reference to herself and the cricket as *pustiak* (trifle) could connote humility; however, since the evaluative appellation involves another, the speaker could well mean that they are both hollow on the basis of the word *pustoi* (empty), and they can therefore resonate with music and the sounds of speech to create true art through life. In other words, they can serve as hollow resonant instruments for the sounds of song.[17] In Akhmadulina, crickets live near or in the walls of homes, hence the connection of the cricket with the recurrent motif of a home. Admittedly, crickets produce a greater frequency of chirps with a rise in temperature; therefore the speaker brings them into her cozy winter haven.[18]

In her ongoing struggle for genuine art, the persona composes in solitude

17. No such definition of "pustoi" as "resonant" is recorded in any dictionary of Russian, including the *Seventeen Volume Dictionary of Russian* (*Slovar' sovremennogo russkogo iazyka*), 17 vols. (Moscow: AN SSSR, 1950–65). Akhmadulina may well be giving her own striking interpretation of the word for the given context.

18. P. Antokol'skii traces Akhmadulina's cricket to Charles Dickens. See his foreword to Bella Akhmadulina, *Stikhi* (Moscow: Khudozhestvennaia literatura, 1975), 4. But Akhmadulina's source, other than Pushkin, is most probably Keats's poem "On the Grasshopper and the Cricket," in which:

> The Cricket's song, in warmth increasing ever,
> And seems to one in drowsiness half lost.

(The Complete Poems, 94)

Wallace Stevens's poems featuring a cricket, "A Quiet Normal Life" and "Le Monocle de mon oncle," as mentioned by Helen Vendler in her seminar on Wallace Stevens at Harvard University in the fall of 1991, trace the tradition through Keats and Emily Dickinson to Milton and Latin literature. Vendler perceives the origin of the candle in the first poem to be Shakespeare's *Merchant of Venice*.

in winter with an occasional cricket for company, and she also travels to the South alone. Mention of a spouse or family occurs in connection with a northern locale, such as the home by the metro station "Aeroport" ("Airport") in Moscow. The poem "Family and Household" ("Sem'ia i byt"; 120) lists the acquisitions needed to form a family and a household for the persona and her husband: a child, a dog, a bird, a candle, and a cricket. Yet until the collection *The Garden* Akhmadulina never names her real husband in the text of the poem; the only names are in dedications. The cricket in her household is humanized through a simile showing that it has possessions and even a cart for transporting them; the chirping sound is compared to the scraping of the cart's iron, and from there, Akhmadulina develops a vivid simile:

> In a moment of magic the candle lit up by itself:
> a cricket was coming to us, dragging (its) most delicate
>   grinding sound,
> like a covered cart with a cricket's belongings.

> В миг волшебства сама зажглась свеча:
> к нам шел сверчок, влача нежнейший скрежет,
> словно возок с пожитками сверчка.

> (120)

These enumerated objects are all connected with "living life." Accordingly, the cricket, like the candle, remains at home as part of the necessary literary decor for composing in winter. Since the persona does not create at home— mostly in "another's home" or a private place for herself—she need not take them away with her. Elsewhere in her verse, the cricket's song has a sad ring, namely, in the text to the television film *Green Meadow* (*Lug zelenyi*) during the Artist's preparation of his canvas when he sees strings and a bow and recalls a concealed orchestra sounding like a chirping cricket: "In his memory was stranded an orchestra, sad, like a cricket" (247). Conceivably, with all the previously mentioned belongings in mind, the speaker brings to bear the Russian saying "Znai sverchok svoi shestok" (Let a cricket know its hearth), meaning that one must know one's station and place in life, an artist in particular: "I dreamed of it totally inappropriately— / the cricket that had forgotten its hearth" (248).

In the light of reverence for the past, it is small wonder that the speaker is attracted to archaic flowery language, as in the poem "Ancient style attracts me" ("Vlechet menia starinnyi slog"; 38) with its assertion "I would give up my horse for half a moment with the man beloved by me" and its patent allusion to Shakespeare's "My kingdom for a horse." It evokes the force of love expressed in "Lot's Wife" ("Lotova zhena") by Lot's wife in Akhmatova's lyrical interpretation of the biblical episode: "Who had given her life for a single glance" (160). When Akhmadulina's speaker, with her experience and knack for work and rhyming, becomes carried away with stilted language to the detriment of honest art and feelings, and when through writing she has drained herself of accumulated experiences, she falls mute. Muteness does not mean that she cannot write poetry at all, for the long-standing habit of stringing line to line and or rhyme to rhyme is ingrained in her—it is second nature. Rather, it signifies that no original, meaningful verse is created.[19] In the poem "How long I haven't had enough sleep" ("Kak dolgo ia ne vysypalas' "; 134) the persona explains in her argument with a "literary specialist" that prevarication in verse is punishable by muteness:

> He knew: if a lie is not muddle-headed,
> it will not defile the lips,
> I knew: muteness punishes
> for prevarication of the word.

> Он знал: коль ложь не бестолкова,
> она не осквернит уста,
> я знала: за лукавство слова
> наказывает немота.

> (136)

It was shown above that, whatever for ordinary people in everyday life does not exist and is perceived as a void, in Akhmadulina can acquire form, characteristics, tangibility, as it were, but on the negative algebraic scale: her unborn self whose very chance for birth is questionable in *My Genealogy* is a surprisingly tenacious nonbeing, with a will and a voice. Consequently, a

19. In this connection it is curious to note Akhmatova's use of muteness ("nemota") for Mandel'shtam without elaboration: "In music O[sip] was at home, and that's an extremely rare quality. Most of all on earth he feared his own muteness, calling it asphyxia. When it came upon him, he rushed about in terror and devised some absurd reasons to explain this calamity. ("Pages from a Notebook. Recollections. A Novella about O. E. Mandel'shtam," *Zvezda* 6 (1989), 22. On muteness in Akhmatova, see Chapter 4.

description as "minus" is justified.[20] To be sure, muteness is perceived by people as no voice; still, mute persons do utter inarticulate, incohesive sounds, a fact Akhmadulina takes into consideration when depicting a physical muteness with a sound all its own. Because the sound of muteness is like iron and uneven, it can torture the throat with its bloody abrasion:

> The sound of muteness, iron and uneven,
> tortures my throat with a bloody abrasion,
> I begin to speak—and I stain my handkerchief with
>   blood.
> Into the silence buried as into the earth.

> Звук немоты, железный и корявый,
> терзает горло ссадиной кровавой,
> заговорю—и обагрю платок.
> В безмолвие, как в землю, погребенной.
>   ("Word"—"Slovo"; 82)

Similarly, in the poem "Muteness," the speaker's voice is construed as a tangible object, rather independent of her body, so that it can be *led* away, leaving in its wake a gaping wound: "Who was so powerful and clever? / Who led my voice away from my throat?" (83). Muteness is so severe that when the persona tries to shout to be heard, a round cloud of steam, as in cold weather, forms around her mouth. It probably forms from the wound's blood. Akhmadulina's use of similes shows that the comparison holds true for the simile's tenor. Tangibility is achieved through the simile: "I shout, but, like steam from my mouth, / muteness has circled my lips." Muteness is also tangible in the poem "To Visit with the Artist" ("Gostit' u khudozhnika"; 105). It can be more severe than springtime writer's block following a productive winter. At one time the muteness lasted as long as a year

---

20. The notion of the self parting with the state of non-being to be born is articulated in Akhmatova's "Northern Elegies. The First" ("Severnye elegii. Pervaia"), no. 634:

> So this is when we thought of being born
> And, unerringly measuring the time,
> In order not to miss any unprecedented spectacles,
> We parted with nonbeing.

> Так вот когда мы вздумали родиться
> И, безошибочно отмерив время,
> Чтоб ничего не пропустить из зрелищ
> Невиданных, простились с небытьем.

("Something Else"; 84). Importantly, although written in verse, this poem constitutes, in the estimation of the persona, mechanical writing and rhyming—not genuine art:

> That's not what I mean. Already old in me is
> the habit of placing word after word.
>
> My hand knows this sequence.
>
> Я не о том. Во мне уже стара
> привычка ставить слово после слова.
>
> Порядок этот ведает рука.
>
> (84)

Objecting to insincere art, the speaker seeks to return to an erstwhile situation when her voice was mischievously bold and capable of true laughter and true sobbing as the verse required. The cure is found in the poem "Sunday" ("Voskresnyi den' "; 85–87), advancing the notion that concentrated work can saturate muteness with sound. After completing work and experiencing the languor of finding the next project, a state concurrent with muteness, the speaker anticipates the return of her voice. Her oxymoron, "merry hunger," is worthy of Akhmatova:

> And, like smoke, that has eclipsed the depths of pipes,
> deep in (my) throat originates voice.
> Insatiable work sneaks toward me,
> enduring a new and merry hunger.
> Muteness awaits satiation with sound,
> gaping with its emptiness, like a birdhouse.
>
> И, словно дым, затмивший недра труб,
> глубоко в горле возникает голос.
> Ко мне крадется ненасытный труд,
> терпящий новый и веселый голод.
> Ждет насыщенья звуком немота,
> зияя пустотою, как скворешник.
>
> (86)

Muteness as a void is compared to an empty birdhouse. Showing that birds can be living inside, the simile serves as preparation for the feeding and singing images to follow, as well as for development of the bird image, which I discuss further in Chapter 5. Here, paper is visualized as a white gaping opening demanding the persona's ministration. Inviting, safe, and wordless, it incorporates all possible nuances hidden in its whiteness. The image develops into the open mouth of a hungry fledgling begging to be fed through the lips of the persona, who implicitly assumes the role of the nurturing parent bird. Again, there is here the motif of the persona merely being an instrument for the verse in natural Russian speech, as being the musical instrument's strings and the ballerina earlier dancing to the tune of another, i.e., physically embodying the musical ideas.[21] This other being is probably living nature expressed through poetic speech. Through her vocal apparatus, the persona merely provides the necessary muscle for speech to originate:

> Speech hurries in order not to perish in silence,
> to accomplish the birth of sound and then
> to forget me forever and to leave me.
> For it I am only a pipe that will pipe.
> Let it pipe and cheer up the neighborhood.
> And for me again—to sleep, as if to die,
> and to awaken in the morning, as if to be resurrected.

> Речь так спешит в молчанье не погибнуть,
> свершить звукорожденье и затем
> забыть меня навеки и покинуть.
> Я для нее—лишь дудка, чтоб дудеть.
> Пускай дудит н веселит окрестность.
> А мне опять—заснуть, как умереть,
> и пробудиться утром, как воскреснуть.

(87)

It can be seen that for Akhmadulina's early persona art is often created when the artist loses personal control to inspiration of her body and mind, be it in dance or in song rendered into poems. This concept is confirmed in the poem "In the vacant rest home" ("V opustevshem dome otdykha") with the words "you will not be able to control your own body" ("ne sovladeesh'

---

21. Note that for Yeats the art form closest to poetry is dance in "Among School Children." W. B. Yeats, *The Collected Poems*. Definitive edition, with the author's final revisions. New York: Macmillan, 1956, 212–14.

so svoim zhe telom"). The rest home is empty now—conceivably, it is winter and the persona wishes more of the same for her body, this veritable "live beast of nature":

> And in future play, know no muteness!
> In deep solitude, in winter,
> I will make merry to my heart's content amid the
>   emptiness,
> crampedly and noisily inhabited by me.

> И впредь играй, не ведай немоты!
> В глубоком одиночестве, зимою,
> я всласть повеселюсь средь пустоты,
> тесно и шумно населенной мною.
>
> (89)

Furthermore, in the piece "Night" ("Noch' "; 127), the speaker shows that on a snowy winter night in an empty house under candlelight, objects acquire their own voice with which to implore her to sing of them:

> the (small) voice of an object grumbles and begs,
> its soul wants to be celebrated
> and only with my voice.

> бубнит и клянчит голосок предмета,
> его душа желает быть воспета,
> и непременно голосом моим.
>
> (127)

Here too muteness torments: "what pain—under the torture of muteness."

Arrogance in the speaker toward others gives rise to muteness in the piece "It's not the same as twenty years ago" ("Vot ne takoi, kak dvadtsat' let nazad"; 200–201). She confronts her younger self, or double: "in monstrous chains of muteness / you will bemoan your guilt toward them" (201). In the third poem of "Tarusa," which is also included in *The Secret*, the boundaries between the senses are obliterated through the persona's equation of auditory and visual muteness:

> And a fish's muteness—
> is it not a shout, not heard, but visible,
> clotted in orange near its mouth?

А рыбья немота—
не есть ли крик, не слышимый, но зримый,
оранжево запекшийся у рта?[22]

(207)

The physical pain of muteness is underscored through the word "clotted," which connotes dried blood on a wound and reverberates with the carrying off of her voice in an earlier poem.[23]

Thus, the process of poetic creation for Akhmadulina's early persona is highly orchestrated. Her creative powers need certain preconditions to function—summer fluidity and development, as well as color and autumn

22. The image of the mute fish's visible shout is reminiscent of the Nobel Prize Laureate Poet, Joseph Brodsky's (b. 1940) early poem "Fishes in Winter" ("Ryby zimoi"), in which fish are portrayed as swimming silently without light and being unable to shed tears. Also, poems about fish stick in the poet's throat like a fishbone and injure it, possibly causing it to bleed:

> Fish
>   are always taciturn,
>   because they—
>   are silent.
> Poems about fish,
>   like fish,
>   stick in
>   one's throat.

> Рыбы
>   всегда молчаливы,
>   ибо они—
>   безмолвны.
> Стихи о рыбах,
>   как рыбы,
>   встают поперек
>   горла.

Iosif Brodskii, *Stikhotvoreniia i poemy* (Washington, D.C.: Inter-Language Literary Associates, 1965), 26.

23. In *The Garden* the speaker will invoke a succession of surrogate muses, all taken from nature, which will graduate to "the guiding sound" as her means for creative writing (49); in this greater awareness of sound, she comes closer to Akhmatova's awareness of sound in the process of creating verse, as in her poem "Poetic Creation" ("Tvorchestvo"): "There arises one all-conquering sound" ("Vstaet odin, vse pobedivshii zvuk"; *Stikhotvoreniia i poemy*, no. 333). Walter Jackson Bate's comment in *John Keats* (Cambridge: Harvard University Press, 1964), 73, concerning Keats's breakthrough on writing about the lack of a subject is faintly evocative of Akhmadulina, whose speaker may have chosen a subject but at the precise moment of writing lacks inspiration and true insight to produce a poem, as will be seen in subsequent chapters. On 4 November 1990 when I mentioned noticing the spirit of Keats in some of her work, Akhmadulina replied: "Da, ia ego chitala so slovarem. Naverno, chto-nibud' ostalos' " ("Yes, I read him with a dictionary. Something could have possibly been retained").

rain with chills, to gather and to assimilate impressions and emotions. There-after, given proper conditions—a snowbound house for concentration of impressions, solitude, a white notebook, night, a candle, a chirping cricket—and the proper attitude, she is able to present luminous poems, her personal refraction of nature and life in art.

3

The Key to the Secret

> The wandering earth herself may be
> Only a sudden flaming word,
> In clanging space, a moment heard,
> Troubling the endless reverie.
> —W. B. Yeats

Bella Akhmadulina's most cohesive collection of verse to date, *The Secret: New Poems,* marks a sophisticated stage in her artistic development in which the poetic endeavors of her lyric persona find unusual articulation and reflection. Observing a degree of continuity with the preceding poetry, the collection features at least fifteen poems from previous collections. Fourteen of the poems are found in the collection *Dreams of Georgia,* the most extensive cumulative collection of Akhmadulina's original verse, prose, and translations of the early period. Although the opening poem in *The Secret* expounds on the secret, or mystery, the gradual illumination of which occupies a great deal of the collection, there is no poem bearing the title "Taina."[1]

As it stands, the collection is intricately interwoven thematically and structurally. Some poems are linked openly and sequentially, with their titles clustering around a given theme, such as the moon, day, space, or the bird-cherry tree. In others, the coda of one poem frequently anticipates the subject of a subsequent piece, and often the theme enters following its debut as a motif, as in the final stanza of "The Coffee Imp" ("Kofeinyi chertik"), in which the speaker says, "I will go down to pay my first respects to the Oka" (22), and the next poem "Squabblings and Reconciliations"

---

1. Bella Akhmadulina, *Taina. Novye stikhi* (Moscow: Sovetskii pisatel', 1983) and *Sny o Gruzii* (Tbilisi: Merani, 1979). Henceforth all references to Akhmadulina's poems by page number only are to her collection, *The Secret.*

("Prepiratel'stva i primireniia") which begins with: "Down toward the Oka, sloping through the forest, / saving the *pervotsvet* from trampling" (23).[2]

In still other poems a fleeting image, as it were, foreshadows an imminent motif, which will not be fully developed in the collection, such as "I hang like a flock of news" ("Traveler"—"Putnik"; 17). The image reappears from another facet in a subsequent poem "Moon over Tarusa" ("Luna v Taruse"; 19), in which bats are figuratively named "krylatye myshi" (winged mice). The normal name for a bat is "letuchaia mysh' " (flying mouse). Yet the overall image evolves into that of thoughts as butterflies (to be discussed in Chapter 7). Another example of an isolated echo sounds in the poem "Line of Work" ("Rod zaniatii"; 41)—"my line of work is unclear"—to be followed up in the concluding poem, "We began together: the workers, winter, and I" ("My nachali vmeste: rabochie, ia i zima"; 123), while, in effect, the entire collection exemplifies the speaker's occupation.

Unlike the work of her early period, *The Secret* centers almost exclusively on the leitmotif of poetic creation. In the period preceding *The Secret*, only certain poems focus on this topic. Now an entire collection scarcely departs from it. Still, the actual newness of this move lies in the direction of the leitmotif's development. Previously, in poems on poetic creation the impressions, experiences, and observations garnered from the energetic, multicolored summer ambience were contemplated with the onset of autumnal rain and the flu. This enabled the poet to withdraw temporarily from her friends and obligations to absorb summer impressions. In winter all the colors of nature merged into their all-encompassing color—white—through the arrival of frost, the freezing of water, and the restriction of mobility. The color white harbored within itself all the possible colors of the rainbow, which made available their intense exploration. The persona-poet crafted her po-

---

2. I retain certain Russian words, such as "pervotsvet," in the original because their monosemantic translation before the proper explanations would hamper the analysis. The pertinent pages from the collection *The Secret* are marked in the text. I translate "taina" as "secret" for the sake of the opening poem "I have the secret of wondrous blooming," in which there is mention of a key. Elsewhere, "taina" can also denote "mystery," which Akhmadulina herself prefers. "Mystery" links the poems more readily with Fedor Tiutchev and with Keats. On this association with Tiutchev, see the review by Vladimir Novikov, "Bol' obnovleniia," *Literaturnoe obozrenie*, no. 1 (1985): 52. One wonders, moreover, if Akhmadulina is familiar with the works of Henry David Thoreau, of whom Joyce Carol Oates writes "Of our classic American writers Henry David Thoreau is the supreme poet of doubleness, of evasion and mystery." "The Mysterious Mr. Thoreau," *New York Times Book Review*, 1 May 1988, 1. The fascinating topic of the garden in Russian literature is addressed in Norman W. Ingham, "Turgenev in the Garden," in *Mnemozina. Studia litteraria russica in honorem Vsevolod Setchkarev*, ed. Joachim T. Baer and Norman W. Ingham (Munich: Wilhelm Fink, 1974), 209–28.

etic images, encased, as in a cocoon, in a warm snowbound house with a cricket for "artistic" company, as well as for literary continuity with Pushkin, Keats, and others, and a candle for tangible continuity with the heritage of the past. Love lyrics were conspicuously absent in the early thematic group of poems on poetic creation, and what was a trend for a specific group now becomes the rule for the entire volume. Exceptions are minor.

The purpose here is to study the lyric persona of Akhmadulina on the writing of poetry first as expressed in the collection as a whole and then in the programmatic opening poem, "I have the secret of wondrous blooming."

Two-thirds of the collection addresses the theme of Tarusa, a town on the Oka River in Russia that serves as the site for the speaker's artistic creativity. After Tarusa, the speaker moves briefly to other places—Moscow, Gagra, Riga, and Leningrad—before returning home to Peredelkino, the writer's colony near Moscow, where her best creative efforts result, ironically, in writer's block in the concluding poem, a transformed resonance with the early poetry. What is more, the first third of *The Garden* is again situated in Tarusa, after which the speaker moves North and the theme of the Symbolist poet Aleksandr Blok (1880–1921) becomes important.

As already mentioned, while the persona in this collection is not pluralistic, nor do she and the person and poet Akhmadulina ever merge completely. Yet she remains very close to the artistic interests of Akhmadulina, unlike the numerous personas of the young Anna Akhmatova or even the varying personas of Akhmadulina's earlier poems. Still, where personal interests are concerned, the speaker focuses sharply on her art and hardly ever touches the private aspects of the person Akhmadulina. Indeed, there is no mention here of parents, a husband (even in the poem dedicated to Boris Messerer's studio, unlike in *The Garden;* 111), children, or dogs. Humor continues, although it is not as boisterous as before (compare the earlier *Chills*); instead it graduates to a forceful irony and to "fun and games." Although the opening untitled poem presents in capsule form the highlights of the creative process that will unfold in the collection, Tarusa is not mentioned in it. The poet works toward her theme of Tarusa through the following poems, "The Garden" ("Sad"), "The Night of the Falling Apples" ("Noch' upadaniia iablok"), and "A deep gentle garden sloping to the Oka" ("Glubokii nezhnyi sad, vpadaiushchii v Oku"), and enters it in "Tarusa," a cycle of six poems. With Tarusa develops the theme of the poet Marina Tsvetaeva. Poems to her include both old and new ones; however, only those former poems to Tsvetaeva are included here that comprise an integral whole with the present themes of Tarusa and poetic creation. Significantly, the cycle "Tarusa" in *The Secret* has been enlarged by three poems.[3] Through Tarusa, then, Akhmadulina retains in her verse an awareness of Tsvetaeva and draws from it inspiration for work.

Tarusa is more than a literary symbol for Akhmadulina. In private conversation in 1983 she informed me that she really could not compose at home in Moscow or in Peredelkino (hence the writer's block there), and that she was soon to leave for Tarusa following readings in Leningrad, Riga (with the poet Bulat Okudzhava), and in Moscow early in January of 1984. In fact, creation in Tarusa merely continues the line of writing evolved in Akhmadulina's previous verse, where for the purposes of writing the speaker consistently creates in a home away from family ties. Her earlier "snowbound house" is replaced here by encasement in nature, to which she needs a window, and by imaginary placement in the past. In the early poetry the candle and the cricket helped her to recall garnered impressions. Now through walking trips and gazing out the window at a very special time she culls the impressions for creating with the help of nature in the broadest sense.

The connection with Tsvetaeva is made explicit through a dedication to her in the "Tarusa" cycle and through an epigraph from her poem "The Garden" ("Sad") used in Akhmadulina's poem "The Rider Garden" ("Sad-vsadnik," 79). Significantly, it is the only epigraph in the collection. The epigraph, as pointed out to me by Akhmadulina, was misprinted in the 1983 edition and should read:

> For this hell, [not "year"]
> for this delirium
> send me a garden
> in my old age.

> За этот ад,
> За этот бред
> Пошли мне сад
> На старость лет.

---

3. The three new poems are "Morskaia—tak idi v svoi moria" "Sea-ling [sea thing]—then go to your seas"; 12), "Rastaet sneg. Ia v zoopark skhozhu" ("The snow will thaw. I will go to the zoo"; 13), "Kak znat', vdrug—malo, a ne mnogo" ("How can one know, what if little, and not much"; 13). Among the deleted poems to Tsvetaeva are "Uroki muzyki" ("Music Lessons"), "Biograficheskaia spravka" ("Biographical Information"), "Chetvert' veka, Marina, tomu" ("It has been a quarter of a century, Marina"); *Sny o Gruzii*, 96–101.

In its previous publication in *Dreams of Georgia* (206–7) the "Tarusa" cycle bore no dedication to Tsvetaeva.

Tarusa is where for twenty years the Tsvetaev family rented the Pesochnoe estate. The town figures in Tsvetaeva's prose and in two poems, "The Ferry" ("Parom") and "Autumn in Tarusa" ("Osen' v Taruse");[4] they capture the ambience of the place and the time as well as the relationship between Marina and her younger sister Asia. Tsvetaeva describes Tarusa extensively in a biographical prose work, on the neighboring sisters "The Kirillovnas" ("Kirillovny"; 1:77–84).[5] These sisters, called only by their patronymic in the familiar peasant fashion, were members of a religious sect who lived on the very edge of Tarusa. Since in summer they were always working in their garden, they seemed to live only in their garden and orchard, hidden by willows and elderberry bushes. Tsvetaeva clarifies the impression, "The garden gobbled up the house" (2:78). Above all, Tarusa represents a place of emotional stability for Tsvetaeva, one closely connected with family and childhood. It was the place where she would have liked to have been buried:

> I would like to lie in the Khlystian Cemetery of the Flagellants of Tarusa, under an elderberry bush, in one of those graves with a silver dove, where the reddest and largest strawberries in our parts grow. But if this is unrealizable, if not only can I not lie there, but even the cemetery no longer exists, then I would like to have placed on one of the hills which the Kirillovnas used to climb to visit us in Pesochnoe and which we climbed to visit them in Tarusa a stone from the Tarusa quarry:
>
> here, would like to lie
MARINA TSVETAEVA.
>
> (2:84)

Akhmadulina echoes this sentiment in her poem "A Finger to the Lips" ("Palets na gubakh"): "Here SHE wanted to sleep" (75). Tarusa, then, constituted a place of imagined future rest for Tsvetaeva, if conditions permitted a real return—but they did not.

Tarusa has yet another attraction for Akhmadulina—it is a place colored

---

4. See Marina Tsvetaeva, *Volshebnyi fonar', Vtoraia kniga stikhov* (Moscow: Ole-Lukoie, 1912), 42–43.

5. Marina Tsvetaeva, *Sochineniia v dvukh tomakh*, compiled by Anna Saakiants (Moscow: Khudozhestvennaia literatura, 1980), 1:77–84.

by Tsvetaeva's green eyes. Thrice repeated is the opening line of the first poem in the "Tarusa" cycle:

> What a greenness of eyes is typical of you, however.
> Even a myriad of soles—cannot trample such grass.
> From the slope onto the Oka you once gazed:
> on the bed of the Oka lies and looks an emerald.

> Какая зелень глаз вам свойственна, однако...
> И тьмы подошв—такой травы не изомнут.
> С откоса на Оку вы глянули когда-то:
> на дне Оки лежит и смотрит изумруд.

Tsvetaeva's emerald eyes have impressed themselves on the brilliant greenery.[6]

Further, as noted in Chapter 2, there is no figure of the Muse in Akhmadulina's verse. With the conspicuous absence of a classic Muse and with the persona's probe into nature on the Oka, with the simple life there and art the collection comes close in attitude to that of Boris Pasternak toward nature as defined by Anna Akhmatova: "All his life long, nature was his full-fledged Muse, his secret interlocutor, his Bride and Beloved, his Wife and Widow—it was to him what Russia was to Blok."[7] In other words, in this collection, and in the theme of creation specifically, Akhmadulina comes close to Pasternak's art as understood by Akhmatova, with the exception of the reference to youth: "I just now understood the most frightening thing about Pasternak: he never reminisces. In the entire cycle "When it clears up" ["Kogda razguliaetsia"] he, already an old man, does not once reminisce about anything: neither his family, love, nor youth" (3:152).

Nor is Akhmadulina overly concerned with personal reminiscences. She is too busy entering the historic past and reconstructing important lives. What is more, Pasternak seems obsessed with specific current time. Indeed, in *Poems and Narratives in Verse* (*Stikhotvoreniia i poemy*) his first poem begins with the name of a month and concerns writing: "February. To get ink and

6. Note that in Akhmatova's poem "An unprecedented autumn built a high cupola" ("Nebyvalaia osen' postroila kupol vysokii"; no. 267) the words "the water became emerald-colored" ("izumrudnoiu stala voda") appear to prefigure Akhmadulina's image, which, however, refers to Tsvetaeva's eyes. Anna Akhmatova, *Stikhotvoreniia i poemy*, compiled by V. M. Zhirmunskii (Leningrad: Sovetskii pisatel', 1976), no. 267.

7. Anna Akhmatova, *Sochineniia*, 3 vols., ed. Gleb Struve, B. Filippov, and Nikita Struve, 2d ed., enlarged (Munich: Inter-Language Literary Associates, 1969–83), 3:152.

to cry!" ("Fevral'. Dostat' chernil i plakat'!").[8] He seems to use the months to convey his feelings: "to write violently about February." Akhmadulina, who never dates her poems by the year or by dates at the end of the piece (Tsvetaeva always does, Akhmatova often does, Pasternak sometimes does), is, nonetheless, similar to Tsvetaeva and Akhmatova through her acute awareness of time as months or the date, which she takes as a topic for her verse. She not only titles certain poems, using the day of the month, "Following the 27th Day of February" ("Vosled 27 dniu fevralia"), "The Day of March 12" ("Den' 12 marta"), "Following the 27th Day of March" ("Vosled 27 dniu marta"), in succession, but she makes the days of the month the main topic of some poems. In the collection *The Garden* three consecutive poems treat three specific days in a more subdued tone: "The 29th Day of February" ("29-i den' fevralia"), "The Eve of March 30th" ("Noch' na 30 marta"), and March 31 in "The Order of Blooming" ("Tsvetenii ocherednost' "). The latter also presents the appearance of long-awaited plants.

Nature, the plants, the moon, space, and even days suffuse the verse-writing process. Like Akhmatova, Akhmadulina distinguishes the process of creating, giving birth, so to speak, to verse and writing down the verse on paper. The difference is that Akhmatova's persona receives ready verse through the medium of the Muse and the various stages of creation preceding it, before writing the verse on paper and firing it to immortalize it and to individualize it, as if to free herself of her own creation. Akhmadulina's persona of the late period, conversely, must write down in verse form through effort the ineffable poetry produced on the basis of daytime impressions by nature in the night to which this vigilant speaker was a witness. There is, then, some effort on Akhmadulina's part, unlike Akhmatova who can say in "Poetic Creation" ("Tvorchestvo") on the final stage of creation following the several stages that precede it: "And simply dictated lines / Arrange themselves in a snow-white notebook" (201). So a poem that Akhmadulina wants to write down can elude her for days, at which time she may reluctantly abandon her quest to articulate a given piece (36). Throughout her efforts at creating verse, nature remains close by; an apple falls on a line of poetry in "The Night of the Falling Apples": "And I wince: an apple has fallen, on the 'NOT'—having placed a stress extrinsically" (7). What is more, a bee alights on a line of poetry; but first it appears and takes life through a simile: "The verse falls

8. Boris Pasternak, *Stikhotvoreniia i poemy*, compiled by L. A. Ozerov, Biblioteka poeta, Bol'shaia seriia (Moscow: Sovetskii pisatel', 1965), 65.

like a bee on the stalks and branches." So the bee in the simile's vehicle turns into a real bee—a way of overcoming the dichotomy of the simile by passing through the metaphor stage into reality: "a bee flew into my line."[9] Petals from a bird cherry tree fall on the poem in "Bird Cherry Last but One" ("Cheremukha predposledniaia"):

> How touchingly the petals
> on your dying day,
> on your fourth one
> fall on these poems.

> Как трогательно лепестки
> в твой день предсмертный,
> в твой четвертый
> на эти падают стихи.

> (70)

Akhmadulina thus maintains a strong interaction between nature in bloom and flourishing poetry; in other words, nature produces fruit, and poetry will also bear fruit.

Notwithstanding all reverential intertextuality with Tsvetaeva and similarities with Pasternak as well as reminiscences of Russian classic writers (Pushkin and Lermontov), Akhmadulina has in this collection raised her artistic voice to a most original note. Whereas the themes in her point of departure—Tarusa, the orchard, the moon, the snowstorm—have been nurtured by important literary predecessors, her development and enlargement of her legacy through her wondrous secret is innovative. The key to a good deal of the secret lies in the collection's opening poem.

The opening poem, "I have the secret of wondrous blooming" ("Est' taina u menia ot chudnogo tsveteniia"), and, indeed, the entire collection, are geared toward the past, toward perceiving the present and even the future through the past. Such an intense and intrusive past obscures some other, traditional aspects of poetry. Hence love for a human falls victim here—there are no love poems, nor is there romantic love in the poems or in the speaker's life within the period covered by the collection. The absence of love for a man is touched upon in the poem "The Moon until Morning" ("Luna do utra"):

---

9. On the dichotomy inherent in a simile, see my "Vehicles for Duality in Puškin's *The Bronze Horseman*: Similes and Period Lexicon," *Semiotica* 25, nos. 1/2 (1979).

What is experience? Nonsense! There is no experience
   for love.
Love *is* the absence of the past.
Oh, how naively I await the moon
on the wane of the twenty-second day of spring.

Что опыт? Вздор! Нет опыта любви.
Любовь и есть отсутствие былого.
О, как неопытно я жду луны
на склоне дня весны двадцать второго.

                           (27)

If romantic love is construed as the absence of that which is past, it stands to reason that love will have little place in a collection strongly laudatory of the past. For while love differs each time, according to the persona, nature repeats itself almost exactly in its renewal, thereby maintaining a powerful continuity in its link to the past. If there is any love lavished in the collection, it is on Akhmadulina's unique conception of the moon and to a lesser extent on the other surrogates to follow. Through this connection with the past both nature and the past become vital to the persona's sensibility. Where earlier Akhmadulina showed her persona's process of assessing and translating impressions of nature and life into her art, she now centers largely on the initial impetus for all her impressions and thoughts: namely, on the budding and growth of nature, the ties with previous art and culture, the very possibility of transmutation into poetry up to the exact moment of committing the poem to writing.

Concealment of the wondrous secret is further augmented by deletion of a stanza during initial publication. Akhmadulina wrote this deleted stanza in the copy that she inscribed to me in November 1983. Thus through deletion the message has been twice obscured in the published version. The imprint B. Akhmadulina, *Poems*, 1988 has published this poem with the formerly deleted third stanza. It has, however, a variation of one word in line two of the formerly deleted stanza three: "ustoiat' " (hold out, resist) has replaced "sdobrovat' " (come to harm), which Akhmadulina restored in the version she added to my copy of *The Secret*.[10] The reasons for the change are unknown to me. Where the poem's opaque message equates nature and life with speech, letters, writing, and literature, conversely, the Oka River distinguishes a live person and living creatures from inanimate nature as evidenced in a retort to the speaker in "Squabblings and Reconciliations":

10. Bella Akhmadulina, *Stikhotvoreniia* (Moscow: Khudozhestvennaia literatura, 1988).

You do not know what you are saying.
You are alive and not yet nature.

—Ты не ведаешь, что говоришь.
Ты жива и еще не природа.

(23)

A live person-poet can in no way affect inanimate nature but can reflect the beauty of fields and of forests, inculcating it through her aortas and turning it into speech, which is the equal of spoken verse, in preparation for its eventual transformation into written poetry. This process creates a second world, which works well enough through reflection. The mood in the poem is that of the final commitment of verse to paper at daybreak; however, the added, third stanza undercuts the assurance. The complete poem [with the deleted third stanza] reads:

> I have the secret of wondrous blooming,
> here it would have been more suitable to write:
>   wonder-filled.
> Ignorant of novelty, yellowing in the old way,
> This flower always cries out for a "iat'."[11]

> Where will I get for it the pleasure of spelling,
> Although it is primordial as the magic of speech?
> What is speech, beauty of fields and you, sylvan beauty,
>   if not the responsive labor of aortas that have imbibed
>   you?

[Only reading-and-writing and you—no other homelands are to be seen. If language is trampled—neither will all be well with you. It's growing light, horticulturist. It's growing light, gardener. Well, I too will reach out to cultivate my notebook.

> This spring I greeted all the plants.
> From inside the earth my midwife's gaze awaited them.
> I have the secret of wondrous blooming.
> And how could it not be? All that is not secret is—
>   nonsense.

11. On line 2, "wonder-filled" ("chudnogo") is spelled "chudnago," in the pre-Revolutionary manner. In 1918 the obsolete letter "iat'" (ѣ) was merged in the Russian alphabet with the letter "e." Tsvetaeva was long a champion of the discarded old orthography.

A joy is the *pervotsvet* to the sight and hearing.
Say, "Hey, *kliuchiks!*" and it will show up right away.
It will not blame you if you tease it: *baranchiks!*
     zheltukha!
And the would-be learned do honor and call it a
     bukvitsa.

O my *bukvitsa,* I keep reading your primer.
How simple is the alphabet which does not
     comprehend
that even from you I guard the secret;
your gold key will not unlock it.

I outlived the violets and saw off to old age
the ability of the lungworts to portray the sunset.
Even to my bird-cherry tree I did not disclose the
     secret,
under torture of the divinity and to his dictation.

The cherry tree has already blossomed, and the apple
     tree till tomorrow
has left its blossoming . . . and right here, contrary to
empty words, in the window, so close and suddenly
has ripened its blossom at the end of my line.

The verse falls like a bee on the stalks and branches
in order to kiss the floral nectar of names.
I no longer know: which is word and which is floret.
But the whole flower bed of earth is no denser than a
     dictionary.

In retaliation—a bee flew into my line.
The error of greedy lips has bitten into someone else's
     sweetness.
I have the secret of wondrous blooming.
But the lily of the valley will bloom—and I will blurt it
     out.

Есть тайна у меня от чудного цветенья,
здесь было б: чуднАГО—уместней написать.
Не зная новостей, на старый лад желтея,
цветок себе всегда выпрашивает «ять».

Где для него возьму услад правописанья,
хоть первороден он, как речи приворот?
Что—речь, краса полей и ты, краса лесная,
как не ответный труд вобравших вас аорт?

[Лишь грамота и вы—других ни видно родин.
Коль вытоптан язык—и вам не сдобровать.
Светает, садовод. Светает, огородник.
Что ж, потянусь и я возделывать тетрадь.]

Я этою весной все встретила растенья.
Из-под земли их ждал мой повивальный взор.
Есть тайна у меня от чудного цветенья.
И как же ей не быть? Все, что не тайна,—вздор.

Отраден первоцвет для зренья и для слуха.
—Эй, ключики!—скажи—он будет тут как тут.
Не взыщет, коль дразнить: баранчики! желтуха!
А грамотеи—чтут и буквицей зовут.

Ах, буквица моя, все твой букварь читаю.
Как азбука проста, которой невдомек,
что даже от тебя я охраняю тайну,
твой ключик золотой ее не отомкнет.

Фиалки прожила и проводила в старость
уменье медуниц изображать закат.
Черемухе моей—и той не проболталась,
под пыткой божества и под его диктант.

Уж вишня расцвела, а яблоня на завтра
оставила расцвесть... и тут же, вопреки
пустым словам, в окне, так близко и внезапно
прозрел ее цветок в конце моей строки.

Стих падает пчелой на стебли и на ветви,
чтобы цветочный мед названий целовать.
Уже не знаю я: где слово, где соцветье?
Но весь цветник земной—не гуще, чем словарь.

В отместку мне—пчела в мою строку влетела.
В чужую сласть впилась ошибка жадных уст.
Есть тайна у меня от чудного цветенья.
Но ландыш расцветет—и я проговорюсь.

Whereas the verdant grass and plants were connected with the green eyes of Tsvetaeva, the leitmotif of flowering and flowers in the poem is grounded in Tsvetaeva's surname. She is thus present in the collection before obvious mention of her name. Indeed, her name is comprised of the root "-tsvet-," spelled with the obsolete letter "iat' " in the old orthography. It will be recalled that in her poems Tsvetaeva called attention to names, specifically, of Blok, Akhmatova, and her own.[12]

The flower imagery of the surname found subtle expression in such poems of Tsvetaeva as "Love! Love! Both in convulsions and in the grave" ("Liubov'! Liubov'! I v sudorogakh i v grobe . . ."; 1:148) and "I know I will die at dawn!" ("Znaiu, umru na zare!"; 1:149), but the play on the surname is less obvious than for her first name. Akhmadulina again goes beyond her predecessor in this collection. Underscoring the image of blooming in Tsvetaeva's name, she develops it to connote flowering and flowers as the equivalent of letters and verse, and possibly of learning. Her speaker evidently moves toward an understanding of the world as comprised of letters and writing, with their interdependence and interchangeability (compare the bee, the bird-cherry tree, and the apple tree). Inasmuch as nature, despite its cyclical change and renewal, is old, so too are writing and script to the extent that the letters were seemingly dictated to man by nature (without the divine intervention propagated in Old Russian literature or in Classical Armenian literature). Whether the parallel of nature and letters was conscious on Akhmadulina's part cannot be ascertained at this point. Put simply, the introductory poem clearly reflects notions that poetry and script stem from nature and are tantamount to blooming and development.

---

12. Her own first name, Marina ("morskaia"), is reflected in several poems; among the best is "Kto sozdan iz kamnia, kto sozdan iz gliny":

> Some are created of stone, some are created of clay,—
> But I shimmer like silver and glitter!
> My business is faithlessness, my name, Marina.
> I am the perishable foam of the sea.

> Кто создан из камня, кто создан из глины,—
> А я серебрюсь и сверкаю!
> Мне дело—измена, мне имя—Марина,
> Я—бренная пена морская.
>
> (*Sochineniia*, 1:141)

It will be recalled that Aphrodite arose from the foam in the sea. Akhmadulina picks up the sea images in her poem from the "Tarusa" cycle, "Sea-ling—then go to your seas." For the significance of Pushkin's poem "To the Sea" ("K moriu"), and of the sea to Tsvetaeva, see her prose piece "My Pushkin" ("Moi Pushkin"), in which she refrains from spelling out its connection to her first name, unlike in her poetry (*Sochineniia* 2:358–66). For the poems on the names of Blok and Akhmatova, see Tsvetaeva, *Sochineniia*, 1:72, 85–86.

Hence the editor's (or rather, censor's) misconstruing of the original third stanza. Language as nature and literature, the land, its plants and people comprises the speaker's homeland.

In this first poem, the flowers demand the letter "iat' " in their spelling. Their demand is manifested through yellowing in the old way, reminiscent of ancient books, and their adherence to the old without knowledge of the new. At a loss, the persona cannot secure for the flower the pleasure ("uslad") of the old orthography. Correspondingly, she uses the obsolete masculine form ("uslad") where the feminine ("uslada") is the current norm. In the poem, the dual concepts of plants growing in a garden and words growing within the capacious word "sad" (garden, orchard) evolve as closely meshed activities: "The word [garden] is more spacious than the environs" ("Prostornei slovo [sad], chem okrestnost' "; 5). In the collection *The Garden,* the concepts undergo further development and acquire new direction. Further, the striking image of the "Deep gentle garden sloping to the Oka" enlarges through the spilling over of the garden on the river banks to the water the world of change and inspiration to all of Tarusa and, implicitly, to the world and oeuvre of Tsvetaeva. The use of this specific locus evokes the Russian past through the line "Let's remain in the garden of the past century" ("Ostanemsia v sadu minuvshego stolet'ia"; 9). With the garden as the specific environment for cultivating poetry (since the muses lived there) and the nineteenth century as the artistic ambience in which Akhmadulina now has her strongest roots, there emerges a sense of the importance of all the land and its history. Thus is Akhmadulina's poetry of this stage grounded in her visualization of the intermingling of nature and letters as the essence of life and art. Like most poems in the collection, the opening ten-stanza piece, "I have the secret of wondrous blooming," is written in quatrains. The meter is iambic hexameter. In these new poems Akhmadulina eschews obvious novelty in meter and stanzaic form in favor of tradition and uniformity. This poem marshals the prime themes, motifs, and images to be developed and revealed throughout the collection. It inaugurates the title of the persona's secret, which is fairly well guarded, despite measured release of certain aspects in an effort to tease and to spur on the reader's imagination.

Akhmadulina's cherished secret concerns wondrous blooming, not in a newfangled way, but as of old with all the religious awe for something holy; hence the appropriateness of the old Russian orthography for the verses. This blossoming of nature and life, which is translated into verse, recognizes no novelty, no drastic change other than the inevitable winter hibernation; it knows only continuity with an illustrious past: hence the persona's inclination to spell the word "wondrous" as "chudnago" using the *-ago* ending of the old orthography as well as the obsolete letter "iat' " (ѣ) for the word "flower" in the old way. Its color in turn evokes the yellowed pages of a manuscript or a yellowed book which uses the "iat'." The message here is that a flower remains a flower throughout the ages in spite of the newness of each individual flower that appears each new season. The fact that nature's secret is old inspires the persona to use the old orthography. According to the poem, speech, which equals verse obtained through the crucible of artistic talent, arises from nature; indeed, it is dependent on the beauty of fields and woods. The reflection of this beauty results in speech, following its assimilation in the speaker's aortas and, indeed, in her very being. The recording of the verse is another matter; it is treated in Akhmadulina's later poems and is addressed in the subsequent chapters. Under beauty is assumed a harmonious and nurturing essence from which may be culled the essentials for the transformation into art. It can also refer to the overall ambience, as in the poem "A Humorous Epistle to a Friend" ("Shutochnoe poslanie k drugu"), where the speaker asks her friend Bulat Okudzhava, "Why do we enter the beauty of alien places, / of someone else's days?" ("Zachem my vkhozhi / v krasu chuzbin, v chuzhie dni?"; 117).

The restored stanza equates the homeland with reading and writing, and the sources of beauty introduced earlier: speech equals verse, which stems from fields and forests; hence the people, the land with its nature, and the culture through writing and learning. If the language, which probably equals writing, is trampled, then the situation bodes ill for the all-important trinity—speech and the beauties of field and woods. As darkness fades and light grows, the persona reminds the tillers of the land, the "sadovniki" (horticulturists) and the "ogorodniki" (gardeners) to set to work. She too is impelled to cultivate her notebook to create written verse. Accordingly, through metaphor the paper (formerly the parchment) performs the role of her land, or soil, for cultivation—an image not at all new to literature— hence "no other homelands are to be seen." A horticulturist should probably work in the forest, which, due to its trees, is an uncultivated form of orchard, while a gardener should till the open fields to grow certain plants. Their efforts will turn part of these places into cultivated areas.

The first flower to be mentioned is appropriately "pervotsvet," a "joy to sight and hearing." This word can denote either the first early blossoming of plants or a specific low plant with pretty flowers of various colors. The ambiguity in name directs the poem's profile. The "pervotsvet" gladdens the persona who greets all the plants sprouting from the earth. Metaphorically, she performs the role of a midwife to facilitate the timid emergence of the plants, all of which are blooming ones. Other persons, less conversant with the natural origins of true poetry, may call forth the same flower by the name "kliuchiki." Dal"s dictionary defines the word as "a floral bunch or cluster, in which small bellflowers hang on long stalks" (2:123).[13] Further, the word "kliuchiki" in Russian sounds like a key ("kliuch"), possibly the key to the secret. The "pervotsvet," surprisingly, will not mind if it is teased as "baranchiki" or "zheltukha." The many definitions of "baranchik" include "kliuchiki" and white "bukvitsa." "Zheltukha" is listed in dictionaries only as the illness "yellow jaundice," but it could well have the meaning of a yellow flower (one educated native speaker of Russian uses it to mean "dandelion") in some local parlances, and a close variant, the diminutive "zheltushka" has, among other definitions, the meaning "zheltyi-tsvet" (yellow flower).

Now the speaker turns ironic toward would-be learned people who will revere the plant and call it "bukvitsa." The meaning of a letter ("bukva") or written characters peeks out of the plant. In Dal"s dictionary "bukvitsa" is listed as "old alphabet, primer; currently the old Slavic letters are called so to distinguish them from Glagolitic [the original script for Slavic invented in the ninth century by Cyril and Methodius] and from other most recent ones; . . . white *bukvitsa*, . . . *kliuchiki, baranchiki*" (1:139). Addressing the flower "bukvitsa," the speaker insists that she continues perusing its primer, that each flower contains sufficient information to instruct in the basics of life and art, particularly this specific flower. However, the speaker keeps to herself the secret of the simple alphabet—a secret not divulged even to the plant "bukvitsa" itself, a secret that the bukvitsa's gold key will not open or unlock, a reference to "kliuchiki" (keys) is evident here. I will later attempt to unravel the mystery with which the speaker is taunting the plant and her readers.

The principal secret, then, is the blossoming of plants, probably as viewed by a poet. The theme of the poet viewing nature (the moon, space, etc.) through the window unfolds in *The Secret* with a view to poetic creation. Other aspects of the secret will unfold with the progression of the collection, but in the first poem the wondrous blossoming initially focuses on a single yellow flower. With the image of the yellow flower figures the yellowed

13. Vladimir Dal', *Tolkovyi slovar' zhivogo velikorusskogo iazyka*, 4 vols. (Reprint, Moscow: Russkii iazyk, 1978), 2:123.

paper or parchment and use of the old orthography. Akhmadulina employs the masculine form of "uslada," which according to Ushakov's dictionary is bookish and poetic, if indeed the form is not the genitive plural form of the common feminine gender word. It would then mean "orthographies of delight," a less likely rendition than "the pleasure of orthography is as primary as the enchantment of speech." By rendering simultaneous the pleasure of orthography and speech, Akhmadulina equates them more firmly with nature, the twin beauties of fields and woods—and the responsive work of the human body and mind. They impress themselves on the speaker. In effect, she converts visual images into phonetic and ideational ones that depict reflected visual images before converting to visual symbolic images of script, which are letters conveying meaning that in turn equal nature. A full cycle is achieved.

Accordingly, "pervotsvet," which denotes the first early blossoming of flowers as well as a plant with pretty flowers of various colors, is a joy to sight and hearing. It is probably the first flower to be noticed by the speaker in the early spring. Through the phrase "hey, kliuchiks" ("ei, kliuchiki") the speaker hopes the beauty of the woods will induce the appearance of the flowers. She prays that the "pervotsvet" will forgive her for mocking it as "baranchiki" and "zheltukha." By contrast, would-be literate men will call the plant "bukvitsa" out of respect, its name alone elevating it to the pinnacle of learning. So these flowering plants sound like letters or the alphabet—a key to reading and learning—or conjure up the form of letters—"baranchik" in form might be said to equal an "o" (cf. "baranka," a small bagel, or *bublik* in Russian). Furthermore, these plants, "pervotsvet," "kliuchik," "baranchik," "zheltukha," and "bukvitsa," all denote the same flower, as expected from the translations in Dal'. Segal's *Russian-English Dictionary* likewise supports the premise of one flower.[14] It defines "pervotsvet" as "primrose" (the English word's etymology means "first rose"), "baranchik" as "officinal primrose, cowslip" (a common British primrose), and "belaia bukvitsa" as "primrose, cowslip." "Zheltukha" does not have this definition anywhere; it is, however, connected at least visually with the flowers through a definition in Dal' of "baranchiki" as "kotovnik" and "koshach'ia miata," that is, "catnip," which has yellow flowers. Thus in my translation of this poem into English it would have been correct to use "primrose" instead of "pervotsvet," but then one part of Akhmadulina's secret would have been revealed without clarification and

---

14. Louis Segal, *New Complete Russian-English Dictionary* (New Orthography), 3d ed., revised and enlarged (London: Lund Humphries, 1946).

her play on words and nuances would have been lost. Specifically, the use of "primrose" in stanza 5 (4 in the first published version) would have obscured the meaning of "first bloom" and that of the "primacy of Tsvetaeva" inherent in the meaning of the Russian word's two roots "perv" and "tsvet." Moreover, the "zheltukha" reflects the yellow flower image at the beginning of the poem and Tsvetaeva's golden hair.[15]

The mining of esthetic riches may well be for poets alone. Only one close to art and nature, as the lyric persona in Tarusa, can keep perusing the primer with its essentials of life in one flower, which through its many names reaches out to various subtleties of meaning. The gold key to the poet's secret is the plants and life, the observation of nature that only a poet can transform through artistic cultivation into written words and verse.

A poem in progress evokes the process of a bee culling nectar from the flowers as shown in the simile in the poem "I have the secret of wondrous blooming." In literary terms the image evokes Osip Mandel'shtam (whose poetry figures later as a tome; 60), which in turn evokes classical literature, as Kiril Taranovsky discusses in his "Bees and Wasps: Mandel'štam and Vjačeslav Ivanov."[16] Words and floscules ("sotsvet'ia") merge, as in a simile, but the entire earthly flower garden is no more rich than a dictionary. So soil equals a flower garden ready for the poet to cultivate in preparation for making available the information through the instrument of her verse. Akhmadulina parallels the classic image of the poet/bee and honey/poetry, but the bee is not the verse since now the persona develops her simile into an extended metaphor, making both the bee and the verse tangible. The bee bites into someone else's sweetness, metonymically connoting nectar or honey. Figuratively, it probably denotes the verse legacy of other poets, which Akhmadulina propagates through allusions and intertextuality. At this point the speaker stops abruptly, despite the soothing structural encircling of line 1, lest the lily of the valley bloom before she is prepared for it and she involuntarily make a lapse of the tongue. A somewhat ironical, even ominous ending to a serene beginning.

Thus "pervotsvet" gladdens the eye and ear as would the delicate sounds

---

15. It is noteworthy that Pasternak makes use of the meaning behind a plant's name in his poem "Devochka" ("Young Girl"), which links the plant's name "drema" with its meaning of drowsiness. See Pasternak *Stikhotvoreniia i poemy*, 115. Moreover, Akhmadulina names the flower "drema" in her poem "The Order of Blooming," in *The Garden* (29).

16. In Kiril Taranovsky, *Essays on Mandel'štam* (Cambridge: Harvard University Press, 1976), 86–87.

of gentle new plants, stirring in the air and in the wind, as well as chirping birds, animals, and insects; it also conjures up a specific plant whose image is augmented through the other names for it to follow; what is more, it evokes Tsvetaeva. Playing on the ambiguity of polysemy in the words, Akhmadulina crafts her dual, though comparable imagery. What seems like teasing or sophistry is actually the name for the plants "pervotsvet," "kliuchik," "baranchik," "zheltukha, "bukvitsa"—all of them flowering ones—that in fact signify the same plant—the primrose. "Bukvitsa" is probably the primrose's most "literary" name, since it sounds like a letter of the alphabet. An early cultured flowering plant, it lends itself to being a primer, as it were, of plants and nature. More familiar flowers follow in the poem. Their presence emphasizes flower semantics for the previous panolpy of plant names, which in the proper context denote only one plant, but each of which can locally signify several others. The familiar flowers are the violet, the lungwort (so obviously linked to Mandel'shtam), the bird-cherry tree (a favorite of Pasternak, Esenin, and Pushkin) that has blossomed, as well as the apple tree that will blossom later, and the lily of the valley whose blooming threatens disclosure of the secret. Actually because these are all one plant, although each plant can signify several others locally, this fact of one that can branch out makes one wonder if Akhmadulina is not trying to promote the notion of one body of universal poetry on earth with different, local variations for better appreciation within a given country or language. The flowers in nature with their sweet nectar mingle with the written poetic line: "where the word is or where the floret is." The names, i.e., the words of the flowers, contain nectar to which the verse, like a bee, can apply itself. As revenge for her verse falling upon the branches like a bee to kiss the flowery nectar of names, a real bee flies into the persona's line of verse. Reality, it would seem, forces entry into art even after its transformation into verse. Ostensibly, the persona resists, possibly, because as possessor of the secret of wondrous blooming, she fears a lapse of tongue with the flowering of the herald of spring, the pure lily of the valley.

Ultimately, Akhmadulina's collection of verse, *The Secret*, marks a new stage in the development of her verse through concentration and intensification of the theme of poetic creation. Nature, comprised of letters, assumes a leading role through its alter ego—verse, the multifarious artistic refraction of speech, learning, and culture.

Following the speaker's disclosure that the secret to art, learning, and letters is nature herself and the poet's ability to make use of it through multilevel communion with nature, the next stage to the disclosure becomes the speaker's attempt to create verse at night by observing the moon, a veritable Muse in the context of creating verse at Tarusa. The following chapter traces the speaker's tense relationship with the moon in her quest for ever more distinctive poetry that will reveal the innermost secrets of nature and in the process capture its unusual ephemeral beauty.

4

The Moon as a Medium for Art

Inspiration

I waited
Pen in hand
For the Muse
To visit me . . .

Meanwhile
I penned
These words
To kill time!

Whereupon the Muse
Arrived and said:
"I see you did not
Need me after all . . ."
—Mischa Kudian

Anyone who reads or writes on the moon in literature may well wonder whether there is anything left to be said on this pervasive topic, that is, until becoming familiar with Bella Akhmadulina's collection *The Secret*.[1] A preview of some crucial moments in the treatment of the moon in literature will serve toward appreciating the innovation introduced by this poet. "It all began with the moon," as Akhmadulina so aptly puts it; that is, her inclination toward verse concerning the particular subjects in this collection, and her inspiration for it, which she appears to have exhausted for the time being.

Following an overview of the moon in literature, the focus of this chapter will be the moon's role and symbolism in Akhmadulina's untold "secret" as well as its function in advancing the secret from another aspect. It will be studied on the basis of six consecutive poems in *The Secret*. The first part of

1. Bella Akhmadulina, *Taina. Novye stikhi* (Moscow: Sovetskii pisatel', 1983).

the secret, as seen in the previous chapter, lies in speech equaling the beauty of field and forest through plants that were identical to writing and the transformation of speech through the creative labors of the poet as well as her comprehension of the primer of life transforming into art as its due and deserved state. Following the introduction of the garden, of the town of Tarusa, and of the Oka River in the collection, the moon's first appearance is noted at midnight in the poem title "Moon over Tarusa" ("Luna v Taruse"). Thereafter, it figures prominently in a sequence of five more poems with its function intensifying to a state of virtual crystalization, namely, in "The Coffee Imp," "Squabblings and Reconciliations," "The Moon until Morning," "The Morning after the Moon," and "February Full Moon." In *The Garden*, which continues the waning Tarusa theme, several more poems address the moon, notably "Why does he pace? I like to alone" ("Zachem on khodit? Ia liubliu odna"; 45–48), "To the Moon from a Jealous Person" ("Lune ot revnivtsa"; 16–17), "The Eve of March 30" ("Noch' na 30 marta"; 26–27), and "The Guiding Sound" ("Zvuk ukazuiushchii"; 49). While the Tarusa theme as the locus of sojourn for the speaker is concentrated in the collection's first part, it turns up later as well. The focus here will be on two of the moon's aspects: its function in creating verse and the quality of the artistic moon, i.e., the appearance of a different one each night.

Throughout the ages man has looked up at the moon, studying it, admiring it, and fearing it. Through study he has learned to measure time by it. In folklore the moon serves magical purposes. In literature it has comprised part of the nightscape, particularly in the Romantic period. It has enhanced feelings of love and beauty as well as mystery, and in the Gothic tale it has served as an aid to magic or to witness the horrors. The roles of this celestial body and satellite to the Earth are many.

The role of the moon in English literature has been studied by Roger Wray in his essay "The Moon in Literature." The important thing about the moon, he maintains, is that "she shares our secrets—secrets that are too good to tell. The moon may be 600,000 times less brilliant than the sun. If so, it matters nothing. The vital difference between them is that the sun is epic while the moon is lyric. . . . The supreme point is that the sun is masculine and the moon feminine. . . . The sun gives light; the moon gives illusion."[2] Obviously, in Russian literature the feminine quality of the moon is enhanced by the grammatical gender of "luna" in contrast to the masculine, often more poetic word for the moon "mesiats," which also means

2. Roger Wray, "The Moon in Literature," *The Atlantic Monthly*, March 1922, 367.

"month." Wray continues on man's perception of the moon: "Always there is this association of glamour and witchery with moonlight; and as long as the moon endures, the common people will believe in that elusive beauty which restores the illusions banished by day. . . . But literature reminds us that the moon is a big symbol, a toy left over from some primeval revelry, a lamp more magical than Aladdin's" (368).

Part of literature since its very dawn, the moon has had diverse roles in English literature. Richard S. Salant in his essay "The Poet's Harp: A Study of the Moon in the Poetry of Wordsworth, Coleridge, Shelley, Byron, and Keats," places as epigraph the words from Keats's *Endymion*—"The sage's pen—The poet's harp."[3] Tracing the image of the moon in the works of these poets, Salant finds that Wordsworth, lover of the complete and the fulfilled, most often saw the full moon, plain and clear. Wordsworth's is the generic moon: full, soft, gentle, very moral, and good. It is the moon that all good people see. It is the voice of the common man. Coleridge's moon is more intense, its rays burn; it is restless. Coleridge finds the peculiarities, the deviations from the usual in the moon. He is a sensational colorist. In constant sharp motion, Coleridge's is a "journeying moon." Moonlight is a source of magic for him. In Shelley's moon all independence between the external object and man's emotions disappears. Veiled behind clouds, feminine, and tenuous, its light has the power of filling the poet's world, his poetry, and his soul. Moonlight makes all things ethereal. Shelley perceived the waning moon as a symbol of death. He writes not about but as the moon. Byron brings the moon to earth through sheer admiration of its beauty. For Keats the moon is connected with poetic inspiration. The moon is the very source of his poetry; he called the moon "maker of sweet poets." For Keats its light "let loose those subconscious promptings which are the genesis of all poetry." The moon was Keats's "tutelary goddess," the embodiment of his ideal love. Akhmadulina begins from here.

Salant maintains that while before Romanticism, others wrote of the moon—Homer, Sappho, Lucretius, Virgil, Cynewulf, Chaucer, Sidney, and Shakespeare—for the English Romantics it was an intense moon, the very stuff of which poems are made, and reached further into the heart of poetry. In the moon they sought a release from worldly things; they sought the infinite. Poets attached to the moon their personal philosophies and emotions ("The Poet's Harp," 29).

3. Richard S. Salant, "The Poet's Harp: A Study of the Moon in the Poetry of Wordsworth, Coleridge, Shelley, Byron, and Keats" (Thesis, Harvard University, 1935).

The diverse role of the moon in Russian literature remains to be more fully defined in scholarship. Vsevolod Setchkarev, in his *Studies in the Life and Works of Innokentij Annenskij,* comments on the poet Annenskii's approach to the moon in his poetry: "There is no doubt that the moon and its uncertain light have a constant appeal for Annenskij. The moon is often connected by him to Hekate, the enchantress of Greek popular religion, and *koldovat'* is the verb he uses most often to characterize its influence."[4] The scholar then draws a parallel between Annenskii's poem "The Moon" ("Mesiats") and Shelley's poem "The Moon." Apart from the moon's uncertain light, Setchkarev observes its yellow and sickly nature in Annenskii (107). Akhmadulina's unusual perception of the moon is innovative for any literature. In her collection *The Secret* she develops the function and symbolism of the moon, drawing on the classic legacy of Pushkin in particular. Perceiving the moon like Keats as the very source of her poetry for certain poems in the collection, Akhmadulina charts her own path of discovery through the moon's tutelage.

The moon in "Moon over Tarusa" seems to serve as the boundary between the days (*sutki*—a twenty-four-hour period); the contrast of sunlight with the moonlight is a further subdivision. Only in the moonlit period is the new day conceived and nurtured; namely, during this particular time from midnight until dawn; whereas the official demarcation between the days remains the mundane changing of the date on the stamp in the post office. This mechanical procedure takes but a moment at midnight, yet in the poet's mind the time from midnight to dawn constitutes a period free from the confines of the previous day as well as of the following day, a sort of "no man's time." Midnight, the magical moment for the moon, opens the poem:

Twelve o'clock. The tenth day of July
has been exhausted, the eleventh has not been begun.

Двенадцать часов. День июля десятый
исчерпан, одиннадцатый—не почат.

(19)

4. Vsevolod Setchkarev, *Studies in the Life and Works of Innokentij Annenskij* (The Hague: Mouton, 1963), 94. See also my article "Moon over Akhmatovaland: With a View toward Pushkin," in *The Speech of Unknown Eyes: Akhmatova's Readers on Her Poetry,* ed. Wendy Rosslyn, 2 vols. (Nottingham: Astra, 1990), 2:303–13.

In terms of imagery Akhmadulina's moon with its streaming beams is a flowing, flaming body, physically close and emotionally more needed than the flame in the candle immediately before her. All told, the moon imagery conjures up a nighttime variant of the Oka River, whose brilliance reflects on the candle and on the speaker. The glaring moonlight burns her eyes covered for protection by her palm and colors her skin with the "tan of mermaids":

> of the moon that singes my eye through my palm,
> that colors my skin with the tan of mermaids,

> луны, опаляющей глаз сквозь ладонь,
> загаром русалок окрасившей кожу,

Enveloping her forehead in a silver frame, it shines eerily like phosphorus. The reference to mermaids and to whiteness in moonlight tacitly evokes Pushkin's unfinished drama in verse "The Mermaid" ("Rusalka"), in which the moon "warms" the mermaids:

> In a merry group
> From the deep bottom
> We swim up at night,
> The moon warms us,

> Веселой толпою
> С глубокого дна
> Мы ночью всплываем,
> Нас греет луна.[5]

Pushkin's presence will gradually build up to a crescendo at the collection's conclusion, whereas Tsvetaeva's presence will reach its apogee in the middle of the collection before slowly fading away prior to the concluding poem with the advent of winter and the end of bloom and growth in nature's flora.

For Akhmadulina's persona the moon pours forth a creative fire, conceivably through its beams: "my hand-wrought fire" ("moi rukotvornyi ogon' ") . . . "shines the feat of my soul" ("svetitsia podvig dushi"). A simile likening the moon to a Christmas tree ornament brings out the

---

5. A. S. Pushkin, *Polnoe sobranie sochinenii v desiati tomakh,* ed. B. V. Tomashevskii (Moscow: AN SSSR, 1962–66), 5:444.

festiveness of the scene that promotes new life as well as its restriction of
the season to Christmas:

> All night long for an unknown goal
> senselessly shines the feat of the soul,
> as if on the branch of a Christmas fir
> someone hung a ball for beauty and left.

> Всю ночь напролет для неведомой цели
> бессмысленно светится подвиг души,
> как будто на ветку рождественской ели
> повесили шар для красы и ушли.

It appears that in compliance with the spirit of yore (and Akhmatova's usage in
the poem "Excerpts from the Poema of Tsarskoe Selo 'Russian Trianon' "—
"Otryvki iz Tsarskosel'skoi poemy "Russkii Trianon" "; no. 632),[6] the
speaker refrains from using the then current term for a Christmas tree,
"novogodniaia elka" (literally, "a New Year's fir"). Bathed in the moonlight,
the poetic speaker herself tries to compose verse:

> Accomplice and sycophant to the moonlight,
> I watch how on the paper a line
> lives by itself.

> Сообщник и прихвостень лунного света,
> смотрю, как живет на бумаге строка
> сама по себе.

> (19–20)

The self-creating poetic lines, apparently induced by the moonlight,
bring to mind the lines in Akhmatova's poem "Poetic Creation" ("Tvorchestvo"; no. 333)—"And simply dictated lines / Arrange themselves in the
snow-white notebook" ("I prosto prodiktovannye strochki / Lozhatsia v
belosnezhnuiu tetrad' ")—as well as Dante to whom the Muse dictated
verse in the words of Akhmatova in her poem "Muse" ("Muza"; no. 301)—
"I say to her, 'Was it you who dictated to Dante / The pages on hell?' She
answers, 'I did' " ("Ei govoriu: 'Ty l' Dantu diktovala / Stranitsy ada?'

6. Anna Akhmatova, *Stikhotvoreniia i poemy*, compiled by V. M. Zhirmunskii (Leningrad:
Sovetskii pisatel', 1976).

Otvechaet: 'Ia' "). In Akhmatova and Akhmadulina alike, the verse emerges after midnight. Yet while in Akhmatova the final dictation by her Muse was preceded by several stages of requisite preconditions, which are like religious passions that the persona underwent, in Akhmadulina the verse of this period often originates in the moonlight with the speaker as observer and only later as assimilator and artistic "chronicler."[7] The process of observing the verse self-create in Akhmadulina, labeled "bezdeistvie" (inactivity) for her due to the moonlight taking charge, is stronger, more powerful than an individual action and sweeter than the fact of the completed verse. It is somewhat akin to Dostoevsky's famous words on discovery in progress being more fulfilling than its result: "Columbus was happy while he was discovering America and not when he discovered it."

Akhmadulina's speaker seems to become the moon's moon; that is, just as the moon shines with light reflected from the sun, she too reflects the moon's light in the state of creating verse:

> I torment the trusting mind of the fisherman,
> when, having kindled the wax star,
> I soar upwards in the timbered mortar of the balcony,
> having surrendered to the glow as if to work.

> Я мучу доверчивый ум рыболова,
> когда, запалив восковую звезду,
> взмываю в бревенчатой ступе балкона,
> предавшись сверканью, как будто труду.

The state is quite similar to glowing from the moon. Her candle glows like a Christmas tree ornament ("zapaliv voskovuiu zvezdu") as she sits on the balcony observing the moon. Also, the persona basks in the glow of the moonlight. She therefore reflects the moon twice or more powerfully—by glowing in its light and by writing down verse created under its auspices.

At dawn, having shared through affinity and wakeful presence the night-time labor and ordeal of the moon ("trud i mytarstvo"), the exhausted persona snuffs out her candle, a veritable crystal ball, a magical tool for enlisting the moon's aid in the ultimate poetic creation. Sharing the moon's

---

7. See Anna Akhmatova, *Sochineniia v dvukh tomakh,* ed. V. A. Chernykh, 2d ed., corrected and enlarged (Moscow: Khudozhestvennaia literatura, 1990), 1:471. It indicates that in reality Akhmatova the poet created in her mind and wrote down a fairly polished version only.

labor and ordeal alleviates the speaker's own poetic efforts. Thus now, by contrast to previous collections of verse, the persona burns and glows, evoking Annenskii's line in the poem "Dear One" ("Milaia")—"For grief even at night the road is light" ("Goriu i noch'iu doroga svetla")—a line taken up by Akhmatova's speaker in certain of her key poems. The speaker's state of glowing in Akhmadulina is, however, the burning of the moon's "heat" and light, implausible though it may sound to the practical mind. It probably derives initially from Pushkin's short poem "The Mermaid," in which the mermaid's two appearances coincide with the moon in the clouds. The first time it is "krasnyi mesiats," in which the poet uses the older, more poetic word for the moon to correspond with the older meaning of the adjective as "beautiful," which in modern Russian means "red" and for the modern reader presents an ambivalent beautiful-red image. The second appearance uses the current word for moon "luna": "The moon went among the clouds." Here the whiteness of a mermaid's skin almost casts off a milky glow similar to the moon:

> And suddenly . . . light as a nocturnal shade,
> White as the early snow of the hills,
> A naked woman emerges
> And silently sits by the banks.

> И вдруг . . . легка, как тень ночная,
> Бела, как ранний снег холмов,
> Выходит женщина нагая
> И молча села у брегов.

> (1:363–64)

As far as the treatment of the creative process is concerned, there is much dissimilarity between Akhmadulina and Akhmatova. In the latter the Muse is most frequently an indispensible stage between prayer to the Muse—an ancient Greek deity—and the song to be transformed into written finalized verse. The Muse is a helper in the creation of poetry. In Akhmadulina, on the other hand, there is no Muse, no ancient Greek deity.

In the following poem, "The Coffee Imp" ("Kofeinyi chertik"), coffee dregs become the lyrical persona's accomplice—"soobshchnik-gushcha." The dregs unleash their own black imp—"chernyi chertik," who plays tricks on the speaker. The poem that is coming into existence, or being, grows pensive with this mood, that is, with its pensiveness encompassing the window, the remoteness of the snow and the ravine:

> The verse pondered over the window, the remoteness
>   of the snow, and the ravine,
> and apparently forgot about the demon in [its/her]
>   mind.
>
> Стих вдумался в окно, в глушь снега и оврага,
> и, видимо, забыл про чертика в уме.

(21)

Having returned from afar (possibly from the moon where it originated), the poem has still not matured, but the speaker leaves it to its own devices, seeing that it knows best. After all, the poem enveloped within itself Tarusa and the night, and extracted her, the speaker, from useless days:

> It [the verse] flew far away, returned, but didn't grow
>   up.
> Let it think what it wants, it always knows best.
> After all, it surmised how to cut out and to steal
> Tarusa, the night, (and) me from useless days.
>
> Он далеко летал, вернулся, но не вырос.
> Пусть думает свое, ему всегда видней.
> Ведь догадался он, как выкроить и выкрасть
> Тарусу, ночь, меня из бесполезных дней.

Whatever its merits, the speaker admonishes the imp to be still:

> Let the verse be silent near its moon.
> While it is implementing its self-creation,
> I like to watch its labor from a distance.
>
> It never troubled me in the least.
> It composes its own—I write down with my pen.
>
> Дай помолчать стиху вблизи его луны.
> Покуда он вершит свое само-творенье,
> люблю на труд его смотреть со стороны.

Меня он никогда не утруждал нимало.
Он сочинит свое—я напишу пером.

Accordingly, here in Akhmadulina the verse self-creates at night with the observing persona sitting by a burning candle with a cup of coffee and with the moonlight pouring on the balcony. The candle allows her to watch the written verse as it appears on the paper and to monitor its progress. Curiously, in one instance verse is perceived as being hatched in nature. The image of verse hatching in nature will be picked up and amplified in the concept of day as deity in subsequent poems, which are treated in Chapter 5. This secret incubation period is possibly compared to the span from midnight to dawn. Verse, then, is grown in the marshy backwaters of haze ("zavod' mgly") by the Oka River:

Who conceived in the sleepless pupil (of the eye)
a backwater of haze, where the word is hatched.

Возымевшей в бессонном зрачке
заводь мглы, где выводится слово.[8]

(24)

Importantly, the persona perceives, gets to know and to understand the real, artistic Tarusa through verse; even her relations with the Oka River will be aired first in verse:

What the squabblings and reconciliations between me
    and the
Oka portend for me,
I'll find out from another line,
not from this poem.

Что сулят мне меж мной и Окой
препирательства и примиренья—
от строки я узнаю другой,
не из этого стихотворенья.

(26)

Indeed, poetry, or better art, is always produced by nature if not around the clock, then all day long, and that which is created by day is "processed"

8. The word "vyvodit' " is used for chicks, tadpoles, etc., where hatching is observed.

(or "hatched") into verbal poetry at night—from midnight to dawn—under the watchful direction of the moon and the inquisitive scrutiny of the speaker. The attitude of Akhmadulina's lyrical ego is evocative of Annenskii. In fact, the magical crepuscular moment in Annenskii—twilight before darkness—when the "lilac mist" comes into play could have prompted in Akhmadulina her own reverse, mirror image of this time of day. She will employ this particular time later in the collection for her unique concept of day.[9] But to transform nature's endeavors into a finite poetic composition, the speaker must subsequently labor in the early hours of the dawn to capture the final, honed results in Russian verse. Thus art and poetry, created continually in and by nature, are infinite. Only precious brief moments are committed to paper by the poet to emerge as individual and independent poems. Her constant efforts notwithstanding, the poet is able to produce a poem only on certain days and under optimal conditions. What is not articulated by her speaker is whether the moon creates in a universal artistic language that the speaker must translate into her native Russian verse, or whether the moon communicates with her in Russian. (One would expect the former were it not for the notion of "Pushkin's moon," which I will discuss in Chapter 9.)

The second function of the moon in Akhmadulina's verse concerns the number of moons. The poems in *The Secret* reveal that the moon is not one for the poet, but many. Indeed, there is one moon for each day that the persona writes about in verse, if not for each day of the month. Just as at this point each poem that Akhmadulina's speaker tries to write by vigilant nightly observation treats a particular day of the month, so too each night and poem has its own moon. Although certain titles of poems display dates, years have always been conspicuously absent at the end of Akhmadulina's poems. Among the few titles containing dates, still without years, are: "Following the 27th Day of February" ("Vosled 27 dniu fevralia"), "The Day of March 12" ("Den' 12 marta"), and "Following the 27th Day of March" ("Vosled 27 dniu marta").

In the poem "The Coffee Imp" the speaker savors observing the process of the poem's self-construction in the moonlight. "The Coffee Imp" continues evolving from the preceding poem the notion of the poem's indepen-

---

9. Setchkarev, in *Studies in the Life*, identifies twilight as an important moment in Annenskii (91). Interestingly, on 26 March 1987, I mentioned to Bella Akhmadulina that I discerned the influence of Annenskii in this collection, along with the four poets she acknowledged; her only reply was, "I like Annenskii very much." Yet the next day in giving an interview to Bruce McCabe of *The Boston Globe*, she listed Annenskii among her influences. See *The Boston Globe*, 28 March 1987, 16.

dence from the speaker-poet: "the line lives all by itself" ("zhivet stroka sama po sebe"). Conversely, Akhmatova had to fire her poems for their independent life (Ketchian, *The Poetry of Anna Akhmatova*, 29–36). There is allegedly little inconvenience to the speaker who merely jots down whatever lines the poems feel like creating for presentation to the world by her speaker. The words "Let the verse be quiet in the proximity of its moon"— move in the direction of the moon being a Muse of sorts, since the verse creates itself in proximity to the moonlight with the poet as an interested onlooker, possibly for better assimilation of what is later to be committed to paper. She thus merely documents and edits in final form that which has already been created: "It composes its own—I will write (down) with my pen." In this way, in certain poems the moon performs, as it were, the role of a surrogate Muse, as well as serves as a catalyst for poetry, where previously in Akhmadulina there was a marked absence of any Muse. Her feeling of emotional attachment to the moon that promotes the process of poetic creation is tantamount to the attitude of most poets toward their Muse. Pushkin and Akhmatova come to mind most readily. For instance, in the poem "To Del'vig" ("Del'vigu"), Pushkin artfully attenuates irony toward his critics and the censor by referring playfully to his Muse:

> It used to be that whatever I wrote
> Never smelled of Rus' for some;
> No matter what I request of the censorship,
> Timpovskii groans about everything.
> Now I barely, barely breathe,
> My Muse is fading from abstinence,
> And rarely, rarely do I sin with her.

> Бывало, что ни напишу,
> Всё для иных не Русью пахнет;
> Об чем цензуру ни прошу,
> Ото всего Тимковский ахнет.
> Теперь едва, едва дышу,
> От воздержанья муза чахнет,
> И редко, редко с ней грешу.

$$(2{:}34)$$

In fact, as mentioned earlier, there is no romantic love for a person in this collection nor does romantic love coexist with the theme of poetic creation in any of Akhmadulina's early poems. In the collection *The Garden,* on the other hand, the speaker articulates love for Akhmadulina's husband Boris Messerer in the poem "I gift you this notebook" ("Dariu tebe siiu tetrad' "; 74).[10] In it the poetic speaker and the poet come very close together. Also, the speaker distinguishes between her own personal moon and the one shining over Boris's studio in the Arbat district of Moscow in order to unite the speaker (who merges with the poet as much as a fantastic speaker can) and Boris in an embrace:

> I correlate my moon
> with the moon known in the Arbat,—
> it results in an embrace
> with you. I love you.

> Соотношу мою луну
> с луной, известной на Арбате,—
> и получается объятье
> с тобою. Я тебя люблю.

If there is any love in these poems, other than for literary antecedents, it is lavished on the moon with a hint later for day. In the poem "The Moon until Morning" ("Luna do utra") the persona negates any advantage from the experience of previous romantic love insofar as each time it differs:

> What is experience? Nonsense. There is no experience
>   of love.
> Love is precisely an absence of the past.
> Oh, how unpracticed I await the moon
> on the wane of spring's day of the twenty-second.

> Что опыт? Вздор! Нет опыта любви.
> Любовь и есть отсутствие былого.
> О, как неопытно я жду луны
> на склоне дня весны двадцать второго.

(27)

With the moon as the object of her love, the speaker's nerves grow shaky and raw:

10. Bella Akhmadulina, *Sad. Novye stikhi* (Moscow: Sovetskii pisatel', 1987).

What can I call the behavior of my nerves?
They tear with their teeth any epithet.

Как поведенье нервов назову?
Они зубами рвут любой эпитет.

This coming to life of the nerves as a realized metaphor is reminiscent of Akhmadulina's early narrative poem *Chills*[11] and of the young Vladimir Maiakovskii's *A Cloud in Trousers* (*Oblako v shtanakh*) where his lyrical ego awaits his love Mariia.[12]

At this time the moon becomes endangered by a golden threat ("opasnost' zolotaia")—evidently the rising sun:

Over there,
on that side is the golden threat.
Get away from it! Following on my heels
a whirlwind pursues, flapping the table's covering.

The flurry of frightened sheets
I catch artlessly, as if a blizzard or a flock.
The top of the scorching heat breathes
fire from the forests—
much stronger and more vividly than I know.

Вон там,
в той стороне опасность золотая.
Прочь от нее! За мною по пятам
вихрь следует, покров стола взметая.

Переполох испуганных листов
спроста ловлю, словно метель иль стаю.
Верх пекла огнедышит из лесов—
еще сильней и выпуклей, чем знаю.

(28)

The images of the sheets and of the blizzard will be taken up in earnest in Chapter 6.

Given the fact of the moon's changes in color and shape through its

11. Bella Akhmadulina, *Sny o Gruzii* (Tbilisi: Merani, 1979).
12. Vladimir Maiakovskii (1893–1930) was a poet of the Revolution who discarded the exclamatory style of his early lyrics for a declamatory verse acceptable to the Soviet regime.

phases as viewed from earth, Roger Wray comments on the artistic reflection of the moon's changes in literature:

> There are hundreds of moons of varying phase and color, and every one of them suggests a different feeling. . . . It is common enough to hear of a yellow moon. . . . Hardy talks of a "chrome-yellow" moon . . . the more distinctive color gives a more exact emotion. It gives one a rich feeling that evades definition. Hugh Walpole speaks of an "apricot-tinted moon," and yet again of "the pale primrose of a crescent moon." . . . Compton Mackenzie has described "an ivory moon shimmering in the blue dusk." . . . Oscar Wilde . . . describes a "honey-colored moon hanging in the indigo dusk." ("The Moon in Literature," 368–69)

Conscious of the interrelation between heavenly bodies, Akhmadulina's speaker perceives the sun in the moon, since the sun "feeds" the moon: "Like a changeling moves the moon, / having enfolded the irreversible heavenly body" (28). The speaker hopes to repay the sun's largess in "fueling" the moon by returning new poems to it in the morning, but no more than one poem each morning. The portrayal of the slowly rising sun is lovingly minute in detail:

> (And, by the way, there, beyond the glimmering line
> of both the moonlit night and of the poem,
> I will meet the sun hidden from sight
> that exudes this redness.
>
> With all its full-bloodedness having nourished the
>   moon,
> It will remain all day in pale absence.
> I saw! I will repay its debt
> with the poems that arrive after these.)
>
> (И, кстати, там, за брезжущей чертой
> и лунной ночи, и стихотворенья,
> истекшее[13] вот этой краснотой,
> я встречу солнце, скрытое от зренья.

---

13. Akhmadulina is playing on the etymology of the word "istekat'," which literally means "to flow out," hence "to bleed" or nourish with its lifeblood, as well as "expire" and *elapse*," as in time. For the sun it also means the "past sun."

> Всем полнокровьем выкормив луну,
> оно весь день пробудет в блеклых нетях.
> Я видела! Я долг ему верну
> стихами, что наступят после этих.)

True enough, another stanza addresses the sacrifice of the sun in nourishing the moon. And the rising moon changes color with attained height—to a pale weightlessness:

> Immediately the moon changes color
> to a dull silver and a special one.
> Or in order to move up is it simply
> convenient" to turn paler and more weightless.

> Немедленно луна меняет цвет
> на мутно-серебристый и особый.
> Иль просто ей, чтоб продвигаться вверх,
> удобно стать бледней и невесомей.

Since each day has its own moon, the persona can declare: "My moon has waned forever," while for ordinary people she can specify their acquaintance with one, solitary moon: "You are illuminated by an eternal but different one" ("Vy osiianny vechnoi, no drugoiu").

At this point Akhmadulina introduces the concept of varying moons, the normal one in the sky for all people versus that available to her, the poetic persona. Thus for others there is the permanent one moon, while hers, for this night, as we will see, has been exhausted forever. Hers appears to be separate, to have become isolated, and then lost forever. Once her moon has been depleted, it can be established as a sort of deity of the day (of the twenty-four-hour period). Everything is set for humanizing the next moon as dictated by its grammatical feminine gender. Sure enough, in "February Full Moon" ("Fevral'skoe polnolunie"; 33) the formless moon is humanized to the extent of becoming a woman, especially in view of the image "a toady-star was huddled near it" ("pri nei iutilas' prikhvosten'-zvezda").[14] Here too

14. Although in Charles E. Townsend, *Russian Word-Formation* (New York: McGraw-Hill, 1968), 201, and in the Ozhegov *Defining Dictionary of the Russian Language* the gender of such words in Russian—hyphenated apostrophes—is based on the gender of the first word, there is here in Akhmadulina an instance of the final word determining the gender, hence the feminine and not the

the first, masculine, word affects the overall compound word, thereby tacitly suggesting a masculinizing effect although the dominant second, feminine, noun actually directs the feminine form of the verb. The speaker is extremely busy immortalizing in art her observation of nature. Each poem must have had its own moon in this sequence as seen in the poem "Following the 27th Day of March" ("Vosled 27 dniu marta"):

> And everything that nature did later
> by entering into open collusion with me,
> without skipping a single sunrise,
> I sang of under a different moon.

> И все, что дале делала природа,
> вступив в открытый заговор со мной,—
> не пропустив ни одного восхода,
> воспела я под разною луной.

(48–49)

Further, it will be seen that each day that the speaker writes about, or tries to write about, must have its own moon; on March 11 she asks day: "And where is your moon?"

It appears that each poeticized day, i.e. each day on/or about which the speaker attempts to write a poem (and in this large sequence of "moon poems" she crafts a poem for a given day) possesses its own moon—the moon that rises at the end of that day. During this time the speaker must seek to assimilate artistically with the help of the moon the possible events that will comprise her new poem. It must be composed before the sun rises high in the sky, preferably before daybreak, in the short interim period between moon and sun. She has scrupulously observed the movement of the moon in the night sky by proceeding from window to window all night. After eight o'clock in the morning her observation point returns her to the initial spot to await final inspiration. Indeed, for three nights she has foregone sleep in favor of her fervent vigilance over the moon:

---

expected masculine. It probably points to new usage or to folk usage in Tarusa. As in a simile in which the tenor and vehicle's doubling effect produces a visual dichotomy, the image hinges on duality inherent in combining the two nouns. See my "Vehicles for Duality in Pushkin's *The Bronze Horseman*: Similes and Period Lexicon," *Semiotica* 25, no. 1/2 (1979): 111–12.

All night around the windows I go after the moon.
Here's the last (window). A little past eight.
Having escorted it [the moon] to the bright distance,
I'll return to the first window—[and] I wait.

Всю ночь вкруг окон за луной иду.
Вот крайнее. Девятый час в начале.
Сопроводив ее до светлой дали,
вернусь к окну исходному—и жду.

(35)

The notion advanced here is that each moon must disappear and never
return the same again in space. The persona probably hopes that the form
and essence of this particular moon will be finalized in her poem. When it
does return, the moon is probably obscured by clouds in much the same
pattern as previously, albeit behind the obstructions the moon itself continues to undergo its change of phases:

Five days ago having seen
the shapeless moon's untidy triangle,
I sneered: the repeater is bold
who has made up these pits and angles.

Пять дней назад, бесформенной луны
завидев неопрятный треугольник,
я усмехнулась: дерзок второгодник,
сложивший эти ямы и углы.

(33)

The speaker displays her awareness of the moon's various shapes in its
phases by animating the moon and separating its visible and invisible half-
moons as two distinct individuals. The unexpected result is quite witty, if a
somewhat strange way of expressing the further waning (or pining) of the
moon: "The half-moon fell ill without the half-moon." Aware that the half-
moon of "the accountant (treasurer) of the heavens" ("schetovod nebes") is
in the moon's possession, the speaker grieves for her own half-moon which
could ostensibly symbolize lost time or the pre-dawn time, if not the fact of
failing to compose poems. In *The Garden* the theme of serving the adored
moon still figures in the humorous poem "Why does he pace? I like to
alone" ("Zachem on khodit? Ia liubliu odna"; 45). The moon's waning is

construed as being spent or wasted by the observing speaker. Inability to pen verse for seven days is expressed as "My moonlessness is seven sad days old" ("Sem' grustnykh dnei bezlun'iu moemu").

The moon in "February Full Moon" is a repeater ("vtorogodnik") because it remained, contrary to admonitions ("ne dumai ostat'sia") and returned to the speaker visibly unchanged; it put in a second appearance just like a pupil repeating a grade at school. In this repetition the moon imitates space, a concept for all of nature in its most elevated form, that repeats itself daily, seasonally, and annually ad infinitum.

The moon of a specific day is the possible conduit for creating a specific poem, which is impossible to fashion without the specific moon's proximity. No other day or night or moon will generate that particular poem. For ordinary people, on the other hand, there remains the one permanent moon that rises nightly to set at the onset of the new day. The difference between the ordinary moon and the poetic one utilized by the persona is shown in the poem "I walk along the outskirts of robust spring" ("Khozhu po okolitsam diuzhei vesny"):

> At first in the local moon
> I didn't recognize my own moon but mooniness took
>   pity on me
> And dangled accessibly among the black branches.

> Я в местной луне поначалу своей
> луны не узнала, да сжалилась лунность
> и свойски зависла меж черных ветвей—
> (*The Garden*, 149)

In the poem "The Morning after the Moon" either the moon remains still visible in the sky beyond the wall after daybreak, or if the moon has "set" behind the wall, much like the sun behind a mountain, the memory of its image lingers in the speaker's mind and vision. Now there is no moon nor any traces of it having been there due to the elasticity of space which closed the spot where the object once stood: "There is no moon nor any evidence, / that it actually was there. Space is forgetful" (31). For this disappearance the persona develops the notion of an elastic, as it were, all-engulfing space, much like air in the atmosphere, that fills in or occupies any space vacated by an object, such as the moon leaving the sky during the day. With no traces remaining of the moon's previous presence, memory too is erased. The poetic version of space is predicated on visual perception from the earth.

It seems that five poems address the time period from midnight to seven in the morning with differing dates (19–32). The first poem, "Moon over Tarusa" deals with the period between July 10 and 11—midnight and beyond until the persona sleeps. "The Coffee Imp" treats time after three in the morning, and, because of snow, is closer in season to early spring. The poem "Squabblings and Reconciliations" centers on very early morning and follows the previous poem. The piece "The Moon until Morning" treats the end of March—probably a day or more after the previous poem. In it the speaker awaits the appearance of the moon until after four o'clock in the morning. The poem "The Morning after the Moon" follows the previous poem; the time is probably March 23 until about 7 a.m.

The concept of the pupil ("uchenik") in stanza 4 contrasts with the would-be learned ones ("gramotei") of the poem "I have the secret of wondrous blooming." Although the pupil could be any pupil of nature, it is most likely the poet herself.[15] It could also allude to would-be poets whom she addresses ironically. An echo of Tsvetaeva's cycle "Pupil" is audible here (1:151–55).[16] Akhmadulina exhorts this pupil in the next two lines: "Learn, learn, vain pupil, and in being a pupil don't connive to remain" (or to repeat). Merely because the pupil exists, he or she should not expect to remain, since all things pass and are forgotten, except in art. And just as the moon's presence quickly turns to absence, so too mankind must feel the all-too-swift passage of time in this transient life and remain humble. In fact, Akhmadulina the person believes this and practices it:

> From very early childhood which coincided with the pre-war period I remember a balloon [or ball] that was helplessly tangled in branches, huge orange petals of a bouquet of poppies which blew off at the first gust of wind . . . This sense of the frailty of everything in the world is still strong in me today, and I believe that in this sense-despair there is some kind of instructiveness. Well, even in the fact that beauty is not something that we must necessarily possess, that any possession at all is somehow not secure.[17]

In the concluding stanza of the preceding poem, "The Moon until Morning," the speaker says: "And again I have to gaze at the morning— / more

15. I believe that is what Akhmadulina told me herself in March, 1987. The notion of a failed student, literally a "repeater" ("vtorogodnik") is pertinent here.
16. Marina Tsvetaeva, *Sochineniia v dvukh tomakh*, compiled by Anna Saakiants (Moscow: Khudozhestvennaia literatura, 1980), 1:151–55.
17. Interview with Bella Akhmadulina, in *Ogonek*, no. 15 (1987): 9.

tenderly and more uneducatedly than before" ("I snova nuzhno utro ozirat'— / nezhnee i negramotnei, chem prezhde"). With these words in mind, it is easier to assume that the pupil refers to the speaker herself as well as to some would-be poets who must humbly observe and record in their art the grandeur and majesty of nature as transmitted to them by nature herself.

When the moon leaves the sky, space ("prostranstvo") fills its area with a thick fog and the multiple span of chirping in the process of acquiring food, success, and the love of feathered ones. The world, open and receptive toward spring, is so suffused with chirping birds that the prepared speaker through metaphor perceives in "The Morning after the Moon ("Utro posle luny") this early dawn as having a bird's sensibilities: "O dear world, opened for spring, / how is your little bird's heart to be preserved?" ("O milyi mir, otverstyi dlia vesny, / kak uberech' tvoe serdechko ptich'e?"; 32). Aware that the world is ready to welcome spring, just as space has welcomed the migrant and wintering birds, the speaker hopes that hunters will be sufficiently reluctant, if not lazy, to screw up their eyes to take aim at the myriad birds that they (he) would not fail to shoot. Bird imagery, mostly metonymic, will lead through the metonymic three dots ("mnogotochie") of the woodpecker (a humorous effective introduction) to the animated negated simile-metaphor of the bird-catcher ("ptitselov"):

> Is it possible to dispute the bird-catcher
> who enigmatically pronounced that to return
> a word to its snare is more difficult than to return a
>   sparrow to it?
>
> Возможно ли оспорить птицелова,
> загадочно изрекшего, что слово
> вернуть в силок трудней, чем воробья?

Accordingly, danger in the guise of hunters and trappers abounds for the feckless birds. The birds probably symbolize spoken, enunciated words, if not poems. Akhmadulina's use and development through periphrasis of estrangement is predicated on the well-known Russian saying: "A word is not a sparrow; if you utter it—you cannot catch it" ("Slovo—ne vorobei; / Vymolvish'—ne poimaesh' "). The lucky speaker ("schastlivets") is of no consequence to the woodpecker. Possibly, the woodpecker is a distanced and diluted, if not convoluted image of Akhmadulina's more thunderous coeval poets. Its drumming frightens the not fully awakened magpies ("soroki"), again depicted through metonymy: "sleepily the magpie panic took wing" ("sprosonok vzmyla panika soroch'ia"). Humor is obvious when the persona returns to her desk, happy not to be pursued by the woodpecker, unlike the insects that comprise its meal. In Chapter 5 the bird image, as we shall see, assumes a new slant.

Then in assessing at the desk just what she has, the persona recalls her promise to the sun to repay the moon's debts, that is to compose verse. Her observations concerned the former moon, the fog, and the non-event of the sunrise. Not having found the means to nurture the "multihue" of the day ("mnogotsvet'e") insofar as the moon has exhausted all colors, the speaker solemnly pales, probably out of remorse at her failure to keep her promise to the sun. Currently, in trying to write down in finalized form the poetry witnessed and experienced in the moonlight, the persona discovers a lack of tangible objects in the process. Nature's loss of memory inhibits her further. In her possession are only the former moon ("byvshaia luna"), the fog, and the non-event of a sunrise explained later as an "insufficiency of a sunrise" ("voskhoda nedostatok," 36)—possibly during a fog or mist. The usual, expected riotous color of day has been exhausted by the moon whose predawn color of milky white contains within itself all imaginable colors. Accordingly, day without a sunrise pales before the all-encompassing brilliance of the moon until the sunrise in the perorating line. Day lacking sunrise comprises predawn non-color, discernible to the speaker in any color:

> The insufficiency of a sunrise
> was compensated for me by the predawn non-color,
> which I expose in any color.

> Восхода недостаток
> мне возместил предутренний не-цвет,
> какой в любом я уличаю цвете.

This color extracts a state of mind conducive to artistry and penetrating observation to which the persona returns at a given, easily fleeting time:

> I'll return to where I stand: in non-color
> [colorlessness].
> It is cautious and fears the evil eye.

> Вернусь туда, где и стою: в не-цвет.
> Он осторожен и боится сглазу.

(39)

Non-color turns out to be but an ardent instant of "mezhdutsvet'e" (intercolor or mesocolor; 40). Among the poems ancestral to this concept of creating verse during an unusual hour is Fedor Tiutchev's poem "The Vision" ("Videnie") which begins: "There is a certain hour, in the night, of the world's silence" ("Est' nekii chas, v nochi, vsemirnogo molchaniia"), continues with: "Then night deepens [thickens] like chaos over the waters" ("Togda gusteet noch', kak khaos na vodakh"), and ends with "Only the Muse's virginal soul / Is troubled by the gods in prophetic dreams" ("Lish' Muzy devstvennuiu dushu / V prorocheskikh trevozhat bogi snakh!")[18] Of further relevance is the opening to Tsvetaeva's second poem in the cycle "Pupil," which repeats the same three words of the epigraph from Tiutchev. Tsvetaeva's opening line goes on to compare the certain lofty hour to one of learning: "There is a certain hour [which is] like a castoff load" ("Est' nekii chas—kak sbroshennaia klazha"; 1:151).

An important concept in this collection is the "return" of objects, in fact an original artistic offshoot of cyclicity in Akhmadulina's verse, to name but one. The gist here is that objects or phenomena may return and thus live more than once through their registration or recording on paper in verse. This happens to the balcony, first mentioned in "The Moon until Morning" (28):

> Here where I live there is—I wouldn't call it: a
>   balcony—
> rather a cluster of dilapidation, an excrescence of
>   disintegration, or
> a wooden likeness of clouds,
> a formation of touching decay.
>
> Onto all this I come out.

> Здесь, где живу, есть—не скажу: балкон—
> гроздь ветхости, нарост распада, или
> древесное подобье облаков,
> образованье трогательной гнили.
>
> На все на это—выхожу.
>
> (28)

---

18. F. I. Tiutchev, *Lirika*, 2 vols., ed. K. V. Pigarev (Moscow: Nauka, 1966), 1:17.

Later in the poem "The Morning after the Moon" the speaker makes a subtle comment on her device of mentioning in passing an object in one poem, then returning to it more fully in another when it is already familiar. She comments on how much she appreciates meeting again an object sung in her verse, such as the balcony:

> How I love to meet once more
> an object sung by me, but in the role of an eyewitness.

> Как я люблю воспетый мной предмет
> вновь повстречать, но в роли очевидца.

An object once sung by her in verse, on repeated encounter, exists twice, as it were, and doubles with the poetic description. This doubling concept can cover even a day—unwittingly the pre-spring day lived twice—once in a poem and once earlier in nature. Existence in the poem secures immortality for it. Such multiple returns are in store for sheets of paper, for the hatching image, the snowstorm, the repeater, and for their artistic transformations from poem to poem.

At times the persona's attitude toward the moon turns iconoclastic with humorous overtones, as seen in "February Full Moon":

> No, I did not lie. . . .
> It [the moon] forgot, or did not know the one
> whose name is a secret. Foolish moon!

> Нет, я не солгала. . . .
> Она того забыла иль не знала,
> чье имя—тайна. Глупая луна!

(33)

So the image produces less than a half-moon. Another instance of rebellion or insubordination is found in the statement: "I won't take any old moon. / I want my own! I am not its sublunar slave" ("Ia ne voz'mu luny kakoi ni est'. / Svoei khochu! Ia ei ne rab podlunnyi"; 33).[19] That the word slave ("rab") refers to the speaker becomes evident in the poem "Line of Work," in which she employs "the slave snapped back" ("rab ogryzalsia") to connote herself

---

19. Compare Pushkin's use: "So long as in the sublunar world / At least one poet is alive" ("Dokol' v podlunnom mire / Zhiv budet khot' odin piit"; *Polnoe sobranie*, 3:373).

in a malevolent mood (39). In "The Guiding Sound" the speaker elaborates on awaiting the guiding sound under a full moon and jealously guarding their relationship:

> I won't share my moon with anyone,
> nor will it love another.
>
> Ни с кем моей луной не поделюсь,
> да и она другого не полюбит.
>
> (*The Garden*, 49)

Although the moon at night resembles a rounded flame, having in the last five days reached its full phase of the full moon ("v usloviiakh polnolun'ia"; 37), on certain days, however, (if not always) toward the ephemeral time—crepuscular predawn—its light turns into the non-color needed to write down these particular poems in their final form: "I'll return to where I stand: to non-color" ("Vernus' tuda, gde i stoiu: v ne-tsvet"; 39). Oddly, the "non-color" of the moon will later turn into the "non-color" of the day. This state of color is "the timid moment of intercolor" ("puglivoe mgnoven'e mezhdutsvet'ia"; 40), a mixture discernible in any color (add the fog and subtract unobstructed sun or light), prepared for poets by a pharmacist who forbids people to ponder his recipe. The pharmacist and "that one" (*tot*) seem to converge.[20]

Occasionally the speaker finds an extension of the moon's early morning non-color through the lack of apparent sunrise on a misty day. Because the sun's color is delayed, the composition time for the persona is extended. Not only can the speaker stand in non-color—a kind of early morning dusk remote from ordinary life and its concerns, often bathed in moonlight or delayed sunlight—but she can single out the "timid moment of intercolor," possibly the moment between the non-color of the moon and the "golden danger" ("opasnost' zolotaia"; 28) of the sun, which affects "the multihue of day," thus putting an end to finalizing the poem. The felicitous choice of "non-color," then, assumes that "all colors are exhausted by the moon" ("vse tsveta ischerpany lunoiu"; 32) through its neutral milky-white color, which at this predawn hour turns almost nonexistent or a transparent hue, if not into a luminous quality before sunrise.

---

20. For the masculine "tot," see also in *The Secret:* "Where does that one live whose name is a secret?" ("Gde obitaet tot, ch'e imia—taina?"; 34).

A moon that fails to communicate to the persona a honed poem to record in final polished form at daybreak vanishes without a trace. Such a moon cannot be immortalized by a poem that never materializes. The speaker then experiences guilt over the loss: "I am the destroyer of moons and suns" ("ia pogubitel' lun i solnts") for she cannot wait too many days to write down the poem from the previous day in nature that refuses to "come" to her for finalizing. No option remains other than to abandon the quest. Conceivably, the poem eludes her at daybreak due to earlier insufficient polishing by nature under the watchful eye of the persona. Unless the creative process attains a certain refinement in nature, the speaker cannot produce her own artistic reworked creation, a poem. With the passing of time, the poem in progress in nature loses its clarity in the memory of the speaker, hence its ultimate transformation must be abandoned. Without any moon whatsoever, no poetry of this particular type can be created or even hoped for by the speaker: "Moonlessly and fruitlessly flowed the days" ("Bezlunno i besplodno dni tekli"; 39).[21] The fruitless period will later be defined as seven days: "My moonlessness is seven sad days old" ("Sem' grustnykh dnei bezlun'iu moemu") in "Why does he pace. I like alone" ("Zachem on khodit. Ia liubliu odna"; 48).

The opening stanza of the poem "Line of Work" (36) is, in all likelihood, the first instance in literature of addressing a poem that due to its own obstinacy will not be composed. Instead, it becomes a non-poem true to Akhmadulina's own trend: "You're being stubborn. You don't want to be. Farewell my poem . . ." ("Uporstvuesh'. Ne khochesh' byt'. Proshchai moe stikhotvoren'e . . .") It will be recalled that Akhmatova created poems that she later burned in order to render them permanent: "How you pleaded, how you wanted to live" ("Kak ty molila, kak ty zhit' khotela"; no. 421). Akhmatova addresses a poem that existed only to be burned later for ultimate preservation independent of the poet. In Akhmatova the negative prefix *ne-* used with a noun usually refers to something that is absent currently but can emerge under propitious conditions, namely nonmeetings and other similar concepts. In Akhmadulina too, the *ne-* in early works bore the same connotation, for instance in her poem *My Genealogy* her yet unborn self speaks to her ancestors, seeking to influence events toward the actualization of her own birth. The unborn self confronts her Italian ancestors:

21. There appears to be some reverberation here with Pushkin's line in "I remember a wondrous moment" ("Ia pomniu chudnoe mgnoven'e"; *Polnoe sobranie*, 2:267) that reads "without a divinity without inspiration" ("bez bozhestva bez vdokhnoven'ia") and is quite appropriate seeing that the moon serves as inspiration and Muse for Akhmadulina's speaker in these poems.

He is surprised and says:
"Scat, scat!
Who are you?
Disperse, weak fogginess!"
I say,
"I am a certain something.
I am a wee bit,
a little trifle of future life.

And I don't exist. But how I want to be!

Он удивлен и говорит:
—Чур, чур!
Ты кто?
Рассейся, слабая туманность!—
Я говорю:
—Я—нечто.
Я—чуть-чуть,
грядущей жизни маленькая малость.

И нет меня. Но как хочу я быть!
(*Dreams of Georgia*, 262)

What is more, the future rose of summer is evident in a comparison in its promise and through the existence of roses in previous summers, for cyclicity ensures reappearance and bloom:

. . . In this way the unbloomed rose of the coming
    summer
is visible to us
through its absence and the promise of color.

Так будущего лета
нам роза нерасцветшая видна
отсутствием и обещаньем цвета.

(38)

Given the unfinished poem's failure to originate, the speaker's thoughts on the previous day are swept under the broom like fallen bird-cherry tree petals, no longer of any use (36). Akhmadulina's image of petals transforms into strewn scraps of paper containing the unacceptable labor of five nights, one scrap for each night:

> So flies my thought about it
> under the broom like bird-cherry scree.
>
> Sadly I look about at the petals—
> the scraps of my five-night scribblings.
>
> так и летит мой помысел о нем
> черемуховой осыпью под веник.[22]
>
> Печально озираю лепестки—
> клочки моих писаний пятинощных.
>
> (36)

Having wasted five moons and suns, the speaker, in a seeming reversal of Akhmatova's burning poems, burns the five scraps of paper from each night with the help of her fellow-conspirator, the stove ("pech'-soobshchnik"), all the while wishing that the heavens could read the words in the incoherent smoke. A fool, a nitwit (compare "the repeater"), to have grown overbearing, she imbibed the dictation of the heavens and is now writing to the heavens about the constellations Sirius and Orion. Her solitude in nature ensures for the speaker deeper penetration into her personal resources and into the relationship between nature and art. With the coming into prominence of the morning star Venus (stanza 24) the moon fades out: "Few visible qualities remained in the moon." The speaker regrets Venus's appearance since there will never be a repetition of this particular moon:

> There is no return for it. Each moon is different.
> And eternity did not meet twice with the same one.
>
> Ей нет возврата. Рознь луне луна.
> И вечность дважды не встречалась с ней же.
>
> (39)

22. The verb "osypat'sia" refers to leaves and blossoms falling from trees and plants, but according to the dictionaries, the noun formed from it denotes the geological notion of "scree." Akhmadulina may be using a dialect meaning, or she may have coined this logical usage of "that which falls from plants."

According to the speaker, in Russian literature the moon is the creation of Pushkin, at least as far as she or his influence on her is concerned. Hence the specification in the collection's concluding poem "We began together" ("My nachali vmeste") that in October, only Pushkin dominates the Russian poetic mind and nature. With the two famous opening words inevitably evoking Pushkin's poem "Autumn. An Excerpt" ("Osen'. Otryvok"), Akhmadulina allows her coda to be suffused with the spirit of Pushkin's verse:

> October has arrived. There's more of Pushkin all
>   around,
> to be exact, only he remains in the mind and in nature.
>
> Октябрь наступил. Стало Пушкина больше
>   вокруг,
> верней, только он и остался в уме и природе.
>
> (123)[23]

Now permeated with the poetic world of Pushkin, the October moon returns, as it were, to its role as predictor of the weather for the practical common person represented in the poem by the construction workers:

> How well Pushkin's moon has turned out today!
> Gloriously turbid and enormous, obviously indicating
>   severe frost!
>
> Как Пушкину нынче луна удалась!
> На славу мутна и огромна, к морозу, должно
>   быть!

23. In her poem Akhmadulina has omitted the particle *uzh*. Pushkin's poem opens as follows:
   October has already arrived—already the grove is shaking off
   The last leaves from its bare branches:
   Autumn cold blew, the road freezes over.

   Октябрь уж наступил—уж роща отряхает
   Последние листы с нагих своих ветвей;
   Дохнул осенний хлад, дорога промерзает.
                          (*Polnoe sobranie*, 3:262)
A brief mention of the moon appears in stanza 2: "in the presence of the moon." Late autumn gives way to winter.

What commenced as an elevated artistic trinity in the poem "I have the secret of wondrous blooming"—speech (*rech'*), beauty of fields ("krasa"—an obsolete word often used by Pushkin), and sylvan beauty—has within the collection through development of contiguous themes and motifs advanced toward the practical to commingle with the everyday and the recurrent—I, the workers, and winter.

Akhmadulina has, then, introduced two major aspects to the moon in her verse. First, the moon acts as a catalyst, or Muse of sorts, for nature to create art in its presence at night under the watchful eyes of the creative speaker, herself a poet. Second, the moon in this poetry differs substantially from the single one in nature that returns nightly for the eyes of all other persons. Indeed, there is one moon for each twenty-four hour period, or for each day and night. Not all these moons can craft a poem, ready to be "transcribed" by the lyric persona, although each one contributes to the ongoing artistic process. Only a few select moons end up with honed verse in the right shape for the persona to finalize as a poem in Russian.

Just as the moon's presence quickly turns into absence, so too man must feel the all-too-swift passage of his life and must remain humble. In expounding on the passing of time in her interview with the Russian magazine *Ogonek,* Akhmadulina stresses that a poet cannot abstract himself from the moment or from history: "And happiness lies in the fact that someone coincided in time with you on this earth, and you coincided with him in time. I am consoled by the fact that there are people who understand poetry subtly and powerfully, people with whom we coincided in time and for whom I write and live" (10).

Once several poems have been composed and the moon's potency for inspiring the creation of more original verse wanes, the lyric persona turns elsewhere for her metapoetic topics and for help from a surrogate Muse; namely, she turns to day as deity, the topic of the following chapter, where the force of Pushkin's "Autumn" will serve as a major influence.

5

Day as Deity

The astronomer
scanning the skies,
looking for the meaning of time,
. . . .
found the fountain of light
and the source of rhythm
and called for the poets.
　　　　—Diana Der Hovanessian

In the collection *The Secret* the concepts of day and space come into play simultaneously with the wane of the moon's potency, or influence, for fashioning poems in the three consecutive pieces to be addressed here: "Following the 27th Day of February" ("Vosled 27 dniu fevralia"), "The Day of March 12" ("Den' 12 marta"), "Following the 27th Day of March" ("Vosled 27 dniu marta"), and the independent piece "Raphael's Day" ("Den'-Rafael' ").[1] Day and space are conjured up on the threshold of spring; an example is the poem "Following the 27th Day of February." At this time, space displays an indifferent attitude toward the poetic speaker:

> . . . the point is not the poems
> but unrequited affection toward space.

> дело не в стихах,
> а в нежности к пространству безответной.

(42)

It is, however, day that will acquire prominence first. Put in practical terms, the speaker has been unable to produce verse for five consecutive nights, her desperate vigil notwithstanding.

---

1. Bella Akhmadulina, *Taina. Novye stikhi* (Moscow: Sovetskii pisatel', 1983). The poem "Raphael's Day" was not included in any collection; see Bella Akhmadulina, *Izbrannoe. Stikhi* (Moscow: Sovetskii pisatel', 1988), 328.

Addressing day as a deity in the next stanza, the speaker urges "day-deity" ("den'-bozhestvo") to engulf her by entering her being for its preservation throughout the night:

> Day-deity, here I am, enter me,
> I alone am your nocturnal refuge.
>
> День-божество, вот я, войди в меня,
> лишь я—твое прибежище ночное.

If the speaker can harbor within her being this day-deity, she will have more inspiration and ample time for creating the desired poem. Besides placing days within the expected categories of time and space, Akhmadulina brings out the ancient approach to day as deity in certain of these poems in an attempt to round out the portrait. To this end, she saturates a number of poems with various aspects of day. Accordingly, she singles out day in the titles: "Following the 27th Day of February" (42), "The Day of March 12" (45), "Following the 27th Day of March" (48), and "Raphael's Day." She thus makes day the principal theme in the three consecutive pieces. The three poems create an impression that each Day (the word is capitalized five times within the lines in the poem "The Day of March 12") is in possession of divine powers, like any mythological divinity, and hence a fine temporary substitute for the Muse. Day is called "day-deity" twice in the piece "Following the 27th Day of February" and once in "Raphael's Day," but not in "The Day of March 12" or "Following the 27th Day of March" as the divineness of Day is to be phased out in the poetry in preparation for the next theme in the subsequent sequence of poems. In other poems a specific day figures in the corpus of the piece: March 9 in "The Mercy of Space" ("Milost' prostranstva"; 53); and March 9, 10, 11 in "The Sternness of Space" ("Strogost' prostranstva"; 56). In the poem "Rafael's Day," Day is depicted as perfection and as a foreigner from Italy, the country of origin of the Stopani family on Akhmadulina's mother's side of the family, as noted in *My Genealogy*. The English text of the three opening stanzas reads:

> Newcomer-Day, don't stand on the rosy hill!
> Don't let the dawn coarsen your features.
> Why did you descend to the ravines and to me?
> I recognize you. You are from Urbino.

Day-Deity, go to your Italy.
It is still winter here. Our people are being
    mischievous.
An envious hunchback,[2] I gaze at you
and my secret anger kisses the hem of your robes.

Oh, as if the pox on my cheeks and the decay in my
    chest were not enough,
the brush too is foolish and the colors disobedient.
Day-Perfection, begone! Get away from sin!
Here shepherdesses always put knives in their
    corsages.

Пришелец День, не стой на розовом холме!
Не дай, чтобы заря твоим чертам грубила.
Зачем ты снизошел к оврагам и ко мне?
Я узнаю тебя. Ты родом из Урбино.

День-Божество, ступай в Италию свою.
У нас еще зима. У нас народ балует.
Завистник и горбун, я на тебя смотрю
и край твоих одежд мой тайный гнев целует.

Ах, мало оспы щек и гнилости в груди,
еще и кисть глупа и краски непослушны.
День-Совершенство, сгинь! Прочь от греха уйди!
Здесь за корсаж ножи всегда кладут пастушки.

Once Italy comes into play, why not make it Urbino (Urbin)—the birthplace of the divine artist Raphael and the birthplace of the Renaissance?[3] Here the day-deity even performs a miracle before its retreat: "But the dead oak bloomed amidst the level valleys."[4] In form and in miracle working the

2. The hunchback figures in Raphael's art.
3. Sam Driver interprets the new child image as the result of this birthplace, as noted in private communication. Note that in Keats's poem "Great spirits now on earth are sojourning" Raphael appears: "A meaner sound than Raphael's whispering." John Keats, *The Complete Poems*, ed. John Barnard, 3d. ed. (London: Penguin, 1988), 75.
4. In private communication Felix Roziner recognized this as a reference to a poem by A. F. Merzliakov (1778–1830), which has since become a famous folk song. Beginning on a lonely oak, it advances the theme of loneliness and longing for the beloved in a foreign land so appropriate for "Den'-Rafael' ":

image sounds more biblical than classical, possibly by dint of the language and the biblical themes in Raphael's art that it is mirroring. Furthermore, the day's beauty in the poem reverberates with that of March 12.

The mention of Raphael's Day is also probably an allusion to a series of murals that Raphael has painted on the Days and Hours, as can be seen in Rachel La Fontaine's *The Days and Hours of Raphael:* "The Days and Hours of Raphael are in the Hall of the Popes, Borgia Apartments, Vatican, and are thought to have been designed by Raphael and painted by his pupils, Giovanni da Udine, Giullio Romano, and Perino del Voga."[5]

Each day in Akhmadulina—at least each day immortalized in its own poem—has a moon of its own with different phases. This moon helps nature create poetry, which the speaker tries to crystallize in a poem. Occasionally, her poems may succeed in encompassing a day's moon within themselves, as expressed tentatively in the lines:

> . . . in the quagmire
> of the past day. It will be easier for them to catch up
>   with its moon
> in fire than in a basket.

> в трясине
> былого дня. Его луну догнать
> в огне им будет легче, чем в корзине.
>
>   (39)

In the poem "Following the 27th Day of February" the date figuring in the title is not the actual day for which the given poem is attempted. The real

---

Amid level valleys,
On the smooth heights
Blooms (and) grows a tall oak
In mighty beauty.

Среди долины ровныя,
На гладкой высоте
Цветет, растет высокий дуб
В могучей красоте.

See *Pesni i romansy A. Merzliakova* (Moscow, 1830).

5. Rachael A. La Fontaine, *The Days and Hours of Raphael. With Key to the Hours* (New York: The Grafton Press, 1905), 17. Musya Glants has brought to my attention the fact that Catherine of Russia commissioned Italian artists to paint reproductions on canvas of all these days and hours in the Hermitage, in a long narrow room.

day that wants to be, i.e., to come into poetic being, is the following day, February 28, presented here periphrastically. Although the year is not mentioned, it is obviously not a leap year seeing that the day after February 28 marks the beginning of spring—March 1 in Russian popular tradition. The speaker conveys sadness at the imminent arrival of spring, a time when she has trouble writing.

The previous poem "Line of Work" named four heavenly bodies—a star, Sirius, a constellation, Orion, and two planets, Jupiter and Venus—as if in preparation for the concept of day as a divinity. Three "fires" accompany the moon in "Following the 27th Day of February"—Sirius, Jupiter, and Saturn. The poem concludes with the juxtaposition of the two planets:

> Outside my window Jupiter and Saturn
> are neighbors. It is said to mean trouble.
>
> В окне моем Юпитер и Сатурн
> сейчас в соседях. Говорят, что—к бедам.[6]

Saturn in conjunction with day as deity evokes Roman mythology where the former was the sower and the Roman deity of the harvest. (There is reason to believe that the poems are the harvest here.) In later legends Saturn was perceived as the repeated devourer of his children—the days, months, and years.[7]

6. On 25 March 1987, in private conversation, Akhmadulina informed me that the phenomenon of Jupiter and Saturn coming unusually close together actually occurred in 1981. Folk belief holds it to herald misfortune.

7. Compare Gertrude Jobes on Saturn in her *Dictionary of Mythology, Folklore and Symbols*, 3 vols. (New York: Scarecrow Press, 1961): "Thus he was lord of time, and the spirit of action, and his name became the source of the word Saturday. [This is important because it is a *day* of the week.] Saturn is a death planet, sixth in distance from the sun, ruler of Capricorn, lord of Saturday. In astro-mythology it typifies duration, the finite within the infinite. Bringer of inertia and mourning. [Cf. Akhmadulina's words "k bedam."] Evil to be born under; its children are cowards, ignorant, perfidious. It represents a melancholic intelligence. Protector of the treacherous. Represented by the color black" (2:1403). In connection with black, compare the wearing of black by Akhmadulina in the years that these poems were written. She was dressed entirely in black the two times I visited her in Peredelkino in 1983. In Boston in 1987 she wore black, in subsequent years the colors were modified to gray, black, and white probably in keeping with the end of the period for *The Secret*. Compare also Jobes, 1:418, on Day: "Enlightenment, growth, principle of good, prosperity, . . . surety, wisdom. Symbols of day are the morning star, sun, white. . . . The word is derived through the Latin *dies* from the Sanskrit *dyaus*. Dianus, a form of the Latin deity Janus, derives from the same root." Jobes also states that Saturday is a day of danger and death; a day of finalities (1:419). It is interesting that in Andrei Voznesenskii's recent poem "Madonna—37" there is reference to Saturn devouring his children. Sam Driver has pointed out that Goya's painting of Saturn devour-

In Akhmadulina the notion of the day-deity being resurrected is possibly akin to living twice, initially as the day February 28 while remaining unaware of it, and once more in verse. Toward this end the persona requests that the day-deity linger awhile in the window. After six o'clock in the evening when day goes down in a burst of red-blue sunset to be reflected on the icy window pane, the speaker invites the day-deity to enter her being, to take temporary refuge within her as its only possible nighttime haven just as she requested earlier for the moon. An exhortation—"Arise" ("Voskresni zhe")—makes it do as bidden. Once "resurrected" the once great and beautiful ("velik i lep") one is urged to arise grandiose ("velikolepnym"), for in her mind she will repeat and fill as if with smoke or steam ("vozdymliu") the image of its first light in her left window. It is interesting to note that the poet indulges in her beloved play on words by defamiliarizing "velik" and "lep" through a pun. She ends with unaware day having lived twice.

In stanza 5 the speaker appears to be evoking the planet Jupiter, one of the three fires, or stars, which accompanied the departing moon. Jupiter is the Prince of Light, with white being sacred to him. As Lord of Thursday (a day that the mystics define as one requiring courage and willpower; Jobes, 1:419), Jupiter can signify the day in question through its evoked presence. The three suns are symbolic of earthly fire maintained by heavenly fire as shown in the concept of the speaker as refuge for the heavenly body—the sun—which rises from the waters, causing the waters to assume the form of steam that will fall back to earth as rain (Jobes, 1:897). Compare Akhmadulina's locution "vozdymliu" ("I will fill with smoke").

Poems about some days stubbornly refuse to materialize, such as the one on February 10 which the speaker attempted to write down until February 15, but ultimately had to abandon. Her attempt is so fervent because the face or personality of each day is unique to it alone; and putting the experience down in poetry is desirable for securing this unusual moment in eternity. Indeed, the personality of each day has its own contribution to make. February 27 in the title as a definition of the actual day is a cold one. For February 28 the persona appears to be observing a taboo in not naming it, rather, she employs descriptive appellations, "Following the 27th Day of February," "the day before spring," "day-deity." She obviously hopes that it

---

ing his sons is Voznesenskii's main source for this image, an observation supported by Voznesenskii's programmatic poem "Ia—Goia" ("I am Goya"), in Voznesenskii's *Rov. Stikhi, proza* (Moscow: Sovetskii pisatel', 1987), 17.

will cooperate in the act of creating verse. Importantly, at the end of each day, certain days are able to enter the persona's being for nighttime refuge and for prolonged existence, possibly like the sun continuing "to shine" on earth through the reflected sunlight cast by the moon. The lyrical ego calls this rainy day "wonderful" (48), for in her early works rain served merely as a prelude to winter creativity.

The capitalization of the word Day enhances its position as a deity; however, the past day is not capitalized, conceivably because the current day is stronger and now in power or reigning at the moment. It remains unclear whether there is an annual one-day return of each day-deity or whether a specific day-deity exists only once in time, always to be replaced by new ones, much like Akhmadulina's special moon. This day, March 12, differs from all its March siblings in personality and in face. Being like winter, it is an outcast among the siblings of March. By wanting the extreme or forceful form of everything, this day of March 12 will not settle for mild half-measures, such as a ground wind: it seems to be thinking in the words of the poem:

> What need is there for a ground wind if there is a
>   blizzard?
> Why languish in paltry cold? Here's hard frost.
>
> Зачем поземка, если есть буран?
> Что в бледной стыни мыкаться? Вот—стужа.

Falling victim to a cold, the observing persona blames the illness, to which her human weakness succumbed, on the preceding day of March: "the pre-brother / left me the legacy of fever" ("pred-brat— / ostavil mne nasled'e likhoradki"; stanza 7). March 11 prepares the way for stormy March 12 by being frigid, as shown later in the poem "The Sternness of Space." Quickly, as if in response to the past day's anger, the speaker recants to assume the blame for her illness:

> Past day, forgive me, I lied!
> Your genius is kind. I myself, fool that I am, caught
>   cold
> and saw off your wings into the distance
> on the chilly wings of illness.

Минувший день, прости, я солгала!
Твой гений—добр. Сама простыла, дура,
и провожала в даль твои крыла
на зябких крыльях зыбкого недуга.

(46)

The speaker apparently fears that unless the potent day is appeased concerning its brethren, it will not allow her even to contemplate writing about it. This deity, the past day March 11, possesses wings. For the day's wings the poet uses the poetic plural form "kryla"; the illness too has wings for which the modern form "kryl'ia" is employed. The contrastive use of the plural forms (juxtaposition) could be related to the antiquity of the wings for the classical deity as opposed to newness of wings for the persona and a recent passing illness. Obviously, wings in literature often symbolize creative artistic power, such as Akhmatova's "And from childhood I was winged" ("A s detstva byla krylatoi"), in the poem "You don't love, you don't want to look" ("Ne liubish', ne khochesh' smotret' "; no. 58) which in terms of syntax and morphological form is echoed by Akhmadulina. Hence wings coupled with the flu for Akhmadulina's poetic persona suggest a state of artistic inspiration for it, in effect a prerequisite in Akhmadulina, one that allows the persona to compose poetry within the poems. It also recalls Akhmadulina's early poem *Chills*.[8]

Accordingly, March 12 differs dramatically from all other days in this month, with its unrelatedness to the other days augmented through the disruptive simile of the cuckoo's nest. In fact, this day of March 12 is a guest, or rather a foundling, in the month of March. Possessing differing features, its beauty does not typify March, nor can there be comparison to the month, for the day's face and character resemble winter. While winter's thawed snows were streaming down the hills in the form of water, winter laid this day like a cuckoo's egg under the feathers of "Mother Warmth," probably an appellation for spring. The bird image is obvious here. An adopted day is then called "narechennyi syn," that is, adopted by March or by Mother Warmth (stanza 4). So the poetic image of the winged deity transmogrifies into a winged bird, parallel to the numerous changes of the

---

8. Anna Akhmatova, *Stikhotvoreniia i poemy*, compiled by V. M. Zhirmunskii (Leningrad: Sovetskii pisatel', 1976). Also, fever can indicate creativity in Akhmatova as well; see my *Poetry of Anna Akhmatova: A Conquest of Time and Space* (Munich: Otto Sagner, 1986), 22–26. *Oznob* is found in Bella Akhmadulina, *Sny o Gruzii* (Tbilisi: Merani, 1979), and in Akhmadulina, *Oznob: izbrannye proizvedeniia* (Frankfurt: Posev, 1968).

gods in classical mythology. Moreover, her pondering in "Line of Work" on whether she is adopted or an orphan of space, a crucial query within the secret, leans, at this point, in the direction of being adopted:

> Am I the adoptee or total orphan
> of space, gazing at me from all sides?
>
> Приемыш я иль вовсе сирота
> со всех сторон глядящего пространства?
> (40)

This day, preserved through the night within the speaker, will be followed by, or crowned with, so to speak, a half-moon: "I can already see and hear, / how in the sky shines exactly half a moon" ("Uzh vidno mne i slyshno, / kak bleshchet v nebe rovno pol-luny"; 47). On this night after the storm, as a result of her illness, the persona appears to have retired to bed, or she could have taken to her bed with the storm raging and could have awakened at seven o'clock in the evening during sunset:

> I woke up. I went out. It was seven o'clock.
> There was something audible in the sunset.
>
> Проснулась. Вышла. Было семь часов.
> В закате что-то слышимое было,

Sadness grips her at the wane of Day:

> (My) tear admires the demise of Day.
> (There's) severe cold: you can produce a tear but won't
>   be able to pour it out.
>
> Скончаньем Дня любуется слеза.
> Мороз: слезу содеешь, но не выльешь.

So the legacy of March 12—the deep freeze—remains through the night and, ostensibly, into the next day.

An impression is formed that each day possesses unique divine powers, like any mythological divinity. Indeed, it will be recalled that in mythology the days are the children of Saturn (some say of Cronus). It will be mentioned in a later poem. This particular poem ends with the ambiguous "bozhii den'," which literally denotes "God's day" thereby corroborating the divinity image in the reader's mind. Yet because the expression is usually a fixed epithet in Russian, its "mythological" meaning is neutralized. Further, unlike other specific references to this particular day, the word is not capitalized. It could refer to any and every day, as in the idiom "kazhdyi bozhii den' " (every single day) or the saying "iasno, kak bozhii den' " (clear as day). By allowing it to refer to any day as well as to March 12, the speaker renders all, or many, of the days "omniscient and all-seeing" ("vseznaiushch i vsevidiashch"). Yet omniscient and all-seeing is the epical Gilgamesh of the eponymous Assyrian epic, himself a demi-god who, it will be recalled, chopped down the sacred cedar of Lebanon, a conifer. The title in Russian reads *Epos o Gil'gameshe. (O vse vidavshem)*. The epic begins:

> About him who has seen all to the edge of the world,
> About him who has known seas, crossed all mountains,
> About him who has vanquished enemies with his
>   friend,
> About him who has perceived wisdom, who has
>   penetrated all:
> The sacred he has seen, he has known the secret.

> *О* всё видавшем   *до края* мира,
> *О* познавшем *моря,   перешедшем* все *горы,*
> *О врагов покорившем*   вместе *с другом,*
> *О постигшем* премудрость,   о всё
>   *проницавшем:*
> *С*окровенное видел он,   тайное *ведал,*

Similarly, this day-deity of March 12 through its howling snowstorm and ferocious winds uproots and breaks coniferous trees: "strokes the fir tree against its fur, bends pines" ("gladit protiv shersti el', gnet sosny"). There appears to be a tacit, unspecified, as it were, parallel here. In *Gilgamesh* the goddess's anger over the chopped trees results in the death of Gilgamesh's friend Enkidu.[9]

To sum up and validate the perception of day as deity the following must be borne in mind. First, in mythology the days as well as the months and years

9. See I. M. D'iakonov, trans., *Epos o Gil'gameshe: o vse vidavshem* (Moscow: AN SSSR, 1964).

were the children of Saturn, whereas in Akhmadulina this role is consigned only to the days, that is, the days are the children of a given month. And Saturn, as a hint, put in an appearance in the preceding poem. The relation of the months to Saturn in Akhmadulina, meaning whether they are gods who would have greater power, is left unclear. Also left vague is whether there is an annual ("ocherednoi") one-day return of each day-deity (for example, of March 1, 12, or 22) or whether a specific day-deity exists only once in time (such as March 1, 1988) to be replaced by new ones in subsequent years. Second, Akhmadulina shows the paternal role of the months towards the days in several ways: in line one by refuting the kinship of one day with the remainder: "The days of March are not related to one another. / The twelfth is a guest or foundling in it." Lines 3 and 4 further refute the relationship by referring to alien features in the guest or foundling:

> There are alien features in its beauty,
> and you can't call to March today, "Hey, March!"

> Черты чужие есть в его красе,
> и март: «Эй, март!»—сегодня не окликнешь.

Third, stanza 2 furnishes the reason for this day's foreignness—in character and in face it resembles winter and not spring (as noted earlier, in the Russian popular tradition spring commences on March 1, so the entire month is spring): "The day has turned out like winter in character and face." Line 2 shows why the day is alien and a foundling, since the foundling day was surreptitiously placed by winter in the spring month of March as the thawed snows of winter flowed down from the hills:

> when its [winter's] snows began to flow down from the
>   hills,
> it [winter], like a cuckoo egg,
> laid it [day] under the feathers of Mother-Warmth.

> когда с холмов ее снега поплыли,
> она его кукушкиным яйцом
> снесла под перья матери-теплыни.

In other words, in flowing past on the way out in March (in the guise of spring) winter slipped the day (its progeny) into the nest under the feathers of Mother-Warmth as if it were a cuckoo egg. Once we have the bird image, our minds resort to birdlore. Indeed, cuckoos slip their eggs into the nests of other birds, and under the feathers of other birds, with the result that the larger and stronger cuckoo hatchling pushes the indigenous chicks out of the nest to their deaths in order to be tended exclusively by the adoptive parents.[10] Thus through a simile the foreignness of the day-deity assumes the image of an adopted bird as well. The bird image with its feathers and wings prepares the reader for other wings that will appear.

In stanza 3 the lyrical persona through sleepless vigil observes the arrival of Day's will and form (a roundabout, periphrastic, way of saying Day), so strange to these parts:

> I did not send my eyes off to sleep today—
> and how clever I am that I did not fall asleep!
> I saw the will and form of Day
> come here although it does not hail from here.

> Я нынче глаз не отпускала спать—
> и как же я умна, что не заснула!
> Я видела, как воля Дня и стать
> пришли сюда, хоть родом не отсюда.

Note that in the poem "Rafael's Day" the foreignness becomes actual, with the day arriving from another country, whereas here the foreignness is that of a species.

In stanza 4, in an attempt to prevent the dawning of the Day March 12, the month of March addresses it by its true relation to itself (the month): "O adopted son, / I am frightened, do not rise, don't." A final characteristic of the deity is evident when the past day leaves on wings in stanza 8. Day as a segment of time, like time, has wings. Obviously in classical mythology the goddess of day (but of all days) was Hemera, and Akhmadulina was probably influenced by this image. Also evident is an echo of Eos (Aurora), goddess of dawn, who flies on wings or in a chariot. Importantly, these are females in charge of all days, whereas in Akhmadulina each day is a male to conform to the masculine gender of the word day ("den' ") in Russian. Wings for time are well known in literary symbolism; for example

---

10. The Brockhaus-Efron Encyclopedia describes the European cuckoo's qualities thus: "The cuckoo either lays its eggs directly in the nest or lays an egg on the ground and then in its beak transfers it to the targeted nest. The fledgling for the most part pushes its stepbrothers out of the nest." *Entsiklopedicheskii slovar'*, ed. I. E. Andreevskii (St. Petersburg: I. A. Efron, 1895), 15A:949.

Akhmatova shows time as having wings in her poem "A swanlike wind blows" ("Veet veter lebedinyi"; no. 253):

> Only the wing of time
> Overshadowed with snowy glory
> My serene brow.
>
> Только времени крыло
> Осенило славой снежной
> Безмятежное чело.

Illness, too, has wings in this poem, possibly due to the fact that in early Akhmadulina illness marks the beginning of her creative period through isolation from family and friends.

The question arises as to why the month of March fears the foundling day? Presumably, the foundling day is stronger, like the cuckoo chick, and presently in total control. This day, March 12, which differs from all its March siblings in nature and in face is like winter, and hence it is an outcast among the siblings of March. Craving the extreme or forceful form of everything, this day of March 12 will not settle for mild (inane perhaps) half-measures, such as ground winds, when a blizzard offers much more force. It ostensibly wants to overthrow the newly established order of warmth in favor of frigid weather (much like the intrusive cuckoo chick).

The speaker apparently fears the past day, benevolent though it may seem, for its ability to deprive her of a poem in progress. Through the illness and the wings that it supplies for her, the speaker is able to follow the day of March 11 and to get physically closer to it, presumably, for better depiction in her verse. It was mentioned that March 11, the past day, possesses wings as well, like the deity it is; to refer to its wings the poet uses the poetic plural form "kryla" (pinions). The illness too has wings, for which the modern plural form "kryl'ia" is employed. While the old versus the new forms of the word "wings" distinguishes the day from the illness, the difference can probably be explained through age; admittedly, the deity is thousands of years old, hence the obsolete grammatical form; on the other hand, the speaker is young and modern, hence the contemporary grammatical form. Moreover, Akhmadulina may be following Pushkin's example. Pushkin likes old and new forms in proximity in the same poem, such as "golova"— "glava" (head), "gorod"—"grad" (city), and "kholod"—"khlad" (cold): "Autumn cold breathed . . . Russian cold" ("Dokhnul osennii khlad . . . russkii kholod").[11]

Thus, wings coupled with the flu for Akhmadulina's lyric persona suggest inspiration, which is in effect a prerequisite in her verse, one that allows the persona to compose poetry within the poems. In the early poetry, catching a cold in autumn signified a welcome isolation from friends and responsibility in her special world of poetic creation; moreover, it was a time to formulate poetic images before producing the actual verse in winter.

Akhmadulina introduces here the important concept of the evanescent quality of perfect beauty, an unusual view at best—"to be on the brink of absence" ("byt' otsutstviia na grani")—hence its expression in the "non-light" ("nesvet"—never articulated as such) and "interlight" ("mezhdu-svetie") of the moonlight. The concept is evocative of Annenskii's striving for the ideal, yet unattainable beauty. As Setchkarev affirms in *Studies in the Life:*

> Unlike the ordinary man, he [the poet] feels the presence of Beauty, he is forced by an inner compulsion to reflect it, to shape it—and he can produce no more than a suggestion of it. This impossibility to do justice to an intense feeling always leaves a drop of poison even in the greatest artistic achievement. And still the unresolved sounds ("nerazreshennost' raznozvuchii") which do not unite in harmony have a charm of their own, because they are striving for the harmonious ideal. . . . Through Poetry he can at least hope to catch the lights of Beauty shining through its dense veil.[12]

An evolvement of the investigation occurs in Wendy Rosslyn's book *The Prince, the Fool and the Nunnery,* which connects this aspect with the Platonic doctrine of *anamnesis,* "according to which the soul, whilst in its pre-existent phase, has a vision of the Ideas; once the soul is joined to the body, the vision is lost to it and only the memory remains, to be reactivated in this world by the sight of that which is beautiful and true and good."[13] This day,

---

11. On Akhmadulina's language, see Sofiia Liubenskaia, "O poeticheskom iazyke Belly Akhmadulinoi," *Russian Literature* 17 (1985): 159. There is mention of the Old Church Slavonic and Russian forms of words alternating in one text in the nineteenth century tradition of Zhukovskii, Batiushkov, and Pushkin.

12. Vsevolod Setchkarev, *Studies in the Life and Works of Innokentij Annenskij* (The Hague: Mouton, 1963), 61–62.

13. Wendy Rosslyn, *The Prince, the Fool and the Nunnery: The Religious Theme in the Early Poetry of Anna Akhmatova* (Brookfield, Vt.: Gower, 1984), 59.

March 12, preserved through the night within the speaker, will be followed by, or crowned with, as it were, a half-moon (47).

The waning day sings the quiet song of several voices, with the loudest being the voice of the reigning day, the day in power, "Farewell, you were loved by me" (stanza 11). The words sound much like Annenskii as reflected through Akhmatova in her early poem "Imitation from I. F. Annenskii" ("Podrazhanie I. F. Annenskomu"; no. 40), in which abstract love, evocative of Annenskii, is not as powerful as Akhmadulina's emotions for the moon. Thus the wistful, almost Romantic note in the love for the day-deity with its possessiveness and possession, echoes Annenskii and Akhmatova as magnified through Akhmatova's "Imitation from I. F. Annenskii" (Ketchian, *The Poetry of Anna Akhmatova*, 121–37). In fact, after the speaker's overt love for the moon the situation with the other surrogate muses is often ambivalent due to jealousy and a stronger emotion, as it were, on their part.

The color of departing day, albeit indescribable, is slightly more rose-hued than "neskazannost" (loosely equivalent to "indescribability, untoldness"):

It's impossible to say what the color was like. But the color
was a tiny bit more pink than indescribability.

Нельзя сказать: каков был цвет. Но цвет
чуть-чуть был розовей, чем несказанность.[14]

(47)

As in Symbolism there is a hint of Perfect Beauty (possibly connected to Akhmadulina's earlier "uniqueness"—"edinstvennost' "; 39), however elusive or barely present:

Here's the lot of perfect beauty:
barely to glimmer, to be on the brink of absence.

Вот участь совершенной красоты:
чуть брезжить, быть отсутствия на грани.

14. This color faintly parallels Annenskii's "lilac mist" ("sirenevaia mgla"), also used in Akhmatova's "Imitation from I. F. Annenskii" (Setchkarev, *Studies in the Life*, 81, 91).

Non-color ("nesvet") is probably a variant of white—the symbolic color of day—a more sublime color than plain white through the nearly visible lack of it. Like white, it possibly contains all colors of the rainbow plus the all-inclusive white, which would render it a "higher," or more saturated color. One feels that it contains some other, unusual color. Untoldness ("neska-zannost' ") is conceivably a desired sublime expression or enunciation rendered impossible for mortal articulation. Through placement of this negating concept (anti-concept, as it were) in a descriptive context and through the device of comparison Akhmadulina concretizes what the nineteenth-century philosophic poet Evgenii Baratynskii (1800–1844) began, what Annenskii and Tsvetaeva took up, and Akhmatova developed in her famous negative concepts, such as non-meeting ("nevstrecha").[15] Also, the departure at dusk of a past day in Annenskii, imitated in Akhmatova, is tangible in Akhmadulina. Akhmadulina, however, places the final departure to a time long after midnight and close to dawn.

The poet then personifies a great dampness ("bol'shaia syrost' "), which enters through the window to warm itself. Transforming into someone vaguely white in departing, it undergoes a grammatical gender change from the feminine of "syrost' " to agree syntactically with the masculine form of "headed back" ("otpravilsia"), elicited by the pronoun *kto*. All in all, it is reminiscent of Annenskii's concept of the lilac mist in its color and watery texture (Setchkarev, *Studies in the Life*, 91, 139). Personification mounts with words denoting human relations and situations, namely, "days are related," "guest," "foundling," "foreign features," "in character and face," "the will of Day and its figure." Capitalization renders its name a proper name.[16] Simile blends with metaphor in Akhmadulina, a rarity likewise noted in Annenskii by Setchkarev, to introduce the spring image of birds hatching eggs. The case, however, is no ordinary incubation of the eggs. The divergence begins with the surreptitious introduction of the notion of "podkidysh" (foundling; literally "abandoned nearby"), after which the image bifurcates through the simile because a simile makes the reader visualize both images, that of its tenor and of its vehicle, simultaneously: "she [winter—feminine in Russian] laid it [day—masculine in Russian] like a cuckoo egg under the feathers of Mother-Warmth." The clever image of the

15. Setchkarev, in *Studies in the Life*, comments on Annenskii's penchant for words beginning with the negative prefixes *ne-* and *bez-* (109–10). Pushkin and Baratynskii liked them as well.

16. Setchkarev shows that Annenskii "likes capitalizations as an emphasis, a personification *on* or *of* abstract ideas. . . ."; "'Den', Noch' and Smert' are nearly always written with capitals, and thus acquire an uncanny life and a most dangerous personality." *Studies in the Life*, 107–8.

cuckoo through which Day is perceived as a foundling promotes humanization that moves in the direction of deification through its human form, so similar to the divine, when March calls it "adopted son" ("narechennyi syn").

In commencing this poem Akhmadulina evokes Pushkin's opening line in the piece "Autumn. An Excerpt" ("Osen'. Otryvok")—"The days of late fall are usually disparaged" ("Dni pozdnei oseni braniat obyknovenno"; 3:262). Pushkin's observation that late autumn is often censured by people, although not by himself, corresponds precisely to Akhmadulina's personal attitude toward the maverick day of March 12, so much like her beloved days of winter, her favorite season for creating verse as evidenced in her early verse. Autumn, on the other hand, is famous as Pushkin's most productive season. Not only the opening line of his poem but the simile of the unloved child in a family and the speaker's support of the mistreated child presage Akhmadulina's simile of the cuckoo egg and the hatchling for the month of March. The speaker's compassion for a child unloved in its family comes from stanza 5 of Pushkin's poem "Autumn. An Excerpt":

> The days of late autumn are usually disparaged,
> But it [autumn] is dear to me, dear reader,
> With its quiet beauty, shining meekly.
> Thus an unloved child in his own family
> Attracts me to him.

> Дни поздней осени бранят обыкновенно,
> Но мне она мила, читатель дорогой,
> Красою тихою, блистающей смиренно.
> Так нелюбимое дитя в семье родной
> К себе меня влечет.

This posture is further evocative of Tat'iana Larina with her quiet demeanor being a stranger in her own family in Pushkin's novel in verse, *Eugene Onegin* (*Evgenii Onegin*). It presages Akhmadulina's simile of the cuckoo egg and the hatchling for the month of March. Of Tat'iana, Pushkin says that she seems alien in her own family:

> Wild, sad, quiet,
> Fearful like a forest doe,
> In her own family
> She seemed like an alien girl.

Дика, печальна, молчалива,
Как лань лесная боязлива,
Она в семье своей родной
Казалась девочкой чужой.
(Canto 2, stanza 25, lines 5–8)

Tat'iana too is fond of gazing out the window like Akhmadulina's persona and feels disaffected from family members, much like an orphan. Having reversed the quiet natures of Tat'iana and of late autumn in Pushkin's depiction to the severe Day of March 12 and the malicious cuckoo chick, Akhmadulina, however, retains the foreignness, or rather the alienation, and the inability to blend in as well as her speaker's love for the maverick Day.

In the event that the inverse parallel with Pushkin may not be readily obvious, Akhmadulina inserts the familiar words "the howling of the storm" ("buri zavyvan'e") from Pushkin's famous poem on a snowstorm, "The snowstorm covers the sky in gloom" ("Buria mgloiu nebo kroet"; 2:288), with a deft retention of his inversion between the two nouns.[17] Other common points are the country cottage and somebody gazing out the window.

Thus in his simile Pushkin has introduced the notion of certain days, sharing similarities, being like children in a family. In Pushkin the family for these days, obtained through the simile quoted above, is part of a season, specifically of late autumn. Akhmadulina uses the classical breakdown of the days in one month as siblings. She probably favors March 12 of this particular year for its coldness, storminess, and for being unlike its siblings in the nest. Even in the following poem "Following the 27th Day of March" the speaker will articulate her collusion with a specific day to retain a trifle longer the coldness of winter. The themes of the orphan and winter figure as well. Like Pushkin in his personal preferences, Akhmadulina for purposes of creating verse often excoriates spring. In the same poem Pushkin admits:

Now is my time: I don't like spring;
A thaw bores me; stench, mud—I am ill in spring;
My blood ferments, my emotions and mind are
    constrained by yearning.

17. This line from Pushkin's poem seems to represent one of Akhmadulina's first memories of speech; compare in her early prose autobiographical piece on her perception of Pushkin "The Eternal Presence" ("Vechnoe prisutstvie"; *Dreams of Georgia*, 466).

Теперь моя пора: я не люблю весны;
Скучна мне оттепель; вонь, грязь—весной я
    болен;
Кровь бродит; чувства, ум тоскою стеснены.[18]

To buttress this parallel and to insure its recognition in the event that it was not discovered by the reader of *The Secret,* in the following collection *The Garden* Akhmadulina furnishes additional clues in stanza 2 of "My Pachevskii" ("Pachevskii moi"; 30),[19] where she cleverly retains the masculine gender by referring illness to her mind ("um"), a masculine word in Russian:

The traitor-mind repeats: "I am ill in spring";
but it is well, and everything is funny for it,
when I go to spy on the field:
what has grown and sprouted in it overnight.

Изменник-ум твердит: «Весной я болен»,—
а сам здоров, и все ему смешно,
когда иду подглядывать за полем:
что за ночь в нем произошло-взошло.

(30)

18. See also in the same vein Pushkin's poem on spring and love:
    Spring, spring, time of love,
    What languid emotion
    There is in my heart, in my blood . . .
    How alien to my heart is pleasure . . .
    All that rejoices and shines
    Bores me and causes languor.

    Give me a snowstorm and a blizzard
    And the wintry long gloom of nights.

    Весна, весна, пора любви,
    Как тяжко мне твое явленье,
    Какое томное волненье
    В моей душе, в моей крови . . .
    Как чуждо сердцу наслажденье . . .
    Всё, что ликует и блестит,
    Наводит скуку и томленье.

    Отдайте мне метель и вьюгу
    И зимний долгий мрак ночей.

(3:39)

19. Bella Akhmadulina, *Sad. Novye stikhi* (Moscow: Sovetskii pisatel', 1987), 30.

Pushkin and Akhmadulina alike, prefer cool weather crispness for purposes of writing. Indeed, in the poem "Following the 27th Day of February" the speaker's words corroborate the choice—for Akhmadulina, "Day before Spring, I feel sorry for my winter," for Pushkin, "And with each autumn I blossom anew / The Russian cold is good for my health" ("I s kazhdoi osen'iu ia rastsvetaiu vnov' / Zdorov'iu moemu polezen russkii kholod." Akhmadulina's flu in her poem was possibly inspired by Pushkin's words on being ill in the spring, seeing that her own speaker in the early works usually catches cold in the fall as a prelude to preparing conducive conditions and a proper state of mind for poetic creation in winter. Conversely, in Pushkin's poem "Autumn. An Excerpt," beginning with stanza 9 and to the end, the theme of creating verse in solitude prevails.

The next poem, "Following the 27th Day of March," underscores the preceding date by the month in the title, echoing the previous but one poem because the speaker wants the two days, one month apart, to fraternize. When the two days separated by one month embrace, the result is a "round number." Having conspired to bring the two together, the speaker now resorts to metaphor, namely, within the closed circle of games and of the circle dance; she whirls about (probably from day to day) with a transparent compass to create a white spacious circle around her that in effect crowns the black forest in the distance. In order to carry out her plans of prolonging the wintry pre-spring period, which is like an interregnum in that anything can be inclined in any direction, through the fraternizing of the tandem tail end days, the persona in stanza 4 exhorts February 27 to return "on angel's wings." The return of the day February 27 on "angel's wings" would signify the continuation of winter, so fervently implored by the speaker. Indeed, she is able to thank February 27 for prolonging winter through the embrace of its kin one month away:

> I thank you for all the favors.
> I requested, don't take away winter!—
> the problems of warmth and of (northern) lights
> you took away with you and removed from the earth.

> Благодарю тебя за все поблажки.
> Просила я: не отнимай зимы!—
> теплыни и сиянья неполадки
> ты взял с собою и убрал с земли.

(48)

Nature, or the days, openly colludes with her, while she in return records nature's activities without missing a single sunrise or moonrise under a varying moon or various moons. The persona's two selected favorite days are February 27 and March 27, ostensibly a period of physically prolonged "pred-vesna" (pre-spring) if not on the calendar, then in fact—a time when winter still actually reigns.[20] It could be her own seasonal equivalent of "non-color" ("netsvet") for colors and the special "no man's time," that is "non-spring" ("nevesna"), created artificially through her entreaties.

The speaker returns to power the protagonist of the poem, February 27, through association with its cohort March 27. At her behest the two days fraternize and probably include (actually "enslave") the days in between as part of the spacious circle. The cementing of one month of days when the weather will remain immutable pursuant to her wishes and the nature of February 27 is termed "our secret celebration" ("nash tainyi prazdnik") and "a round number" ("krugloe chislo"). The pre-spring rain of February 28, which would lean in the direction of true spring in nature, has been thwarted according to the speaker's wishes. Having conspired with the days (February 27) to prolong pre-spring of a wintry bent, the persona observes their antics without missing a single sunrise of which she subsequently sings under different moons. The addressee, following the first three descriptive stanzas, becomes the day of February 27. The current peer ("rovesnik") and rival ("sopernik") of February 27—March 27 itself—hid from the speaker in the gloom:

> Your current peer and rival
> was hazy and long like the times,
> not contemporary to March and lilacky,
> (it) is concealed from me in shrouds of gloom.

> Твой нынешний ровесник и соперник
> был мглист и долог, словно времена,
> не современен марту и сиренев,
> в куртины мрака спрятан от меня.

Insofar as this day truly held the promise of spring, long and "lilacky," she follows it up the hill while the sunset of this day is imbued with "feminine sadness."

---

20. The concept of pre-spring appears in the title of Akhmatova's poem "Pre-Spring Elegy" ("Predvesenniaia elegiia; no. 443).

All this prepares the reader for the feminine image that will be the converse of Homer's deity, the goddess Aurora. Day hides in the mist leaving behind the five petals of her forgotten glove, which fades on the table like a plucked lilac. This image reverses Homer's metaphor. The fingers of the dawn have through metonymy (five petals of a lilac glove) become a glove and are then metaphorized into the petals of a wilting lilac. They bring to mind the earlier five petals or the five scraps of paper with the unrealized poems for each of the five days. Homer's rosy-fingered dawn is evident here: in Russian, "mnogoperstnaia Avrora." Once day as deity has been established, the presence of the goddess Aurora comes as no surprise. The image of the lilac harkens back to the description in neologism of the day as "lilacky" ("sirenev") above, an unusual short-form adjective for this word. In books 2, 8, and 19 of *The Odyssey* dawn arrives early, with rosy fingers. Akhmadulina's addition of the glove in lieu of the fingers allows her to leave the glove as a trace in Aurora's absence and has supplied the color lilac for fading through the simile. Use of the glove could have been motivated by a refraction of Homer's original image where frigid winter necessitates gloves in Russia. Moreover, in the north the dawn may be less brilliantly colorful than in the southern lands of ancient Greece. For a waning day, lilac imagery, as opposed to rose or pink, is appropriate in view of the death or funereal symbolism in the imagery of Annenskii and Akhmatova, for the lilac, both as a color and a flower, and a wilting one in particular, underscores dying or funereal symbolism. Akhmadulina professes:

> The sunset is imbued with feminine sadness.
> Day slowly disappears in the haze—
> the five petals of its forgotten glove,
> like lilacs, wilt on the table.

> Закат исполнен женственной печали.
> День медленно скрывается во мгле—
> пять лепестков забытой им перчатки
> сиренью увядают на столе.

(49)

Two levels of narrative time are brought into play in this poem: the speaker uses "objective time" (stanza 11), that is chronological time that passes in nature within the poem—the fourth hour of a new day has commenced. She also employs "subjective time," the retarded time of her inner creative world through which she can remain within the previous day while objective time passes by: "Again it's past three o'clock of the next / date, but I have not come out of yesterday." There may be a temporal parallel, as it were, to the lyrical ego as related to the writing poet, i.e. the actual writer. As in colloquial parlance, the poet substantivizes without compunction the adverb of time "yesterday" ("vchera"). In Chapter 7 in addressing the theme of the bird cherry, the speaker will develop the notion of two simultaneous temporal levels to depict herself in two centuries at the same time.

The period between the two days, namely, the early hours of the new day when all is still dark, remains the speaker's time for composing verse. The time range echoes Annenskii favoring twilight (Setchkarev, *Studies in the Life*, 91, 108), as well as Tiutchev and Tsvetaeva. At the conclusion of the poem Akhmadulina's speaker clearly demonstrates how the impressions of the next, new morning will be described in verse only later, if at all: "And that which morning will cost me—I will endure. And I will describe it later" ("I to, vo chto mne utro oboidetsia— / ia preterpliu. I opishu—potom"). The span of one day is not sufficient for the creation of verse; and rarely is the night—the time for reassessing and creatively transforming the information—long enough: "A nightly chasing after the days: / poems, cramped is the figure of all the days" ("Za dniami ezhenoshchnaia dogonka: / stikhi—tesna vsekh dnei velichina"). In *The Garden,* three consecutive poems deal with three specific days in a more subdued tone: "The 29th Day of February" ("29-i den' fevralia"), "The Eve of March 30" ("Noch' na 30 marta"), and "The Order of Blooming" ("Tsvetenii ocherednost' "; 24–29). The last one, however, also echoes day as deity ("from the heavens March 31st / all pink, descended"—"s nebes den' tridtsat' pervyi marta / ves' rozovyi, soshel"; 28) and the appearance of plants so ardently awaited in the poem "I have the secret of wondrous blooming."

Quite eerie in the poem is the emergence from the ravine at night of a "great dampness," as well as its subsequent transmogrification into what initially seems to be an imperceptible white unknown human or animal. Dramatically, the persona queries:

> An owl? No! It's a great dampness
> that has emerged from the ravine and has entered the
>   window,
> it warmed itself—and an indistinctly
> white unknown someone headed back.

> Сова? Нет! Это вышла из оврага
> большая сырость и вошла в окно,
> согрелась—и отправился обратно
> невнятно-белый неизвестно кто.[21]

The confusion of the great dampness with an owl already points to a small size and to quick flight before daybreak. The persona's attitude toward it appears neutral. No, this is not a bird, nor is it likely to be the next, incipient day—March 28—seeing that the following stanza addresses the two days, whose fraternizing is the subject of her writing, and the one that has commenced these past three hours. The appellations, "semi-knowledgable spy" ("sogliadatai-nedoznaika") and "newness" ("nov' "), presumably refer to the mist from the ravine. Conceivably, it is the first mention of space, and its premier personification: "here is in my eyes and will remain all day / the total glaze of all-white" ("Stoit v glazakh i prostoit ves' den' / vse-belizny sploshnaia povoloka"; 51). This quotation from the following page dispels notions other than of space. It is "my enamored spy" ("vliublennyi sogliadatai moi")—space. The conclusion anticipates the next sequence of poems on space, which I shall explore in Chapter 6.

In summary, it can be seen that in a continual effort at composing verse in nature and on nature the speaker evokes the ancient concept of day as deity and of the days as the children of a given month. For each day in February and March of that unspecified year that she can immortalize through a poem lives twice, once in nature fleetingly and then in art for a longer time. Hence an artistic prolongation of time, as it were, in addition to briefer mental retardation of time for the purpose of composing. It was, furthermore, seen that the images and personalities of the days vary considerably—some are potent and stern, others are mild. Wings as a motif usher in the notion of the adopted child—here of day—or rather, through simile, of the cuckoo chick. This imagery evokes Pushkin and points to literary sources in addition to the mythological. The power and inspiration for the speaker's creation of verse assumes a new form and another part of the secret unfolds in preparation for the role of space.

21. Typically, "nevniatno" is used for sounds, speech in particular.

6

The Power of Space

"Dawn returns on the SUN's rewinding."
—F. D. Reeve

The themes advanced on the creation of verse in the Tarusa period that have been explored thus far—the moon, day, and nighttime vigil—directed the reader along the path toward discovery of the secret in the town of Tarusa. In the preceding chapter the "spacious" circle of days ready to do the poetic speaker's bidding involved the cooperation of all the days, since they all embraced one another within the enclosing fraternal embrace of the two days, February 27 and March 27. Akhmadulina's theme of space in the creative process, which originated within the poem on the day "Following the 27th Day of March," appears to be independent of previous literary tradition. Five consecutive poems treat it: "The Envy of Space" ("Revnost' prostranstva"), "The Mercy of Space" ("Milost' prostranstva"), "The Sternness of Space" ("Strogost' prostranstva"), "Light and Fog" ("Svet i tuman"), and "Dawn" ("Rassvet").[1]

The poem "The Envy of Space" commencing the theme of space in poetic creation, opens with what could be its disapproval of the speaker's previous doings: "An embrace—now that's an occupation and leisure" ("Ob"iat'e—vot zaniatie i dosug"). Space envies her poems' self-creation and the help rendered her by the days. The attitude could be the persona's assessment after a week has elapsed since the embracing of the two key days, namely, seven. Currently, the hands of support from the embrace have unclasped to reveal remoteness and milkiness: day has given way to space. "Glush'," (a remote secluded place) may be a precondition or prerequisite for the enlargement and all-envelopment of the whiteness that restricts vision if it is not what it creates in itself (through its presence):

1. Bella Akhmadulina, *Taina. Novye stikhi* (Moscow: Sovetskii pisatel', 1983).

> There's a bend here—but you can't discern
> the bend from Parshino to Tarusa.
> All-white's total glaze
> stands in my eyes and will stand all day.

> Здесь поворот—но здесь не разглядеть
> от Паршина к Тарусе поворота.
> Стоит в глазах и простоит весь день
> все-белизны сплошная поволока.

Somehow the all-encompassing white color of the early verse has transformed into an opaque tangible whiteness: "The distance is in white nothingness, proximity is not deep, / it is the apparition of the whites of the eyes and not of the pupil" ("Dal'—v belykh netiakh, bliz'—ne gluboka, / ona—belka, a ne zrachka viden'e"). Mist has become snow.

The explanation for all this is fairly straightforward. The white pieces of nothingness are, in effect, snowflakes, which proliferate the space only to turn into nothingness when melted by virtue of losing their white color to transparency and their form to a liquid state. With so much snow even closeness feels shallow, as if it were the apparition of the whites of the eyes and not the pupils that actually see. The Oka River is nowhere in sight in the whirling blinding snow. Spaciousness becomes a lost concept. Coming right up to the eyes, the snow is even squeezed and tight under the speaker's eyelids. The jealousy of space in being left out finds expression in its hiding under cover of the blizzard the normal occurrences in nature thereby obviating further poems by the persona without its participation and assistance. Admittedly, space does not stunt all her work, only that in which it is not instrumental. Indeed, now her current poem self-creates almost to its dictation (stanza 10). Space brings together both the speaker and her self-creating poem: "(My) sinful forehead and craft / have no fiercer matchmaker than space" ("U greshnogo chela i remesla / net svodnika liutee, chem prostranstvo").

One could say, then, that the poem now self-creates to the dictation or under the dictation of space, particularly during a strong blizzard, that now space serves as a medium for poetry. This affords a new twist to the persona's earlier creative process in the snowbound house and her relations with the moon and day, for previously she was indoors, whereas now she is outdoors or at an *open* window. Yet the poem, and space, refuse to divulge information on her questions to the former:

Well, if you self-create,
tell me: What is the meaning? What is the secret
    command?
Where is Tarusa? where is the village of Parshino?
But, the secretive poem remains silent.

Уж если ты себя творишь само,
скажи: в чем смысл? в чем тайное веленье?
Таруса где? где Паршино-село?
Но, скрытное, молчит стихотворенье.

The poem refuses to undo the handiwork of the blizzard, which has obscured the countryside and all objects to such a degree that the speaker cannot distinguish north from south. All is one big blur and a total immersion into the endless swirling motion of the white snow and its claustrophobic shadows. The jealousy of space is obviously a stance toward the embrace of days opening the poem. It is a jealousy of her seven-day creative absence from the magically detained winter weather of March. To make the persona forget all but her current poem and herself, space possibly triggered the blizzard, which physically narrowed the circle erected during the month of fraternization. Ultimately, all machinations notwithstanding, winter will lead irrevocably to yet another pre-spring.

It was the embrace of the tandem namesake days, February 27 and March 27, which brooked no warming of the weather, that resulted in the dominance of "glush' " and milkiness everywhere. A peak is reached on March 9, as demonstrated in the following poem "The Mercy of Space," which will put an end to the seven-day interim in which the lyrical ego produced nothing. The "glush' " and milkiness conceal from the speaker's scrutiny the landscape and even the turn from Parshino to Tarusa. All day long an "all-whiteness" prevails, so total in every way, that it whitens, then enters the speaker's eyes. In practical terms snowflakes indeed enter the eyes when the wind blows. The distance too is enveloped in white nothingness ("Dal'—v belykh netiakh"), while the phrase "nearness is not deep" signifies that nothing has depth anymore since the swirling snow crowds right up to the lyrical ego and enters her eyes, nose, and mouth, in other words, her body and being. Yet if this is a manifestation of space, it is now space, rather than day or the moon, that will enter the speaker for inspiration and direction in the finalizing of great verse. Consequently, everything is shrouded in mystery, even the most familiar objects and places: "What is beyond the Oka is a secret, and the Oka—/ is merely the knowledge of it or a delusion" ("Chto za Okoiu—taina, i Oka—/ lish' znanie o nei il' zabluzhden'e"). Knowledge or experience could be but a delusion if the present transformation is perceived as an absolute fact on the basis of what is there. In a later poem on the two sisters Ol'ga Ivanovna and Mariia Ivanovna, the notion of "beyond the Oka" will be developed further.

All the while Akhmadulina the poet operates deftly with defamiliarization and periphrasis. Everything is so totally white and voluminous that this whiteness squeezes under her eyelids more audaciously than the control of color by reality. Entrance into this infinite white color is possible only by groping, for this surrounding whiteness is whiter than in nature. In effect, it is a blizzard presented metonymically and metaphorically, and certain images are redolent of the Symbolist poet Aleksandr Blok's (1880–1921) cycle *The Snow Mask* (*Snezhnaia maska*).[2] The speaker perceives a whiteness concurrently with a darkness. Space and the movement of the swirling snow obstruct all objects and the reality that exists without the blizzard. So a motion-filled color white dominates everything else. Instead of saying that outside one has to grope one's way due to zero visibility caused by the thick or heavy snow, she maintains that one may enter this color (only one aspect of the exterior, hence metonymy) by groping. The style of her idiom is convoluted, flowery, and archaic, as in the word "is open" ("otverst"). The speaker does not, however, prowl to find the hidden threshold, again couched in strange language: "I don't prowl the hidden threshold" ("ne ryshchu [unusual verbal government] ia sokrytogo [obsolete] poroga"). In Akhmadulina's early poetry such complicated language, due to what she believes to be its insincerity, would have rendered mute the lyrical persona. Currently, quite the contrary, with her new aides for creating verse—the moon, day, and space—the creative process has changed so that the lofty words inflict no harm. Her name for the opening is "otkryt'e," its plug ("shtopor") is the blizzard, finally specified as such.

The circle within the jurisdiction of winter narrows everything that exists all around to zero visibility. If everything is white, so are wholeness ("tsel'nost' ") and minuteness ("podrobnost' "). Shadow plays a vital role here. The peculiarity of the constricted whiteness, hence its color, volume, and texture, is explained through the striking simile following it:

---

2. See Aleksandr Blok, *Sobranie sochinenii v shesti tomakh*, ed. M. A. Dudin et al. (Leningrad: Khudozhestvennaia literatura, 1980), 2:8–33.

In the hollow under the angelic wing
it is probably this white and this dark.

Во впадине под ангельским крылом
вот так бело и так темно, должно быть.

What makes the simile rare is the fact that instead of comparing the tenor and vehicle by dint of a comparative adverb ("slovno," "kak," "kak budto") or an instrumental of comparison, i.e., A is like B, it uses "tak" (so) in the tenor and omits the vehicle, which is the blizzard specified in the previous stanza, and ends on a problematic note—"most probably" ("dolzhno byt' ")—a device which, while comparing, leaves a margin of doubt. So Akhmadulina employs here what could be termed a "problematic simile." Implied in the simile is a shadowy tinge to the pristine whiteness of the angel's wing (possibly symbolic of day); with the white in shadow, day will be deprived, to a certain degree, of light and brightness. There emerges a cozy hemmed-in quality, a sense of being benignly protected. Indirectly, space is lauded.

Akhmadulina merely creates a semblance of contradiction by characterizing Day March 9 as "a stagnation of snows" ("zastoi snegov"), so cold that the snow has frozen solid, and "a rotation, or whirlwind of snow" ("snega krugovert' ")—note the obsolete form of the root -vert in lieu of the modern Russian root variant -vorot, as in "krugovorot" (rotation, circulation)—the wind is so strong that it swirls both the newly falling snow and whips up the frozen ground snow. The color of the snow can be called white only for short; in effect it is stronger and more nameless than whiteness since flatness ("ploskost' ") is insurmountably ramped through the unmentionable swirls of snow in motion with the deposited snow also lurching upward in the blizzard: "Insurmountable is the ramped flatness" ("Neodolima vzdyblennaia ploskost' "). The Day uses the blizzard to create the image of a horse and even to conjure up a coachman to complete the picture.

Although the coachman in "The Mercy of Space," unlike the coachman deftly tooling the wagon over the protests of the riders in Pushkin's allegorical poem "The Cart of Life" ("Telega zhizni"; 2:164),[3] belongs wholly to the power of the blizzard (a feature of Day March 9), and is at a loss because of it, his horse, later in Akhmadulina seen as Pegasus, foresees ["providit"—

3. A. S. Pushkin, *Polnoe sobranie sochinenii v desiati tomakh*, ed. B. V. Tomashevskii (Moscow: AN SSSR, 1962–66), 2:164.

an archaic, bookish usage] the snowstorm and with its nimble genius runs home safely. The horse, sung by her and now conveying her, vies with those whom she has not sung, where others have, until she hears its voice directly, not secondhand ("ne ot naslyshki"). The compound adjective "vechno-odnozvuchnyi" recalls Pushkin's "monotonous bell" ("kolokol'chik odno-zvuchnyi") and immortalizes Pushkin's image further through the adverb "eternally" ("vechno"). For the expression of all this, the speaker naturally resorts to floweriness in describing the steed: "for the time being, my dear, forever monotonous, / I hear your voice not secondhand" ("poka, rodnoi moi, vechno-odnozvuchnyi, / ne ot naslyshki slyshu golos tvoi"). To compose well the speaker must hear this voice firsthand.

The whiteness of March resembles her ink (that is, its absence from the paper) when it produces nothing. It must acquire color when creating something good. The persona may well have in mind the shadowy color to the white that she introduced in the preceding poem, "The Envy of Space." Into the whiteness through the watchful care of the ink not a spot was carelessly brought in. As usual Akhmadulina the poet moves freely through and between, if not even amid, layers of language, as evidenced by the obsolete high style word "attempt" ("tshchan'e") and the obsolete masculine gender for "hearsay" in lieu of the current feminine form in "the common parlance of hearsay" ("prostorechie naslyshka").[4]

A new simile underscores the speaker's learning aptitude in the collection. She has gleaned from Day (the Day in its entirety) its state indicating a schoolchild that is furtively copying from the work of his peer all the behavior of the snow and the hangover song in the village of Parshino. This simile contains both a tenor and a vehicle. It introduces the motif of the schoolchild to show that the persona at this point in time takes all her topics and inspiration from the entire day, the snow's behavior, and the hangover song in the village of Parshino. No intellect has been wasted on fabrications: the field actually undulated and the blizzard actually raged. Akhmadulina seemingly employs reality stringently and closely, yet with her unique and unusual devices and topics the result is a new, far more daring fantasy than in other writers. Only the phantom reader, whom she addresses, has been invented. The fabrication, addressed and personified, that she needs, since

4. Sofiia Liubenskaia in the article "O poeticheskom iazyke Belly Akhmadulinoi" maintains that "Akhmadulina's poetry is actually saturated with archaisms, Slavonicisms, and "poetic" lexicon. This phenomenon is characteristic not only of Akhmadulina, it is in fact observed in all major poets of the twentieth century, and even in many contemporary poets, but only in Akhmadulina is the concept of these layers of vocabulary unusually high" (159).

the reader has not read the poems on March 9, is a projection into the future, as is her unborn self in her narrative poem *My Genealogy* and the poem that would not come into being in "Line of Work." For the thaw of March 10 she changes from felt boots to rubber ones, an unpoetic detail worthy of Annenskii or of Pushkin's use of the prosaism "organism" ("organizm") in the poem "Autumn. An Excerpt" to which the latter calls particular attention:

> Once more I am full of life—such is my organism
> (Please forgive me this unnecessary prosaism).
>
> Я снова жизни полн—таков мой организм
> (Извольте мне простить ненужный прозаизм).

Through the image of dripping the intensification of the thaw evolves into the shouting drop, which in deference to March sobbingly prophesies. The window fibs brightly about having experienced the recent white murals on "gloom" ("mrak"). Space seems to equal nature as in the elements and the universe since all that was solid and brocade-like, as well as someone's dark-blue, thin voice giggled, namely, all snow and frost has thawed to a blueness so that the end house of Tarusa is visible through transparent Pachevo. The persona hears the laughter of space and of someone else that cleared the snow and is sending light, a kind of being—"uniqueness" or "oneness" ("edinstvennost' "). Or is it the classical divinity Day turned into *edinstvennost'*? Laughter is merciful. Her wristwatch joins her in being surprised. The faint delicate glimmer of a quarter moon enhances the air and light. Even so, a being orders her to sleep. The notion of "power and mercy" ("vlast' i milost' ") is of space here and equals the place of the blizzard. The deity transforms day into space and then into "edinstvennost' " (if the change is not only substitution), a higher being, a deity, almost a god, most probably a modern perception of God.

Not having quite finished with March 9 and 10, the poetic speaker dwells upon them nostalgically into the next day, without empathizing with March's easy dismissal of them as one of many. March 11, addressed in the poem "The Sternness of Space," peeks over the speaker's shoulder into her notebook. The reader should not be surprised, since by now the poetic world of Bella Akhmadulina has furnished numerous phantasmagorical events. Guilt grips the speaker for expending the third hour of this day on the previous one. The day's glance and address enforce its humanizing.

March 11 could be tacitly admonishing her on expending his precious irreplaceable hours on a less worthy sibling. Although still dark, the night is technically part of the new day, but the speaker is willing to sit up until daylight and even longer—until bird-cherry time—in order not to divulge anything unwittingly. The eleventh day's moon, a remnant of his sibling March 10, has disappeared just now; probably it is the moon that carries over into the early morning sky and sometimes, past noon. Now only the speaker's moon shines—the one she has transformed into verse (the verse-grown moon) after the day of springtime reprieve, not the one in nature. Two worlds acquire separate identity—one in nature, the other as reflected and working in her verse.

Stern and abrupt, this new day returns winter to nature:

> But you, I see, are stern. Where water stood,
> you helter-skelter erect ice floes in memory of ice
>   floes.

> Да ты, я вижу, крут. Там, где вода стояла,
> ты льдины в память льдин возводишь впопыхах.

Its sternness carries over to not replying to the persona's quibbles, instead "It fortified the Oka" ("On ukreplial Oku") with ice. Like a wicked wizard, the severe day freezes a bird in flight,[5] a measure of extreme cold, while striving to fashion out of water the lost past: "It checked strictly: is it frosty? / and in flight it killed the weakest of birds" ("On strogo proveryal: morozno li? / i na letu sgubil slabeishuiu iz ptakh"). Using the dialectal word "ptakha" brings to mind "ptashka," and the fact that it is most often used in the diminutive, to designate a small bird. Here Akhmadulina faintly echoes the civic poet Nikolai Nekrasov's (1821–78) famous narrative poem *Red-nosed Frost* (*Moroz krasnyi nos*), in which Frost maintains: "If I want—big rivers / I can hide for a long time under a yoke" ("Zadumaiu—reki bol'shie / nadolgo upriachu pod gnet").[6] Nekrasov's line "I will build palaces of ice" ("postroiu dvortsy iz l'da"; 2:101) echoes Akhmadulina's: "He built from water the demised past, / as if he were resurrecting a temple turned to dust" ("On stroil iz vody umershee byloe, / kak budto voskreshal khram, obrashchennyi v prakh").

5. Anna Lisa Crone has pointed out the connection with Mallarmé here.

6. Nikolai Nekrasov, *Polnoe sobranie stikhotvorenii v trekh tomakh*, ed. K. I. Chukovskii (Leningrad: Sovetskii pisatel', 1967), 2:101.

No longer does the speaker keep count of March's days: having caused her illness, this day irreverently forces her back home:

> When as usual I headed for Pachevo,
> it flung me home like its trifle.
> I no longer keep count of your days, March.
> Here's the singer of your deeds: frozen and sick.

> Когда я, как всегда, отправилась в Пачёво,
> меня, как свой пустяк, он зашвырнул домой.
> Я больше дням твоим, март, не веду подсчета.
> Вот воспеватель твой: озябший и больной.

To recuperate, the speaker will seek out a little nook between the days of March, that is, she will not observe or write for a while. Unfriendly space appears gloomy to her. Its unfriendliness is possibly due to her not composing at present. The persona will write about this "vyrodok iz dnei" (degenerate/black sheep among days) to hail the advent of day twelve. These words are most telling, they recall Pushkin's concept of the poet being different from ordinary men. Akhmadulina's lines refer also to the foundling day of March 12:

> Day—a degenerate of days, although it hails from
>   March,
> alone, like a poet—[is] always an alien in its clan.

> День—выродок из дней, хоть выходец из марта,
> один, словно поэт—всегда чужой в роду.
>
> (57)

Akhmadulina plays on the morphology of "*vy*rodok" ("a degenerate") and "*vy*khodets" (immigrant, a person from somewhere) by nearly equating them because the root in "vy*rod*ok" denotes "to come out into the world, to be born." It stems from Tsvetaeva's play on the word mentioned in Chapter 8.

Despite its own mischievousness, Day will not tolerate jokes or undue familiarity. Capacious space, probably the measureless volume inhabited by each successive day on earth with its moon and its nature, appears at the succession point between the days. Its demeanor is stern:

> How gloomily gazes unsociable space!
> It itself plays pranks but does not tolerate jokes.
> Woe on him who is overly familiar with it.

> Как сумрачно глядит пространство-нелюдим!
> Оно шалит само, но не приемлет шуток.
> Несдобровать тому, кто был развязен с ним.

At night paper and ink beckon the persona to evoke day, while she regrets that day has stepped beyond the midnight boundary. This degenerate day, although of March extraction, represents the one day in the month that, like a poet, remains ever a stranger in its own clan. To herald the advent of the stormy day of March 12, she will write about the departure of this "black sheep among days." Space here is unsociable ("neliudim"). March 11, then, is a solitary and isolated freak, and as in any clan, the poet is different and foreign. This stern petulant day is trying to turn the seasonal clock back to winter, to "resurrect" it, as it were. Out of the recently thawed water this day of March 11 crafts ice as if reconstructing a temple turned to dust. It constricts the streams with ice and torments the trusting willow that had sought to bud. A gusting wind lashes the speaker—a weightless, insignificant object—back from Pachevo. Consequently, this singer of March herself falls ill and seeks out a cozy spot of a few days between the days of March to recover. Meanwhile at night the paper and ink call upon day for poetic inspiration, but this stern day meets a tragic end when departing on March 12. The persona will not glorify it. The repetition here connects with the poem "The Day of March 12."

Imperceptibly, the persona's philosophic sententions wax into humor, then to irony on life and on man's outlook. Her moral emerges—life knows *us*, it is we who are ignorant of life. The shy ignorant person, however, is able to appreciate easily the small wonders of nature where the learned with their excess baggage of information cannot. This thought recalls the poem "I have the secret of wondrous blooming" with its sarcasm directed against the "gramotei" (would-be learned ones). Accordingly, in the next poem "Light and Fog" the persona ponders:

> No matter how long you live, no matter how long you
>   study sciences—
> life knows how to entice and make a fool of you,
> and the timid ignoramous, having said, "This is a
>   meadow,"—
> dumbfounded gazes at a dandelion.

Сколь ни живи, сколь ни учи наук—
жизнь знает, как прельстить и одурачить,
и робкий неуч, молвив: «Это—луг»,—
остолбенев глядит на одуванчик.

An echo of naive discovery sounds in the poem "There was no admission. I was unaware of it and entered" ("Byl vkhod vozbranen. Ia ne znala o tom i voshla"; *The Garden,* 59), in which the ingenuous ignoramus of *The Secret* is apparently teaching his son:[7]

Some kind of dacha, a drowsy hammock, and grass,
and an enamoured voice: "Sonny, this here is a daisy."

Какая-то дача, дремотный гамак, и трава,
и голос влюбленный: «Сыночек, вот
      это—ромашка»,

According to the poem "Light and Fog," man perceives the singular, or the piece, in lieu of the whole whose source lies beyond the heavens. Again, man's obtuse genius comprehends instances yet fails to grasp continuous time, a time signifying a lack of coordination for moments:

In the twinkling of an eye[8] there is the inspiration of
      lips—
in this instant [or "into this instant"] our short-witted
      genius penetrated,
but faced with the second (instant), our experience is
      totally stupid:
continuous time is a discord of instants.

Мгновенье ока—вдохновенье губ—
в сей миг проник наш недалекий гений,
но пред вторым—наш опыт кругло глуп:
сплошное время—разнобой мгновений.

This observation returns the reader to the earlier mention of wholeness and minuteness. While deploring man's inability to grasp mentally the total

---

7. Bella Akhmadulina, *Sad. Novye stikhi* (Moscow: Sovetskii pisatel', 1987), 59.
8. There seems to be here a visual play on "óka" (of the eye) with stress on the first syllable and "Oká" (the river) with stress on the second.

picture of life, the persona also addresses the microscopic and psychological differences within even the smallest and seemingly most "uniform" objects. Hence she advances the philosophical and scientific notion of even outwardly similar objects differing within their own kind. No two drops of water are alike, just as she is unlike anyone else: "The neighboring drop is not the drop's twin, / They are as similar as I and someone else" ("Sosedka kaplia—kaple ne bliznets, / oni pokhozhi, slovno ia i kto-to"). Humans, it seems, mostly overlook significant minute differences as well. Indeed, nothing, even the same object, is the same twice, not even the "shine" of what she is watching from the slope—the "shine" being metonymy for the river: "Two times will not shine in similar fashion / that at which I gaze from the hill" ("Dva raza odinakovo blestet' / ne stanet to, na chto smotriu s otkosa"). Here the speaker alludes tangentially to her philosophical source, the Greek philosopher Heraclitus (540–475 B.C.), who professed that one could not step twice into the same river, because of perpetual motion and changes in the river and person alike.[9] In quoting this premise of Heraclitus, Akhmadulina follows Tsvetaeva, who quoted the Greek philosopher in her essay "Poets with a History and Poets without a History."

As the speaker continues her search for inspiration and the ability to craft a poem, she not only goes out into nature, but while indoors at certain times, she looks out beyond herself. Everything is viewed through the window, an image and activity pivotal to the poets Annenskii and Akhmatova, and interesting in Aleksandr Blok and in Pasternak. The activity produces no positive results for Akhmadulina's persona:

> The wonder of the window is always new to me.
> Its eternal reader and laborer,
> I don't have the courage to know what the letters
>   mean;
> and for the twentieth time now I am a repeater.

> Всегда мне внове невидаль окна.
> Его читатель вечный и работник,
> робею знать, что значат письмена,—
> и двадцать раз уже я второгодник.

>   (58)

Everything is perceived anew, hence "nevidal' " (that which has not been seen before, a wonder). Naturally, the view changes each time she studies it.

---

9. *Encyclopaedia Britannica*, 11th ed., 13:309.

On this day, albeit an artistic reading of nature through the window is thwarted by fog, no matter what, its reader the persona must strive toward understanding nature. For its part, nature seems to be proudly and potently ensuring limited access to its secrets to a select few. Thus the speaker is "vtorogodnik," a failed student, a repeater many times over.

In the poem "Light and Fog," the blue color signifies the appearance of light through the fog, quite important in Annenskii, but slow enough here to make it a time of despondency ("unynie") for pre-happiness. The speaker finds that the expression ("iz"iavlenie") of the abyss is denser than the word. Coming to life, her pen wants to record in art, but all remains unattainable from the fog, or mist ("mgla"). Beyond the dense fog that seems to work like a wall to shield the light lies the anonymous largeness of what in common parlance is called blue. Given the fact that the sun will yet appear, everything is blue and not non-color. The blue of the previous poem has unfolded into dawn. On the background of such a color, the speaker's humble flower, Van'ka-mokryi (Dewy Vanka), all raspberry and ruby, comes to life.[10] The spreading of dawn does not condescend to become friendly with the viewer, namely the speaker, who finds everything in sight utterly inextractable from the mist. Wholly enthralled with the view, she professes not to have the willpower to fear the future, although even the downcast stance of the birches in March presages a special sorrow of pre-happiness. In answer to her announcement of fearlessness for the future, space, momentarily abandoning its self-absorption, suggests sweetly, "Don't lie."

Accordingly, on March 26 the speaker is found at her perennial role perusing the "nevidal' " of the window and working at it. Apart from its regular meaning of "wonder" or "rarity," "nevidal' " probably denotes in a single word "never to see the same thing twice or in the same light." Because the speaker must strive to understand and probes the far depths opening from here, she remains timid before what unfolds through the wonder of the window. Failing to comprehend fully the letters, the persona remains a dummy, a repeater, for the twentieth time. Evidently, "vtorogodnik" is the lyrical ego insofar as at this point she has twice failed to compose a poem in spite of her diligent plumbing of the far reaches open to the window. Still, her awe of nature's wisdom remains strong. Now while it is still dark and well in advance of the dawn, the speaker has set herself to reading nature:

10. The Dewy Vanka is a rose-red flower that always looks dewy, as described to me by Bella Akhmadulina in March, 1987. I believe it was growing in flower pots on her window sill when I visited her in Peredelkino in November of 1983.

Well, today on the 26th day of March,
While still dark I undertook this reading.

Вот—ныне, в марта день двадцать шестой,
я затемно взялась за это чтенье.

In ordinary parlance there is a thick fog. Even so, the expression of the abyss is denser than the word. What unfolds before the persona through the window is a color colloquially dubbed light-blue but which remains anonymously large. Her unconceited flower Van'ka-mokryi came to life on this as if to inspire her with color. Obviously, the plant is potted and its flowers have just opened. Its colorful pageant cannot as yet be matched by the growth of dawn and of light that has not deigned to fraternize with the observer. Everything in sight is inextractable from the mist. There is a special despondency of pre-happiness as if the persona were in love with March (61) in its downcast posture of birches which she does not possess the willpower to fear. They are like the waiting Sleeping Beauty.

The poem "Dawn" treats what appears to be dawn of March 26, the dawn that was only a vague reality in the previous piece "Light and Fog," with which it is connected by title and the opening line:

It grows light earlier than yesterday.
I woke up at six o'clock because
in the window—so close as if within me—
prophesying,
a droplet muttered, tormenting me with its prophesy.

Светает раньше, чем вчера светало.
Я в шесть часов проснулась, потому что
в окне—так близко, как во мне—
вещáя,
капель бубнила, предсказаньем муча.

It could also be March 27, the final day of the enchanted circle of days that were enlisted to detain winter further because in the previous poem the speaker was awake to greet the dawn that never arrived. Now she awakes at six o'clock with dawn in full glory. It could be March 27 since it grows light earlier than on the previous day but it could also be the dawn of March 26. She is awakened by the "muttering" in the window of the prophesying, predicting dripping of thawing snow. Not at all what she wants to hear, its

prediction of spring's advent torments her. Gaining momentum as it bur-
geons into a stream, the water parallels an unvoiced, or unformulated, simile
on the enlargement of dawn and the final establishment of spring. As if
within the speaker ("kak vo mne"), the thin voice of the muttering, racked by
sobs, grows into a stream of sorts and into moaning. Simultaneously the
appearance and change of color resembles a tearing through the shroud of
the mist. Its enlargement heralds and shapes the potency of the dawn. The
transformation touches the water in a glass: "water shows dark-blue in a
glass on the table" ("voda sineet na stole v stakane"). It is probably there to
force bloom the branches that will introduce some aspects of spring into the
lyrical ego's life, the desired ones only, while she retards the others.

    With her sight so perfectly full of the moment, the speaker would prefer
the long-awaited dawn ("zaria") not to appear. There is a saturation with
blueness, of new light, not only in nature but in one's life. Even so, this
persona, the insatiable favorite of this wondrous moment, gazes at the dark-
blue volume of Osip Mandel'shtam's poetry, obviously the Poet's Library
Series edition of 1974.[11] To continue this train of thought and to evoke his
poetry, bee and dark-blue lungwort ("medunitsa") imagery will follow—an
elaboration on the images in the opening poem. The light-blue dreamy
color of the previous poem develops into dawn; the ambience of the dark-
blue water in the glass on the table, the earlier blobs of color, which were the
size and hue of olives, now turn into dark-bluish purple plums, not very
different from the water in the glass. Outside, the birds cast into the snow
are blue titmice ("sinitsy")—with the same prevailing color ("sinii"—dark-
blue) in the name's root. So intense is the blueness that the speaker expects
the pupils of her eyes to be dyed the dark-blue color and she no longer
wants the awaited dawn. It is as if the entire pre-dawn prefigured the
Mandel'shtam volume and a new dawn in modern Russian poetry. The
imagery here may be a reversal of the burying of Russian poetry with the
death of Pushkin, an image taken up by several writers, including Mandel'shtam. Here, the sun rises on Mandel'shtam's verse. Prominent in the
poem is the symbolism of light and dawn in life and culture. Given this new
information, one can conjecture whether in the previous poem the persona
was merely scanning the view from the window or also preparing to immerse
herself in the Mandel'shtam volume. Whichever is more plausible, if not
both possibilities simultaneously, all color concentrates to enhance the Man-

    11. Osip Mandel'shtam, *Stikhotvoreniia,* compiled by N. I. Khardzhiev (Leningrad: Sovetskii
pisatel', 1974).

del'shtam image, to announce, as it were, that his volume (however cropped by the censor) has finally been published in his own country following decades of ban. Yet everything is predicated on understatement.

Space, then, which emerges by emitting a great dampness, assumes tangibility and corporeality, as it were, through a proliferation of swirling snow or a thick fog to encase nature and the lyric persona, goes on to dictate to her. Its mien remains somber and stern, even through its envy, as if it were playing a role. Finally, it allows itself to be seen through a light-blue dawn heralding light and change. The change is not only political but seasonal, for spring must arrive and bring with it the bird cherry—the next instrument of verse in the collection *The Secret.*

7

The Lure of the Bird Cherry

Зацветет черемуха душиста.
—Pushkin

Черемуха мимо
Прокралась, как сон.
—Anna Akhmatova

Popular in Russian song and verse, the widely growing fragrant white, and occasionally pink, bird cherry has appeared in the verse of Pushkin, Akhmatova, Esenin, and Pasternak, among others. The critic Vitalii Vilenkin expounds on the tragic aspect of the bird cherry in the verse of Akhmatova in his study, *In the One Hundred and First Mirror;* namely, in her poems "Way of All Earth" ("Putem vseia zemli") and "From the Cycle 'Youth' " ("Iz tsikla Iunost' "), both of which treat the period of the Russo-Japanese War (1904–5).[1] For Akhmadulina the white petals afford a smooth transition from white snowflakes, which tangibly crowded space in the poems discussed in Chapter 6 and which in turn are derived from the image of white scraps of paper. Three poems furnish the bird cherry's name in the title: "Bird Cherry" ("Cheremukha"), "The Three-Day Bird Cherry" ("Cheremukha trekhdnevnaia"), "Bird Cherry Last but One" ("Cheremukha predposledniaia"); with three more in *The Garden:* "The Demise of the Bird Cherry—1" ("Skonchanie cheremukhi—1"), "The Demise of the Bird Cherry—2" ("Skonchanie cheremukhi—2"), "Bird Cherry of the White Nights" ("Cheremukha belonoshchnaia"), and one implied—"The Order of Blooming" ("Tsvetenii ocherednost' ").[2] The image, however, figures within other poems as well, where it still remains close to that of paper scraps ("like bird cherry scree

---

1. V. Ia. Vilenkin, *V sto pervom zerkale: Anna Akhmatova* (Moscow: Sovetskii pisatel', 1987), 201–2.
2. Bella Akhmadulina, *Taina. Novye stikhi* (Moscow: Sovetskii pisatel', 1983), and *Sad. Novye stikhi* (Moscow: Sovetskii pisatel'. 1987).

under a broom"—"cheremukhovoi osyp'iu pod venik"), and unravels imagery and themes in ever more complex designs and configurations, her objective becomes the subtle melding of present poetry and time with the classic poetry of the past.

As a medium for change in temporality and for inspiration during the creation of verse, Akhmadulina now turns from the moon, the day-deity, and space to the pungent bird cherry. Artistically, these are poems on the ongoing creation of verse; philosophically, they are poems on the changes effected in verse by time; personally, for the poetic speaker the blooming bird cherry serves as a medium for entering and manipulating temporal planes other than her own. Akhmatova achieved comparable results through the artistic use of metempsychosis and of multiple subtexts from other writers within her poetry. The speaker, like the real Bella Akhmadulina, is in retreat to write in Tarusa's rest home for architects, *Dom arkhitektora*, presided over by two sisters, Mariia Ivanovna and Ol'ga Ivanovna. Three periods of time can be singled out during this sojourn:

1. "Do cheremukh" (pre-bird-cherry)—normal earthly time, languid, reflective.

2. Time of forced blooming indoors, resulting in compressed time and space, with the concentrated fragrance.

3. Dual time and space with temporal movement in the direction of the past and rarely to the future, as with the pilot. It is induced through sustained exposure to the hallucinogenic qualities of highly concentrated fragrance.

The normal period of blooming for the bird cherry in Tarusa appears to be fifteen days in mid-May (*The Garden*, 29, 41) in contrast to the three concentrated days of forced blooming in crammed space indoors described in the poems in *The Secret*. Three poems from *The Secret*—"Bird Cherry," "The Three-Day Bird Cherry," and "Bird Cherry Last but One"—are examined here with reference to several related poems in *The Garden*.

The first poem "Bird Cherry" resounds with the earlier poem "The Sternness of Space," in which the persona insists: "I'll sit up until light and longer—until the bird cherry, / in order not to say hastily, how black the night has become" (56) as well as the poem "I have the secret of wondrous blooming." The speaker now elaborates on her previous words:

When (my) enamored mind was enchanted by March,
I said, "To finish my service to night I'll sit
until daybreak and longer—until the bird cherries";
having thought (a little I said): "I'll sit up if God wills I
    live that long."

Когда влюбленный ум был мартом очарован,
сказала: досижу, чтоб ночи отслужить,
до утренней зари, и дольше—до черемух,
подумав: досижу, коль бог пошлет дожить.

(61)

The season is probably sometime in late April or early May if the lilacs are in bloom in Georgia, unless she is imagining it all. By the time the speaker returns to the Oka River and the bird cherry blooms in Russia, it is probably the second half of May or early June—still, the speaker has no qualms about glossing over time. The chosen one of this poem, the bird cherry, rivals Tbilisi in the speaker's favor since it induced her to leave Georgia's Aragvi River for the gloomy ravines of the Volga and its tributary, the Oka. She probably flew the branches in from the South. Now the tree is real, although the petals are as yet unopened, where previously it was comprised of the letters in the word, as mentioned in the poem "I have the secret of wondrous blooming." The later Akhmadulina, who, like Annenskii, uses similes to create extraordinary formulations, finds striking metaphors as well: "Oh, if only I catch backstage at the benefit performance / before coming out into the world its young fright" ("O, tol'ko by zastat' v kulisakh benefisa / pred vykhodom na svet ee mladoi ispug"). Apparently, the words "to live until the bird cherry" ("do cheremukh dozhit' ") refer to being able to compose until this period, hence her fervent prayers. With the bird cherry on the verge of bloom, the speaker has reached its "pre-first," or initial movement. By cutting off some branches, she takes captive, or ensures, the plant's intention to bloom the next morning; in other words, she forces the bloom. In the glass of water from the earlier poem "Light and Fog" they will blossom out into their pungent flowers. So the bird cherry, soon to burst into bloom, is real now and made of flower petals and not of letters alone.

The poem addresses that which yet is not but which is expected to be momentarily, a situation particularly emphasized in the image of the bird cherry that has still to blossom and become real from its idea in words and pictures. The speaker's olfactory sense cannot derive the scent of the flower from the name alone, only the genuine flower connects the fragrance, so crucial to her composing, to the name. Fearful lest she miss the "pre-initial" movement of the bird cherry as it begins bursting into bloom, she cuts off the branches just before the big event. Periphrasis encumbered by defamiliarization expresses the fact at this point: "its intention / to bloom in the morning I have taken captive" ("ee predpolozhen'e / nautro rastsvesti ia zabrala v polon"). The obsolete Russian form "polon" is substituted here for

the current form from Church Slavonic "plen." Obviously, the form emphasizes the practical aspect of capturing. While vacationing in Georgia, the
lyrical ego apparently retained in her memory the image of a pale bush,
vulnerable and shy, as if unloved, tormented, and persecuted. She then
amends the image to being tormented by adoration, obviously hers. The
bird-cherry bush cannot be faulted for what has been predetermined by the
persona. A striking simile, of the kind Setchkarev attributes to Annenskii,
follows: "It [the bush] is not to blame for what I have predetermined. / In
this way the poor child by his father's promise / is already engaged, though
he's not yet born" ("On [kust] ne povinen v tom, chto mnoi predresheno. /
Tak bednoe ditia ottsovskim obeshchaniem / pomolvleno uzhe, eshche ne
rozhdeno"; 61).

To observe the first bloom of the tree as it unfolds, the speaker neglects
her verse-writing. The reader's mind echoes with the primrose ("pervotsvet") in the poem "I have the secret of wondrous blooming." It seems that
she has not written since March. Presumably, she was away in Georgia; now
her interrupted poetic line from stanza 2: "Under the March moon showed
forlornly black—/ like mileposts through a blizzard—the outstretched line"
("Pri martovskoi lune chernela odinoko—/ kak vekhi skvoz' metel'—
prostertaia stroka"), now ends in the perorating stanza with no change. It is
still frozen in time, suspended, as it were: "The forgotten line extended in
time" ("Zabytaia stroka vo vremeni povisla"). Indeed, the persona has
stopped writing on the month of March, having switched her topic now to
late spring and the renewal of nature. To write on Russian spring and the
first bloom of the bird cherry, she eagerly curtails her usual visit to the
Aragvi River in Georgia, as noted in her early poetry. Implied here is the
meaning of only "first bloom" as opposed to the primrose in the poem "I
have the secret of wondrous blooming." The root "black" in the word
"chernela . . . stroka" already anticipates acoustically the bird cherry ("cheremukha"). The humor and irony of the collection continue throughout to
conclude this poem with a challenge to the interpreter and a welcome
comment for the reader: "I am always bored with the seeker of sense, / and
I cannot please him: I (fall) asleep" ("Vsegda mne skushen byl vyiskivatel'
smysla, / i ugodit' emu ia ne mogu: ia spliu").[3] Her aching head metaphorized into a garden and a ravine: the provenance for the ideas, the
receptacle for the images from nature to be metamorphosed: "What's hap-

---

3. Note how she matches in spelling the most accepted pronunciation of the word "skuchen."
Its effect may be not only to please by showing that she is like everybody else in her speech but even
to shock the reader with unconventionality. What is more, it imitates Tsvetaeva.

pened to my poor head" ("Chto s bednoi golovoi?"; 62–63); "there is a hollow there now, in order not to inhibit the plants, / the forgetful ravine and the fainting garden" ("tam vpadina teper', chtob ne stesniat' rasten'ia, / bespamiatnyi ovrag i obmorochnyi sad"). Sleep glues her eyes shut. In general, the speaker appears bored with seekers of sense in poems, her words serve as a warning to the readers of the poem. In the collection *The Garden* Akhmadulina will once again address the insistence on sense in the poem "A Christmas Tree in a Hospital Corridor":

> Long have I been reproached that my works are empty.
> Composer of empty things, I look into the corridor at
>   my compatriots.
>
> Мне пеняли давно, что мои сочиненья пусты.
> Сочинитель пустот, в коридоре смотрю на
>   сограждан.
>
> (63)

If some people seek sense in the empty verse of the composer of empty things, now at least her verse can resound with music where earlier, as discussed in Chapter 2, it was the speaker who was an empty instrument ready for art to play.

Thus in this poem the persona, her mind enamored of March, decides to sit until dawn and into bird-cherry time. The specific time is early in May since April 30 is seen as early for the blossoming in Tarusa, as revealed in the poem "The Order of Blooming":

> This time spring did not try my patience—
> it handed out all its debts with a running jump,
> and sooner than always—on April 30—
> the bird cherry blossomed throughout the
>   neighborhood.
>
> На этот раз весна испытывать терпенья
> не стала—все долги с разбегу раздала,
> и раньше, чем всегда: тридцатого апреля—
> черемуха по всей округе расцвела.
>
> (*The Garden*, 29)

To be sure, in nature the bird cherry blossoms for about fifteen days ("The Demise of the Bird Cherry—1"—"Skonchanie cheremukhi—1"; *The Gar-*

den, 41) in contrast to the three days of forced blooming. The theme of reading and writing ("gramota") returns to echo the poem "I have the secret of wondrous blooming." The speaker pronounced the period to be that of the bird cherry due to the inconceivability of the time period. Yet naming the flower does not induce recognition of its fragrance. The process seems to be one of conjuring up the bird cherry through the written word. The speaker could be tacitly evoking the outstretched branch of the tree as well as its obvious meaning in the lines of "in the moonlight": "Under the March moon showed solitarily black— / like mileposts in a blizzard—the out-stretched line (of verse)." For now this line shall remain suspended in time in the poem's coda. A pale bush emerges a few lines later. To ensure an early blooming of the flowers, the lyrical ego brings home some branches from the sheltered ravine, as shown in the poem "No matter what region I give myself up to" ("Kakomu ni predamsia kraiu").

> and there in the ravine dear to me
> where I would go to get the bird cherry.
>
> и там, где в милый мне овраг
> я за черемухой ходила
> (The Garden, 66)

Although the home environment will force the blooming, the cutting of the branches will result in quicker wilting of this plant that does not cut well. Luckily, the verse promised to remain until true bird-cherry time, to guard, perhaps, the pale, vulnerable bush outside.

Meanwhile, the speaker enjoyed the South with its riotously ("bacchi-cally") blooming lilacs. This time she eagerly gave up the luxury of the Aragvi River in Georgia for the still morose landscape of the Oka. Her return proves to the bird cherry its favored status over the Georgian capital of Tbilisi; its attraction now consists in its petals, ready as they are to turn into words of verse (as once scraps of paper evoked the petals), and not into the dry letters of March. It is almost as if the thought expressed in letters induces the true bloom. The opening of the flowers in the morning is personified as well as treated with imagery. Through metaphor the first opening is quietly linked with the mouth of a fledgling ready to gape, which recalls the image of the cuckoo in Chapter 5:

> The knots of the cramped petals loosen—
> and the yawning of a little mouth wants to know:
> where the freshly damp feed is that it seeks.

Слабеют узелки стесненных лепестков—
и маленького рта желает знать зевота:
где свеже-влажный корм, который им иском.[4]

Now the shyness of the flower as well as its vulnerability emerge in its confusion through the scrutiny of the speaker's face and the lamp: "It has awakened and trembles. Above it are a face and a lamp. / It is embarrassed to blossom in all its beauty and glory." ("Ochnulas' i drozhit. Nad nei litso i lampa. / Ei stydno rastsvetat' vo vsiu krasu i stat' "). Like a young adolescent, the bird cherry is embarrassed to show its full beauty in bloom. While this image of comparing blooming in nature with young persons is not new to literature nor to figurative speech and many examples of it can be found in written works, one wonders whether Akhmadulina was not familiar with Akhmatova's translation of the poem by the exquisite Armenian lyricist of miniature form, Maro Markarian (b. 1915), "The Peach Tree." In Akhmatova's Russian translation Markarian's poem reads:

The Peach Tree

You blossom, my peach tree,
A lass, a wilding-maiden . . .
Who fawns upon you, who clings?
That is the faint mountain breeze.

And you are embarrassed, (you) tremble,
You fear love's initial words,
And your charm—
Is a soundless and silent call.

But you do not gaze at yourself
And therefore you do not know
That in your youthful loveliness
You are perfection in beauty.

I look at you in alarm,
Sighing and secretly sorrowing,
How you remind me
Of something most dear.

4. Akhmadulina successfully spreads out an image over the collection in mounting or waxing motifs, the theme in the process of development and the quieter declining or waning of motifs, as in the present example of the gaping fledgling. Also, the bird-cherry image mounts in the poem "I have the secret of wondrous blooming" through the witnessing of its first bloom, another meaning of "pervotsvet," and finds its declining motifs only in *The Garden* following a revival of the theme in several poems.

Персиковое деревцо

Ты расцветаешь, персик мой,
Подросток, девушка—дичок . . .
Кто ластится к тебе, кто льнет?
То легкий горный ветерок.

А ты смущаешься, дрожишь,
Любви боишься первых слов,
И обаяние твое—
Беззвучный и безмолвный зов.

Но на себя ты не глядишь
И потому не знаешь ты,
Что в юной прелести своей
Ты совершенство красоты.

С тревогой на тебя смотрю,
Вздыхая и грустя тайком.
Как ты напоминаешь мне
О чем-то самом дорогом . . .[5]

The flower's displeasure at being awakened sooner than nature intended in a place almost like a laboratory is intimated through a bald simile: "The blossom, like the nakedness of an awakened eye, / cannot discern: why it was not allowed to sleep" ("Tsvetok, kak nagota razbuzhennogo glaza, / ne mozhet razgliadet': zachem ne dali spat' "). The simile's vehicle evokes the redness of a sleepy eye. It recalls, furthermore, the flower's inner reddish core. Verse, the martyr of love, accepts the disfavor of the flower. The written verse is viewed as a separate entity by the persona, although the writing effort is depicted as a joint venture with her: "Verse, martyr of love, accept its disfavor! / What is the subservience of your and my ink to it!" ("Stikh, muchenik liubvi, primi ee nemilost'! / Chto rabolepstvo ei tvoikh-

5. See Anna Akhmatova, *Iz armianskoi poezii*, compiled by K. N. Grigor'ian (Yerevan: Sovetakan grokh, 1976), 56. Akhmatova's original poem on poetic creation "One More Lyrical Digression" ("Eshche odno liricheskoe otstuplenie"; no. 377, in Akhmatova, *Stikhotvoreniia i poemy*, compiled by V. M. Zhirmunskii [Leningrad: Sovetskii pisatel', 1976]) equates through simile and metaphor blossoming apple trees with newlyweds:

And the apple trees, God forgive them,
As if (newly) from the altar, are in love's tremor.

И яблони, прости их боже,
Как от венца, в любовной дрожи.

moikh chernil!"). Yet the writing of the poem and the observing of the flower are linked with the dangling March line. The theme of the bird cherry continues beyond the pale of *The Secret* into *The Garden* in the poems "How many this little music has" ("Kak mnogo u malen'koi muzyki etoi"; 10) "My Lebedkin" ("Lebedkin moi"; 20); "The Order of Blooming" (29); "The Demise of the Bird Cherry—1" (41); "The Demise of the Bird Cherry—2" (43); "The nearby border of Lapland's summer ice" ("Laplandskikh letnikh l'dov nedal'niaia granitsa" (93); "Space is never playful here" ("Zdes' nikogda prostranstvo ne igrivo" (122–24); "Bird Cherry of the White Nights" ("Cheremukha belonoshchnaia"; 126–28).

At this point the speaker laments: "What's happened to my poor head? What's happened to my head? / In it, like butterflies, swarm trifles" ("Chto s bednoi golovoi? Chto s golovoi moeiu? / V nei, slovno motyl'ki, pestreiut pustiaki"). The image of flying creatures clustering was presaged by the earlier image of swarming bats where the word for "bat" was changed slightly for emphasis and possibly for poetic sound (17, 19). The linking of the bird cherry with the buzzing of bees or of thoughts in the speaker's head brings to mind the nineteenth-century impressionistic miniature lyricist Afanasii Fet's (1820–92) poem "Bees" ("Pchely"):

> . . . The bird cherry sleeps.
> Oh, again those bees are under it!
> And I cannot at all understand
> Whether the ringing is in my ears or on the blossoms.

> Черемуха спит.
> Ах, опять эти пчелы под нею!
> И никак я понять не умею,
> На цветах ли, в ушах ли звенит.[6]

6. A. Fet, *Stikhotvoreniia* (Moscow: Khudozhestvennaia literatura, 1970), 183. Fet is known for the image of butterflies in his verse. Indeed, the satirist Mikhail Saltykov-Shchedrin (1826–89) placed him in the "butterfly" school of poetry. Butterflies, or large moths, home in on light in Fet, as the thoughts probably do for Akhmadulina's speaker at night, in his poem "People are not in the least guilty before me. I know" ("Liudi niskol'ko ni v chem predo mnoi ne vinovny. Ia znaiu"):

> "My heart, like irrational Icarus, from out of the gloom like a
> butterfly to the light,
> To the sacred thought strives.

> Сердце—Икар неразумный—из мрака, как бабочка
>   к свету,
> К мысли заветной стремится.

In this connection Annenskii's poem "Flies Like Thoughts" ("Mukhi kak mysli"), based on a line from the poem "Flies" ("Mukhi") by a lesser known poet of sadness and dissatisfaction with life, Aleksei Apukhtin (1840–93), also comes to mind here:

> Flies like Thoughts
> (*In memory of Apukhtin*)
>
> I am weary from insomnia and dreams,
> Locks are hanging over my eyes:
> I would like through the toxin of poems
> To numb unbearable thoughts.
>
> I'd like to untangle the knots . . .
> Could it be there are only mistakes there?
> In late autumn the flies are so vicious,
> Their cold wings are so sticky.
>
> Flies-thoughts crawl as in a dream,
> Here they've covered the paper, blackening (it) . . .
> Oh, how, dead, disgusting they are . . .
> Tear them to pieces, burn them quickly.

> «Мухи как мысли»
> (*Памяти Апухтина*)
>
> Я устал от бессонниц и снов,
> На глаза мои пряди нависли:
> Я хотел бы отравой стихов
> Одурманить несносные мысли.
>
> Я хотел бы распутать узлы . . .
> Неужели там только ошибки?
> Поздней осенью мухи так злы,
> Их холодные крылья так липки.
>
> Мухи-мысли ползут, как во сне,
> Вот бумагу покрыли, чернея . . .
> О, как, мертвые, гадки оне . . .
> Разорви их, сожги их скорее.[7]

7. Innokentii Annenskii, *Stikhtvoreniia i tragedii*, compiled by A. V. Fedorov, Biblioteka poeta, Bol'shaia seriia, 3d ed. (Leningrad: Sovetskii pisatel', 1990), 79. For the underlying poem "Mukhi,"

It is interesting to make the connection between what folk etymology can deem the two roots "black" and "fly" (*cher* + *mukh*) linked by the soft connecting vowel "e" in "*cher*e*mukh*a" and thoughts like butterflies.[8] Apukhtin and Annenskii alike are suffering from insomnia and overwork.

In Akhmadulina the thoughts swarm in her head, whereas Annenskii's have already reached the paper. Annenskii's flies have sticky wings. The stickiness in Akhmadulina is that of the opening flower, as in leaves that are just bursting out of the bud. But the stickiness mingles with the butterflies and the trifle-thoughts (or trifling thoughts) and her closing eyes as well as the stickiness of a spider's web; drowsiness becomes "sticky drowsiness" ("lipkaia dremota"), in her head and mind the butterflies stick in the gluey drowsiness that hangs between her temples. In fact, comparison with the Russian idiom "eyes are sticking together from fatigue" ("glaza slipaiutsia ot ustalosti") inclines one to consider this locution a realized metaphor in both poets.

Having kept vigil for forty-eight hours (after the first day ["den' "] comes night ["noch' "], then "den'," and finally "noch' ") the speaker becomes transfixed and engrossed to such an extent that she forgets the line of verse now suspended in time from the pre-bird-cherry period. Regretting that the falling of the first petal portends warmth and the end of this charmed fleeting period, she subsequently falls asleep expressing her impatience with the seeker of logic that she cannot, and will not, satisfy. Suspended between logic and humor, the poem reaches an expected but uneasy coda. As illogical as the words may seem due to periphrasis, the expression equals its first blooming viewed as a spectacle: "Oh, if only I could catch at the backstage of the benefit performance / before coming out into the world [also "society"] its young fright." The comparison comes to mind of the nineteenth-century pioneering ballerina Maria Taglioni (1804–84) who made history by

---

not quoted here, see A. N. Apukhtin, *Stikhotvoreniia*, ed. R. A. Shchatseva, Biblioteka poeta, Bol'shaia seriia (Leningrad: Sovetskii pisatel', 1961), 148–49.

8. In Goethe the butterfly symbolizes the possibility of poetic immortality, whereas in Mandel'shtam it equals literary and linguistic resurrection. See Anne Nesbet, "Tokens of Elective Affinity: The Uses of Goethe in Mandel'štam," *Slavic and East European Journal* 32, no. 1 (1988): 119–20. In Annenskii the butterfly is a symbol of inspiration. Vsevolod Setchkarev, *Studies in the Life and Works of Innokentij Annenskij* (The Hague: Mouton, 1963), 63–64, 128. It is also frequent in Tiutchev. See F. I. Tiutchev, *Lirika*, ed. K. V. Pigarev (Moscow: Nauka, 1966), 1:15 and 75. Also curious is the fact that the Greek word for "butterfly" is the same as for "psyche." Moreover, A. E. Anikin links Annenskii's "Flies Like Thoughts" and his prose poem, "Needles-Thoughts" ("Mysli-igly") with Lermontov's "objects-thoughts" ("veshchi-mysli"). See his "*Akhmatova i Annenskii. Zametki k teme* (Novosibirsk: AN SSSR, 1988), 12.

first standing on point. Part of a theatrical dynasty, she performed several times in St. Petersburg.[9] The parallel with the former prima ballerina of the Bolshoi Theater, Maya Plisetskaya, Boris Messerer's first cousin, and the Messerer theatrical dynasty also emerges here. As sleep overcomes the persona, the line that she was writing remains unfinished. The line that in stanza 2 under the March moon resembled a black milepost in its extension, that martyr of love ("terzaem obozhaniem"), is now a forgotten line suspended in time, namely it is not continued.[10] The blooming and dropping of the first petal was carefully grasped by the persona who neglected the previous topic for verse in order to follow the first bloom ("pervotsvet") of the bird cherry.

Many aspects of the poem "I have the secret of wondrous blooming" continue here. Particularly patent is its irony. The speaker ironizes through the words of the moon over those seeking sense in the poem, as the speaker herself is doing. Sense can be attempted only by carefully piecing together the mosaics. Having returned before the blooming, she appears to pick a branch: "It didn't bloom!—its intention / to bloom in the morning, I have taken captive" ("Ona ne rastsvela!—ee predpolozhen'e / nautro rastsvesti ia zabrala v polon"). This occurred on the previous day because the passing of night is expressed by two nominative sentences, a favorite technique of Tsvetaeva: "Yesterday. A little darkness" ("Vchera. Nemnogo t'my"). The buds ("pochki") open, which fact is expressed periphrastically by the words "The knots of the constrained petals are slackening" ("Slabeiut uzelki stesnennykh lepestkov"). Employing the device obscures her meaning as desired. The branch is now in the speaker's room: "It has awakened and trembles. Above it are a face and a lamp." Unless the face implies the sun, it is presumably the persona's face. Rudely awakened from its seasonal slumber, the bird-cherry flower glares with displeasure at the poem: "Verse, martyr of love, accept its displeasure." At least twenty-four hours pass (provided the first night ("noch' ") listed does not refer to the first night already mentioned in the poem) or perhaps forty-eight hours (if the first "noch' " listed means a night after the first to figure in the poem): "Thus a night, and a day, and a night I bend before it" ("Tak noch', i den', i noch' skloniaius' pered neiu"). So the poem "Following the 27th Day of March" left dangling with a promise to describe later, remains incomplete, while

9. See *Teatral'naia entsiklopediia* (Moscow: Sovetskaia entsiklopediia, 1967), 5:40–41.

10. It vaguely echoes the milepost in Akhmatova's *Poem without a Hero* in Vilenkin's interpretation of a poet in general ("Verstovoi stolb [byl] Poetom voobshche"; 227).

images are evoked of lilacs blooming in the South at the beginning of April, approximately one month before blooming in Tarusa: "of that March line" ("toi martovskoi stroki"). The last two stanzas portray the speaker drifting off to sleep.

Strange indeed, the bush is very much like a shy retiring maiden. Its stark black outline in the moonlight pales as the buds unfold to reveal shyness in the morning.

> . . . in front of my face
> shines a pale bush, so vulnerable and timid,
> as if (it were) not loved but tormented and persecuted.

> перед лицом моим
> сияет бледный куст, так уязвим и робок,
> как будто не любим, а мучим и гоним.

Perhaps, the speaker conjectures, it is tormented by adulation. The bird cherry is obviously displeased with the forced early awakening due to being brought indoors and kept in water. Its displeasure is aroused by the poem whose chosen one it is ("izbrannitsa stikha"). The poem becomes a martyr of love for the bird cherry that cares not a whit for all the fawning. (The spotlight on the ink could be to illuminate the flower Van'ka-mokryi.) So whereas in the South—in lush Georgia—the southern lilac bloomed riotously and even "bacchically," in the severe north—in Russia—the northern, more sedate bird cherry, with flowers clustered like a lilac, self-consciously and austerely spurns the adoring love of the poem. The distinction between the two lifestyles, as it were, mirrors two contrasting and alternating periods in the speaker's life—the austere secluded periods of artistic creation versus the periods of relaxation away from the self-imposed restrictions. This obviously echoes the early period in her poetry.

Sleepiness causes trifling thoughts to crowd the speaker's head in a fashion reminiscent of Annenskii's concept of "flies like thoughts": "What's wrong with my poor head? What's happened to my head? / In it, like butterflies, trifles show multicolored" ("Chto s bednoi golovoi? Chto s golovoi moeiu? / V nei, slovno motyl'ki, pestreiut pustiaki"). Butterflies, often white, conjure up the fluttering white petals of the bird-cherry flower as well as the snowflakes in recent poems. Everything seems interchangeable with the passing of time and the establishment of each successive season. Earlier in the collection five petals become white paper, in the morning they turn into five rays, which equal the fingers of dawn, further on they change to snowflakes, later to bird-cherry petals, and finally the butterflies emerge. Their clustering image reflects obliquely the bats in previous poems (17, 19). Typically for Akhmadulina, there evolves a changing succession of interrelated and intertwined images.

The stickiness of newly or nearly opened buds, reminiscent of Pushkin's "Little sticky leaves unfold" ("Raspustiatsia kleikie listochki"; 3:63),[11] is no different than the persona's sleepy eyelids. In her drowsy mind the stickiness turns to spider glue, namely cobwebs, then to a sticky drowsiness between her temples, obviously periphrasis to connote her brain, where the butterflies stick. It correlates to the earlier simile of thoughts.

The forgotten line of earlier verse (50) hangs suspended in time due to her slumbering while the first petal falls—a forlorn indication of impending warmth, a time when the persona usually stops creating verse on these topics. She returns to the topic of being bored with seekers of sense in her verse whom she cannot please. Hence she makes fun while stating her refusal to change her poetry for these people. Her excuse is her slumber. In the poem "A Christmas Tree in a Hospital Corridor" there is an affirmation of censure, as already noted. Having prepared the readers for a possible lack of logic in the poems, she launches the truly illogical one. The topic persists in "The nearby border of Lapland's summer ice":

> The mind is a feature of genius, but it harms talent:
> a poem composed by it [the mind] always lies a tiny bit.

> Ум—гения черта, но он вредит таланту:
> стих, сочиненный им, всегда чуть-чуть соврет.
> *(The Garden, 93)*

There appears to be here a new reflection of the earlier concept of muteness as high-flown, lofty verse without artistic essence and emotion, as in the poem "Something Else."

While the speaker is following the first bloom ("pervotsvet") of the bird cherry, Tsvetaeva, the speaker's mentor and idol of the twentieth century, returns as a theme that the speaker experiences through delirium, allegedly induced by the heady scent of the bird cherry blossoms. In the poem "The

11. A. S. Pushkin, *Polnoe sobranie sochinenii v desiati tomakh*, ed. B. V. Tomashevskii (Moscow: AN SSSR, 1962–66), 3:63.

Demise of the Bird Cherry—2,"[12] the hallucinogenic qualities of the bird cherry emerge. They not only affect her but they create her lyric persona: "I am the hallucinogenic invention of the blossom":

> . . . The pulse of my open temple is nourished
> by a bird cherry infusion.
> It [the bird cherry] is my delirium. But we deserve each
>   other:
> and I am the delirious fabrication of the blossom.
>
> The instrumental potion itself will decide
> what will to foist on my mind.

> Черемухи настоем
> питаем пульс отверстого виска.
> Она—мой бред. Но мы друг друга стоим:
> и я—бредовый вымысел цветка.
>
> Само решит творительное зелье,
> какую волю навязать уму.
>
> (The Garden, 44)

Poems of this type are the possible reason for the misnomer of a "hallucinatory quality" to Akhmadulina's verse in the program for her reading at the historic Tremont Temple in Boston on 21 March 1988. Bella Akhmadulina told me in private communication on 25 March 1987 that the heady fragrance of the bird-cherry blossoms truly effected a lightheadedness in her which served as the impetus for these particular poems. In a similar manner the daisy affects the speaker in the poem "There was no admission" (*The Garden*, 60). Obviously, the effect of smells on writers is well known, such as in the case of rotten apples for Baudelaire and wilting lilies for Annenskii.

In her bird-cherry delirium the persona partly travels backward in time to Tsvetaeva's girlhood in Tarusa. With the locale already the Tsvetaev summer vacation site, the return is partial only, seeing that she simultaneously carries on a spirited conversation with her present landlady. In actuality her illness—the cold (57)—from the earlier, pre-bird-cherry poem has now

---

12. I believe "skonchanie" is used in the regional idiom to mean "death" ("smert'," "konchina"; D. Ushakov, *Tolkovyi slovar' russkogo iazyka*, 4 vols. [Moscow: Sovetskaia entsiklopediia, 1934], 4:228). It could, however, be used here in the obsolete bookish meaning of "end" ("konets" or "okonchanie").

reached the delirium stage through the bird cherry. This time the trip to Georgia may be a figment of her delirious imagination; since she feels hot, she may believe she had been in the South and, again, it may have been real. Or if the time is the beginning of April, the bird cherry may have been delivered by her Georgian friends to cheer her up in her illness. The discussions with the historical Nefedov were summoned by the bird cherry "fumes."[13] Disregarding chronological exactitude under the influence of the bird cherry's diachronic effect, the speaker's neighbor Nefedov has himself been under the influence of the bird cherry for three days. The poem concludes with the fourth day of the bird cherry whose fragrance and cold beauty, in permeating the room, have affected the persona's mind. Mention of the plant as a "beauty" evokes the word "krasa" in the poem "I have the secret of wondrous blooming." The plant is "the flaxen-haired leader of strange thoughts" ("vozhd' belokuryi strannykh dum"). Under its influence the speaker spurts out its nonsense ("bredni") for three days. All the while the white butterfly image hovers in the vicinity. The plants' pernicious or ruinous bloom ("dushepogubnyi tsvet") confuses her.[14] Perceiving the effect, the landlady Ol'ga Ivanovna calls the plant mischievous, "rasten'e-ozornik," for inducing unusual states that require neologisms by Akhmadulina, in this case "glush'" (isolatedness, detachedness), "laziness and langor"—"len' i lunnost'" (the latter is "mooniness," a languid state of observing which brings to mind the white milkiness of pre-dawn).[15]

Notwithstanding the impairment of the persona's reasoning due to the situation ("povrezhdennyi razum"), she slyly makes certain not to be distracted or brought back totally to the present by the landlady's invigorating tea and the honey:

> How refreshing the tea! How wonderfully bitter the
>   honey tasted!
> How cunning I am!—neither the tea nor the honey
> distracted me from the knowledge that Nefedov
> elegantly heavily jumped down from the droshky.

13. In private communication Akhmadulina explained to me that Nefedov had been a kindly landowner in those parts who was still remembered with affection.

14. The actual word is "dushepagubnyi" (pernicious) or "dushegubnyi," but the difference in Akhmadulina is probably derived through folk etymology from the idiom "dushu pogubit" ("to damn one's soul").

15. "Lunnost'" (mooniness), a languid state of observing, which recalls the white milkiness of pre-dawn, is actually Blok's coinage and not Akhmadulina's.

Как чай был свеж! Как чудно мед горчил!
Как я хитра!—ни чаем и ни медом
не отвлеклась от знанья, что Нефедов
изящно-грузно с дрожек соскочил.

At first, the conversation with Nefedov, the learned squire of Pachevo ("Pachevskii uchenyi barin"), revolves on the government of the time and on Tolstoi; later it leads to Tsvetaeva and to Nefedov's acquaintance with the young Marina and her sister Asia. Nefedov leaves as the landlady enters once more. While it lasts, the enterprising speaker lives two lives simultaneously, in two different time periods, an unusual experience in Russian literature. This is not the concept of the double as in the great master of prose Fedor Dostoevskii's (1821–81) novella *The Double* (*Dvoinik*), nor is it metempsychosis as in Akhmatova where the persona experiences other lives, periods, and states without specifying simultaneousness. Rather, one assumes that Akhmatova's persona takes time off through dreams, sleep, etc., from her "permanent" life of the present to visit other possibilities, or that the different lives succeed one another. Here in Bella Akhmadulina there is deft handling, a juggling of sorts, of concurrent "events" where the speaker commends herself, "how cunning I am" ("kak ia khitra," a kind of self-laudatory spying on oneself—*sogliadataistvo*), for partially managing to deceive the landlady. In the present she drinks tea, while in the concurrent past her drink is alcoholic, shown through metonymy "at a meeting of wine glasses" ("pri vstreche riumok"). Even so, the two planes meet through the landlady's inquiry concerning his sanity. Left alone with Nefedov, the persona wants this delirium to continue as a possible means to meet the Tsvetaev girls, but her expectations are not realized within the poems, seeing that the girls' mother is ill with tuberculosis. It could be the years just prior to their mother's death in 1906. To be sure, prior to this point in the collection, the speaker senses and sees Tsvetaeva everywhere, notably, the greenness of her eyes in the lush vegetation and her very name in the blooming of nature. Surprisingly, there are signs of the speaker having served Nefedov some food, which the landlady, Ol'ga Ivanovna, notices. Because Ol'ga Ivanovna knows Nefedov sufficiently to volunteer that he is nervous, her own genuineness in this scene comes under scrutiny.

The fourth day commences with the prevalence of greenness. The theme of insanity continues to permeate the poem along with the speaker's delirium. Slowly an impression is formed that if her delirium is due to illness, then the landlady's mental state is more permanent where Nefedov is concerned, if it is not a more extreme result of the bird cherry. At first it all sounds innocuous, the landlady has left and the persona says:

> O, someone, ask me about it . . .—
> there's no one!—it's all the same to me! let him ask,
> "All is clear about you. But why is Nefedov
> connected to you? After all—he is sane?"

> О, кто-нибудь спроси меня о том . . .—
> нет никого!—мне все равно! пусть спросит:
> —Про вас все ясно. Но Нефедов сродствен
> вам почему? Ведь он-то—здрав умом?

So the idea of questioning *his* sanity is introduced. A ludicrous affirmation of his sanity undercuts effectively her elaborate avowal by maintaining that she is in the same state as he:

> Oh, completely. All his clan
> is known for common sense, and he himself
> has taken an examination in electricity.
> But—his bird cherry is also three days old.

> —О, совершенно. Вся его родня
> известна здравомыслием, и сам он
> сдавал по электричеству экзамен.
> Но—и его черемухе три дня.[16]

Using the same root—*zdrav* (healthy)—in her answer, the speaker resorts to nonsense—that is, that his clan is known for common sense and that he has taken an examination in electricity, which could be a euphemism for electrical shock treatment for nervous disorders. Her elaboration underpins the similarity in their conditions. At the end, to the speaker's delight, the landlady shows her permanent acquaintance with Nefedov:

> "Do you know him?" "Of course, I know him!
> A very kind, noble person, only he's nervous."
> Praise to my three-day bird cherry!
> Congratulate us on its fourth day.

16. Here as in the previous quotation, Akhmadulina employs the emotive dash typical of Tsvetaeva.

—Он вам знаком?—Еще бы не знаком!
Предобрый, благородный, только—нервный.
Хвала моей черемухе трехдневной!
Поздравьте нас с ее четвертым днем.

Even Nefedov's departure fails to remove the presence of the two green-eyed young sisters whose eyes could be gazing at the full moon:

> It [the fourth day] has begun. How green the forests
>   are!
> The waters blazed with a green light.
> Or are these the green eyes of two girls
> contemplating the full moon?

> Он начался. Как зелены леса!
> Зеленым светом воды полыхнули.
> Иль это созерцают полнолунье
> двух девочек зеленые глаза?

Thus the image of the greenness of Tsvetaeva's eyes melding with nature resurfaces from the beginning of the collection for the last time. Accordingly, the moon conspires with the heady bird cherry and with the speaker's understated delirium to add to her experiences, to whisk her away, as it were, from her own time and from personal concerns as well as from the practical mundaneness of her daily life to the life of her poetic idol. All of this cold burning, this loss of mind and time, is fortified through the lacing of four words bearing the same root *gor*. The impression is that Akhmadulina is showing Akhmatova, the master of burning and grieving imagery, that there are alternate ways of burning and losing one's mind and suffering bitterly: in stanza 1 "ty ugorish' " means "to be poisoned by fumes"; here it refers to fragrance or else it means to lose one's wits, which is also relevant in the given context. In stanza 4 the burning imagery is enhanced by possible conflagration in "his house will burn" ("dom ego sgorit"), in stanza 9 by a bitter sensation "how wonderfully bitter the honey tasted" ("kak chudno med gorchil") with the honey possibly made of bird-cherry nectar. Finally, in stanza 10 there is grieving, connected in Akhmatova with burning, "we grieve over gloomy days of the fatherland" ("o mrachnykh dniakh otechestva goriuem"). Granted, Tsvetaeva crafted a narrative poem on the intricacies of this root in her *Poem of the Mountain* (*Poema gory;* 1:366–73).[17]

The tree, then, emerges as a flaxen-haired leader of strange thoughts, revealed to the speaker through confession in the course of three days. It probably disclosed the essence and secrets of nature within its keeping to the enthralled poet, who lovingly terms the thoughts "ravings." Fearing the appearance of Nefedov, the landlady would prefer to refute the tree and its transmogrifications. As intimated in the previous poem, here too one understands that the speaker put the branches in water in her room to force the blooming, but has thereby shortened the blooming period. Happy in her present state induced by the overpowering fragrant blossoms, the persona slyly thwarts the well-intentioned actions of the landlady to return her to a normal state; nothing, however, works, neither the removal of the branches, nor the tea. Deftly, the persona juggles drinking tea with Ol'ga Ivanovna— "the honey made the tea taste bitter"—with conversation in the past.[18] The poetic speaker, then, either imagines the honey is made of bird cherry nectar or, more likely, it actually is. The landlady could be offering her the local honey. The other side of the juggling involves her simultaneous conversation with Nefedov on education, politics, and Tolstoi, despite the state of languor, mooniness (a sort of dreaminess), and mental intoxication induced by her delirium and intensified by the bird cherry. Thus present reality and imagined past reality coexist in one poem at one time. So too the moon, the fourth day, and the bird cherry all advance her poetic activity. Using the newly discovered properties of the bird cherry, the persona possibly "artificially" extends her creative period to May when the Tarusa region bird cherry blooms in reality, whereas in her early period (pre-1980s) she would face writer's block in the early spring.

In the poem "Bird Cherry Last but One" the speaker's fantasies return to the present with projection into the future, as evidenced by talk of the pilot. The fourth day has fully dawned to the strong influence on her mind of the intoxicating bird cherry. The resulting fun and games thrust upon her mind the expansive submissiveness of her spirit in exchange for native regions of slopes and environs, cemeteries and monastery walls, all connected with Tsvetaeva's Tarusa and the past. With the concentrated fumelike fragrance of the bird cherry in hand, the speaker intends to condense its stupefying

17. Marina Tsvetaeva, *Sochineniia v dvukh tomakh*, compiled by Anna Saakiants (Moscow: Khudozhestvennaia literatura, 1980), 1:366–73.

18. The berry of the bird cherry, a bush of the rose family, is edible but bitter, the flowers produce nectar, probably with a bitter tinge. It grows best near rivers. See the *Bolshaia sovetskaia entsiklopediia,* 47:134.

fragrance into a one-time-only essence, into one full inhalation of that which the entire neighborhood breathes in many times: "Everything that the entire neighborhood / inhales—I undertake to inhale at one time" ("Vse to, chto tselaia okrestnost' / vdykhaet,—ia berus' vdokhnut' "). The result of such intense inhaling (almost like pure oxygen) will probably be choking, death, and resurrection, possibly a reward for her good intention: "Let me suffocate, let me be resurrected / and die—let something happen" ("Dai zadokhnut'sia, dai voskresnut' / i umeret'—dai chto-nibud' ").[19] Or else if she inhales what the neighborhood has exhaled, she becomes like a purifying plant that can process carbon dioxide into oxygen; in other words, she approximates the leaves of the bird cherry. More likely, she imbues the lives, thoughts, and essence of Tsvetaeva's beloved Tarusa, the better to concentrate it into verse. Mundane reality becomes art under Tsvetaeva's influence and its residue of green color. It is unclear whether this is a possible stage toward poetic reincarnation.

The persona further pleads with the bird cherry to take possession of her as she is no more cramped than the environs (neighborhood), to make her a slave or a friend (she uses the old form "drugi") or to take her into the ravines and to possess her. There is here an intricate play on verbs and on the accusative case for different meanings—"voz'mi v raby" versus "voz'mi v ovragi." The possession of her person is reminiscent of her early poem *Chills* (*Dreams of Georgia*, 227), in which the chills take possession of her body and mind as of a musical instrument for art, but here it is more a possession of the mind and imagination. In *The Garden* the speaker awaits an elusive "little music" in proximity to the bird cherry in the poem "How many this little music has" ("Kak mnogo u malen'koi muzyki etoi"):

> Heeding the transient bird cherry,
> I especially know how precarious life is.
> But that's not enough for little music:
> it chased all away, yet itself did not come.
>
> Черемухе быстротекущей внимая,
> особенно знаю, как жизнь непрочна.
> Но маленькой музыке этого, мало:
> всех прочь прогнала, а сама не пришла.
>
> (*The Garden*, 10)

19. Note the play on the form "dai," which when followed by an infinitive means "let" and when coupled with a noun or pronoun in the accusative denotes "give," as in the alternately possible "give me something."

The bird cherry will compose for the speaker and will guide her hand in writing. The verbal play on literally taking one to a place versus taking as a person's position or role to be fulfilled toward the subject rejuvenates the idiom here:

> take me as a slave or a friend
> or (take me) into the ravines and take possession of me.
>
> What fantasy will you infuse in me with your breath?
> Free to command,
> what will you compose and what will you write down
> with my hand in my notebook?

> возьми меня в рабы иль в други
> или в овраги—и владей.
>
> Какой мне вымысел надышишь?
> Свободная повелевать,
> что сочинишь и что напишешь
> моей рукой в мою тетрадь?

Wondering what fantasy the bird cherry will waft toward her, she leaves it free to command her, to create and to write with her hand and in her notebook. The persona wants it to perfume the corners of her room: "and for the time being / perfume my corners" ("a pokuda / okurivai moi ugly"). With the intense intrusion of the bird cherry into space, into her senses and her thoughts, come ideas of possible love for the tree: "In the center of a closed circle—/ is love or the eve of love" ("V sredine zamknutogo kruga— / liubov' ili kanun liubvi").

Indeed, the bird cherry has one kind of knowledge that it imparts through the pain-inducing breath of its bloom: hope ("upovanie") and torment. In the stage of initial bloom in the preceding poem, the tree induced an imaginary conversation set in the early twentieth century with Nefedov that also concerns the two Tsvetaev sisters; now slowly losing its bloom, it conjures up contemporary images (ostensibly, for lack of potency)—of an airplane and a pilot. The account is somewhat eerie, with magical words: the bird whose name the speaker keeps secret, as in observance of a taboo, "my precious period, the bane of witchcraft" ("moi zapovednyi srok, paguba privorota"). It is like predicting or sealing the pilot's future, the change in him, his isolation from people while in flight and later for having wings. One senses a tacit comparison with the poet and her wings for creating. The speaker intuits the lack in the present of ertswhile romanticism and only the gloomy beauty of the Caucasus, "the twilight squint of the Caucasus" ("sumrachnyi prishchur Kavkaza"), mediates the boring age. Toward this depiction the speaker furnishes a superb image of the high peaks of the Caucasus as of Gothic architecture:

> Everyone has experienced how imperiously
> the sharp-peaked snow attracts us.
>
> Любым испытано, как властно
> влечет нас островерхий снег.

Akhmadulina is apparently carrying on a dialog with Pasternak here. The description of the pilot in flight in Boris Pasternak's poem "Night" ("Noch' ") develops into an image of the artist who must bear vigil at night by the window in order to create. The concluding four stanzas of Pasternak's poem are particularly pertinent:

> Sleep does not come to someone
> In the wonderful distance
> In the ancient attic
> Covered with tiles.
>
> He looks at the planet
> As if the heavenly firmament
> Has bearing on the subject
> Of his nocturnal concerns.
>
> Don't sleep, don't sleep, work,
> Don't interrupt your labor,
> Don't sleep, fight the drowsiness,
> Like the pilot, like a star.
>
> Don't sleep, don't sleep, artist,
> Don't succumb to sleep.
> You are a hostage to eternity,
> A captive to time.

Кому-нибудь не спится
В прекрасном далеке
На крытом черепицей
Старинном чердаке.

Он смотрит на планету,
Как будто небосвод
Относится к предмету
Его ночных забот.

Не спи, не спи, работай,
Не прерывай труда,
Не спи, борись с дремотой,
Как летчик, как звезда.

Не спи, не спи, художник,
Не предавайся сну.
Ты—вечности заложник
У времени в плену.[20]

Moving into the future with the aid of the bird cherry and out of imprisonment by time, Akhmadulina's pilot will be pronounced ill and will be sent to
a sanatorium where he will drink fierce sleep-inducing peacefulness. Out of
pity for the pilot, the speaker demands to occupy him with another
motion—to save him, to give him a promotion, and to marry him off.[21] The
joking ceases as the persona perceives the fading of the blossoms' breath
and the falling of the petals onto the written poems. She is not certain that in
spring in the bird cherry's native ravines the two of them will meet once
more. Ostensibly, the reason is that spring is drawing to a close. It was fun to
invent a pilot whom they left unharmed, unlike her early poem "Small
Planes,"[22] in which the pilot in question was actually shot down, although

20. See Boris Pasternak, *Stikhotvoreniia i poemy*, compiled by L. A. Ozerov, Biblioteka poeta,
Bol'shaia seriia (Moscow: Sovetskii pisatel', 1965), 463. It is interesting to compare here W. B.
Yeats's poem "An Irish Airman Foresees His Death," in *The Collected Poems of W. B. Yeats: Definitive
Edition, with the Author's Final Revisions* (New York: MacMillan, 1962), 133–34. In fact, in several
instances points of juncture can be discerned between Akhmadulina and Yeats.
    21. Another instance of Akhmadulina's speaker as author becoming a character in an artistic
work is found in her *My Genealogy*. Blok moves into the narrative as "the author," a character
included in the dramatis personae to influence the plot in his play *The Puppet Show* (*Balaganchik*) in
Aleksandr Blok, *Sobranie sochinenii v sesti tomakh*, ed. M. A. Dudin et al. (Leningrad: Khudozhestvennaia literatura, 1980), 1:358.
    22. Bella Akhmadulina, *Sny o Gruzii* (Tbilisi: Merani, 1979), 76.

this fact goes unmentioned in the poem. The image of a pilot over enemy territory could in part stem from the first poem in Tsvetaeva's diptych "Dream" ("Son"), which begins with the lines: "I burrowed in, forgot myself—and how from a thousand—" ("Vrylas', zabylas'—i vot kak s tysiach—"). In it the image of falling is augmented through comparison:

> Vigilantly—like a pilot over enemy territory
> Sleeping—(like) a dream over a soul.
>
> Зорко—как летчик над вражьей местностью
> Спящею—над душою сон.

> (1:276)

The speaker in Akhmadulina extracts a promise that this hour of night will not be a rehearsal of parting with all that is dear to her. She wants to meet again in nature for a second meeting (under natural conditions this time) in one season and location, without the accelerated time and concentrated breath of the branch blooming indoors. This is where the above-mentioned poems in *The Garden* come into play. The appearance is of fun and games.

The poem "Bird Cherry Last but One" evokes the introduction to Pushkin's *Bronze Horseman* in the image of the two dawns in close proximity: Akhmadulina has "The close proximity of sunrise and sunset / crowds my sacred time" ("Dvukh zor' splochennoe sosedstvo / tesnit moi zapovednyi srok") where Pushkin states "One dawn hurries to replace the other / Having given night a halfhour" ("Odna zaria smenit' druguiu / Speshit, dav nochi polchasa"; 4:382). Obviously, the theme of a deranged mind figures in the *Bronze Horseman* in the character of the tragic young man Evgenii. In Akhmadulina the fever and delirium of her speaker from the bird-cherry fumes mask the true tragedy inherent in the theme of Tsvetaeva's early and violent demise and in Nefedov's idiocy. Conversely in the poem "Frantsuzov's Death" ("Smert' Frantsuzova")[23] the fever and delirium are ascribed to the bird cherry and not to the speaker, ostensibly because outdoors in nature the tree is experiencing headiness from its own enfolding fragrance in the enclosed ravine:

> Here's what happened to me, what happened not to
>   me:
> the bird cherry was in fever and delirium all night . . .

23. Bella Akhmadulina, *Stikhotvoreniia* (Moscow: Khudozhestvennaia literatura, 1988), 311.

The bird cherry's conversation became mad toward
    morning . . .

My bird cherry's petals have not yet fallen.
I am going to its ravine without having finished writing
    the poems.

Вот было что со мной, что было не со мною:
черемуха всю ночь в горячке и бреду. . .

Черемухи к утру стал разговор безумен. . .

Черемуха моя еще не облетела.
Иду в ее овраг, не дописав стихи.

In the poem of 1985 "At the foot of the mountain a grieving house, an
unlucky house lives" ("Pod goroi—dom-goriun, dom-gorynych zhivet"; *The
Garden*, 132), a phantom quality is ascribed at night to the bird cherry
growing outdoors in the northern region of Lake Ladoga:

And at night the passerby can see from the road
how the phantom of the bird cherry stands by the
    window
and how the expression of the window is of the beyond.

И ночному прохожему видно с дороги,
как черемухи призрак стоит у окна
и окна выражение потусторонне.

Two stanzas below, the image of a bird-cherry branch ("vetv' cheremukhi")
repeats, only to be reinforced with the reappearance of the repeater who was
the speaker in *The Secret* and now figures as the vehicle of a simile that
serves to wind down several recurring images in Akhmadulina's intricate
internal system of reference (again refers to her?):

The repeater, tired of earthly misfortunes,
looks at the globe just as stupidly and intently.

Второгодник, устав от земных неудач,
так же тупо и пристально смотрит на глобус.

Next the questioning repeater image and the branch merge through periphrasis "the triumph of the questioning branch" ("voprositel'noi vetvi triumf"). The poem prepares for the image of white nights and hence the North in the next poem's title while continuing the speaker's adoring vigil:

> I am tired out at the post of the white nights,
> and the bird cherry is oversaturated with me.

> Я измучилась на белонощном посту,
> и черемуха перенасыщена мною.

Another poem of 1985, "Bird Cherry of the White Nights," returns figuratively to the bitter honey and tea drinking:

> The inhaler and admirer of the bird cherry,
> again I drink the infusion of its soul.

> Черемухи вдыхатель, воздыхатель,
> опять я пью настой ее души.[24]

This northern bird cherry of Sortavala in Karelia remains aloof and unaccepting of the "southern" speaker. So aloof does it remain that the poet employs metonymy through the word "dialect" or "language" ("narech'e"):

> Near non-being
> the bird cherry's dialect replies,
> "Go on your way. I don't love you."

> Вблизи небытия
> ответствует черемухи наречье:
> —Ступай себе. Я не люблю тебя.

And in the poem on the North "So white that it singes my eyelids" ("Tak bel, chto opaliaet veki"), where the bird cherry blossoms even later, the time

24. Bella Akhmadulina, *Izbrannoe. Stikhi* (Moscow: Sovetskii pisatel', 1988), 446. Interestingly, the violet ("fialka"), mentioned here and which figures in the poem "I have the secret of wondrous blooming," is related to the bird cherry. It is obviously linked to the image of Ophelia in *The Garden* (140, 142, 145) and in Tsvetaeva. For a discussion of violets and Ophelia, see my *Poetry of Anna Akhmatova: A Conquest of Time and Space*, verse translation by F. D. Reeve, Slavistische Beiträge 196 (Munich: Otto Sagner, 1986), 121–37.

comes to part with her bird cherry this particular season, prolonged through travel North; yet she deplores the impending separation:

> and the bitter time of parting
> of my bird cherry with me.

> и расставанья срок горючий
> моей черемухи со мной.
>
> (*The Garden,* 123)

Although the bird cherry in the North has finished blossoming, apparently, a fading remnant remains in her crystal vase (if it is not encased in ice during unseasonably cold weather):

> A crystal coffin stood there long,
> and in it the bird cherry slept.

> Там долго гроб стоял хрустальный,
> и в нем черемуха спала.[25]
>
> (124)

The bird cherry, then, serves as a medium for artistic creation in two modes. First, it can alter the velocity of time, that is, the passage of time, from a normal, earthly, "objective" one (for earthlings) to a compressed, concentrated, and accelerated one for forced blooming (for artists). Second, it can alter the direction of time—to the past or to the future, and then time can ostensibly be viewed or briefly frozen. During indoor, forced three-day blooming in cramped quarters, the concentrated fragrance precipitates hallucinations in the poetic speaker, which result in the appearance of parallel dual temporal planes. Consequently, the speaker can deliberately repeat an experience within a much shorter period of time than waiting for nature to return to spring in one year, at first under laboratory conditions, as it were, in preparation for the fifteen-day blooming in nature soon afterward. Indoors, at this stage in the creative process, the bird cherry assumes the task of creating verse. And indoors, away from the natural flow of time and true nature, the process transforms, even distorts. For Bella Akhmadulina, the imaginative reflection of nature and life is what art is all about. It is at this point that the

25. The image of the Sleeping Beauty in nature recalls Fet's poem "The depth of the heavens is again clear" ("Glub' nebes opiat' iasna"; *Stikhotvoreniia,* 367).

speaker abandons the apparent providers of inspiration, the surrogate muses, as it were—the moon, day, space, and the bird cherry—and begins taking her leave of Tsvetaeva who dominates the Tarusa region which served as the venue for most of the verse. All her thoughts and all her aspirations turn to home and to the poet who is her sole inspiration without the need of surrogate muses—Pushkin. This change, as well as the form of her articulated debt to other writers, will be explored in the following chapters.

8

Revered Writers—1

Пусть так—без палача и плахи
Поэту на земле не быть.
Нам—покаянные рубахи,
Нам со свечой идти и выть.
　　　　　　　—Anna Akhmatova

Time unifies
art and artist
in the beholders' eyes.
—Diana Der Hovanessian

While Marina Tsvetaeva's person and verse permeate the first half of the collection *The Secret* through venue, color, blooming, and notions of water, other writers also figure through their verse. With the waning of Tsvetaeva's presence, Pushkin's essence, already noticeable in "Bird Cherry Last but One," becomes prominent as early as in the next poem to be discussed, "Games and Mischief" ("Igry i shalosti"). Although the poetic speaker remains in the town of Tarusa and Tsvetaeva's influence is still felt, Pushkin's approach to verdure darkening—apparently at the end of summer—seems to overrule the formerly bright green color of Tsvetaeva. In the concluding poem of the collection, with autumn drawing to a close, Pushkin becomes all-pervading, and he shows up in *The Garden* with less regularity. It will be seen that other writers also enter the creative scene.[1]

　　The fun and games of the previous piece now erupt in overt games in the poem "Games and Mischief." The notion of a game that the poetic speaker is playing with the reader ("dear friend") in the poems displaying unreal

---

1. Bella Akhmadulina, *Taina. Novye stikhi* (Moscow: Sovetskii pisatel', 1983) and *Sad. Novye stikhi* (Moscow: Sovetskii pisatel', 1987).

fantasy appears as "rules of the game" in the collection's fourth poem "A deep gentle garden sloping toward the Oka":

> Hey, dear friend, here are the rules of the game:
> don't ask why and lure with your hand
> to the deep gentle garden flowing from the hill,
> released by the hill, accepted by the Oka.

> Ау, любезный друг, вот правила игры:
> не спрашивать зачем и поманить рукою
> в глубокий нежный сад, стекающий с горы,
> упущенный горой, воспринятый Окою.

In fact, the games are part of the multifaceted, if not multilayered, secret that the collection is unraveling before the reader. The poem's opening creates an impression that somebody, whose identity is obscured, was either toying with the speaker or teasing her. The weather, once more defined as frosty, shows that the previous poem coerced May indoors through forced blooming of branches in water, in other words, it may still be early April outdoors and too early for natural blooming in the heart of Russia. The title here belies the somber contents of the poem. Although it commences playfully, the familiar "ty" (you) no longer refers to the bird cherry of the previous poem. Immediately space comes to mind:

> It seems to me someone's playing games with me.
> It seems to me I have guessed who it is
> when again, grinning and delicately,
> frost and the sun glanced into the window.

> Мне кажется, со мной играет кто-то.
> Мне кажется, я догадалась—кто,
> когда опять усмешливо и тонко
> мороз и солнце глянули в окно.

This "someone" ("kto-to"), however, is masculine, not neuter, as space would be in Russian. He has, moreover, promised her a rose and, at her insistence, throws the rose of the day to her feet, possibly as a symbol of beauty and freshness. At this point the presence intensifies with mysterious signs and a trace of speech. A horse ("loshad' ") is harnessed to the sleigh, since if *he* wants it to be, how can it not be. Now the speaker specifies that it is a stallion ("kon' "), whose coat is the color of day and of snow, namely periphrasis for the color white. On a magnificent day *he* transformed the mare into a stallion, more specifically, "loshad'," a feminine noun which can denote a horse in general, into the poetic (and masculine) "kon' " (stallion). Together they fly into the blue yonder and the blazing light, fleshing out the mythical substance of the winged steed.

Sensing *his* presence in *his* breath, the persona intuits that they have formed a secret union. Now she seems to be informing *him* about the occurrences in *his* absence, about how strong *his* influence has been on nature, on humanity and on humanity's perception of nature on the basis of *his* vision and *his* songs. *He* being conjured up and becoming a reality probably owes a debt to the persona's acquired ability through bird cherry delirium to conjure up a credible past:

> As you taught—so the verdure turns dark.
> As you liked—so they sing in the hut.
>
> Как ты учил—так и темнеет зелень.
> Как ты любил—так и поют в избе.

The entire day is of *his* making, i.e. a day crafted by him since that is how most Russians, and this poet in particular, view it:

> This entire day, as your own handiwork,
> although given to me—belongs to you.
>
> Весь этот день, твоим родным издельем,
> хоть отдан мне,—принадлежит тебе.

The persona appears to have inherited his perception of day. Even the half-moon belongs to him by virtue of his verse: "And at night—under a morose blue, / under your own half-moon" ("A noch'iu—pod ugriumo-goluboiu, / pod sobstvennoi tvoei polu-lunoi"). Now the half-moon that missed its other half-moon can also be interpreted as one half-moon missing Push-kin's half-moon. There is no need to weep for him who is so real ("sushchii") that he can play tricks on her: "how foolish I am that I cry over you, who are so real that you can play tricks on me" ("kak ia glupa, chto plachu nad toboiu, / nastol'ko sushchim, chtob shalit' so mnoi").

The one behaving mischievously with the persona, he whose mind and will seem to dominate the visual and verbal art of Russia, induces philo-sophic thoughts in the next poem "A Stroll" ("Progulka"), a poem so pivotal to the poet that she also includes it in *The Garden* (37–38) as the only poem carried over from *The Secret,* possibly for smoother transference of Pushkin. Moreover, the personal pronoun referring to Pushkin is now capitalized as it is when referring to Tsvetaeva in *The Secret:* "that is where You are" ("Eto tam, gde Ty"). At first, her place of solitary wandering is unclear, but it could be on the hillside ("kosogor") or the steep bank of the Oka River, because one false move would result in being pulled in or swallowed by the heavenly vault ("nebosvod"). The speaker appears to equate sea and sky, as Akhmatova does, in imitation of ancient times. Either it means that the persona could topple to her death or that gazing too long at the firmament will hypnotize her, or even pull her into it: "How freely I roam, how solitarily. / Stumble—and the heavenly vault will drag you in" ("Kak vol'no ia brozhu, kak odinoko. / Ostupish'sia—zatianet nebosvod"). Be that as it may, the speaker is strolling alone and gazing at the dispersed holdings ("rasseiannye ugod'ia") of Orion, the most magnifi-cent of all constellations.[2] Either physically or only mentally the speaker is carried off to an isolated spot in the firmament. It could, obviously, be a development or subsiding of her bird-cherry delirium: "In the dispersed holdings of Orion / you cannot refrain from the thought about everything" ("V rasseiannykh ugod'iakh Oriona / ne upastis' ot mysli obo vsem"). Suddenly someone questions her: "About what, for instance?" ("O chem, k primeru?"). Stanza 4 shows that it could be Pushkin's spirit: "Dear Pushkin" ("Pushkin milyi"). Life and art follow Pushkin's teachings and precepts, claims the speaker. Indeed, Pushkin's precepts have been imple-mented to the letter: "As you taught—so the greenery darkens" ("Kak ty uchil—tak i temneet zelen' ").

The half-moon belongs to the addressee, since he, Pushkin, has sung of it like no one else. In fact, his existence is so intense that he (or his image in her mind) plays tricks on her. Using the convoluted syntax of the eighteenth century, which Pushkin dispensed with, and placing an enjambment on a preposition at the end of a line, the speaker points out that the only part, or tiny example, of the great mystery of the universe open to man is the fact of

2. Jobes explains Orion: "The most magnificent of all constellations represented by a man wearing a belt formed by three bright stars and a sword formed by three bright stars. Greek sun hero. His hound was Sirius." Gertrude Jobes, *Dictionary of Mythology, Folklore, and Symbols,* 3 vols. (New York: Scarecrow Press, 1961), 2:1215.

his own imminent and definite demise. He can be certain of nothing else. Man's demise, or the fact of it, brings minuteness to infinity, making its "storonnii" (peripheral? or alien as compared to "of the other world"— "potustoronnii") sense closer to man:

> In the midst of the gaping abyss
> is barely revealed to us a small example
> of the great mystery: our own death.

> Разъятой бездны средь
> нам приоткрыт лишь маленький примерчик
> великой тайны: собственная смерть.

Next the speaker takes issue with Pushkin in his poem "Autumn. An Excerpt" because he imagined the inconceivability of the abyss as a terrible grave. Indeed, in comparing the beauty of late autumn to a fading young consumptive woman who continues to smile, Pushkin notes:

> She does not hear the opening of the grave's abyss,
> Crimson color still plays on her face.

> Могильной пропасти она не слышит зева;
> Играет на лице еще багровый цвет.[3]

Rather, Pushkin should, in the speaker's opinion, think of this as the place where he is now, and any place graced by his presence cannot be all that bad. Unlike Akhmatova and Tsvetaeva, who, for the most part, only adore Pushkin, Akhmadulina's disputative persona also questions her idol.

The opening line of Akhmadulina's poem "A Stroll," with its key words in the first person singular "I wander" ("brozhu") and "alone" ("odinoko"), evokes Pushkin's legacy poem "Whether I wander along noisy streets" ("Brozhu li ia vdol' ulits shumnykh"; 3:135) and his solitariness amid the crowd. Akhmadulina's speaker, of course, has evaded a human crowd by climbing a hill, but she too seems hemmed in by the Orion constellation. What for Pushkin is a descriptive first stanza has been condensed within the opening line. Pushkin says:

3. A. S. Pushkin, *Polnoe sobranie sochinenii v desiati tomakh*, ed. B. V. Tomashevskii (Moscow: AN SSSR, 1962–66), 3:262.

> Whether I wander along noisy streets,
> Whether I enter a crowded cathedral,
> Whether I sit amidst reckless youths,
> I fall into a reverie.

> Брожу ли я вдоль улиц шумных,
> Вхожу ль во многолюдный храм,
> Сижу ль меж юношей безумных,
> Я предаюсь моим мечтам.

Although only the word "wander" coincides fully in Akhmadulina, the remainder of her line takes in Pushkin's details for creative interpretation. Akhmadulina's concept "freely" ("vol'no") can exemplify free movement among obstacles of every sort, including nature. Pushkin's persona roams the noisy streets (hence people, horses, voices, and noise), and enters a crowded cathedral (again many people; the sounds include prayers, singing, and chanting). The adjective "bezumnyi" (insane, foolhardy) suggests in Pushkin rebellious youths involved in an uprising.[4] Again, there is noise intimated through arguments. Even so, in all three situations the speaker is able to fall into a reverie, or give himself up to his daydreams. He always remains, in effect, alone mentally and possibly emotionally. Pushkin's mental vision takes in an oak tree—symbol of life—and a valley—ostensibly emblematic of the Valley of Death—which approximate Akhmadulina's surroundings. Both poets treat the theme of death—their own. Hailing the new generation, Pushkin ponders on his place of final rest and wishes that the young would play in the vicinity of his gravesite and that indifferent nature would shine there with eternal beauty; he employs the form "krasa" pointed out earlier:

> And although for an insensible body
> It is all the same where it decomposes,
> But closer to the dear border
> I would, however, like to sleep.

---

4. In the *Bronze Horseman*, as in the press of the time, the word "bezumnyi" was used to refer to the Decembrist insurgents. See my "Vehicles for Duality in Pushkin's *The Bronze Horseman:* Similes and Period Lexicon," *Semiotica* 25, nos. 1/2 (1979): 117.

And by the entrance to the grave
Let young life play,
And (let) dispassionate nature
Shine in its eternal beauty.

И хоть бесчувственному телу
Равно повсюду истлевать,
Но ближе к милому пределу
Мне всё б хотелось почивать.

И пусть у гробового входа
Младая будет жизнь играть,
И равнодушная природа
Красою вечною сиять.[5]

Akhmadulina broaches the subject of one's own death as well, but does so near an abyss. Her resulting feeling is that she—humanity—is part of eternity: "Minuteness has been included in eternity— / its alien meaning has become closer" ("Privnesena podrobnost' v beskonechnost'— / rodnee stal ee storonnii smysl"). Further in the poem she queries Pushkin:

It's also possible to ask: dear Pushkin,
why should the incomprehensibility of emptiness
be imagined as a terrible grave?
Isn't it better to think: that is where you are.

Еще спросить возможно: Пушкин милый,
зачем непостижимость пустоты
ужасною воображать могилой?
Не лучше ль думать: это там, где ты.
                              (*The Garden*, 37–38)

---

5. The will or testament is an old genre in poetry that originated with the Romans of the decadent period. See William Flint Thrall and Addison Hibbard, *A Handbook to Literature*, revised and enlarged by C. Hugh Holman (New York: Odyssey, 1960), 485. It is interesting to compare in this connection Tsvetaeva's wish to lie in the Khlystian cemetery as a theme already introduced in Akhmadulina's line "Zdes' TA khotela lezhat' " (Here She wished to lie). Also noteworthy is Tiutchev's poem referring to the poet Prince P. A. Viazemskii's (1792–1878) animosity toward the young generation and his unwillingness to cede his precedence. F. I. Tiutchev, *Lirika*, 2 vols., compiled by K. V. Pigarev (Moscow: Nauka, 1966), 1:209, 428–30.

Thus her earlier search into minuteness and wholeness, which, drawing on Tsvetaeva's philosophic poem "A Minute" ("Minuta"; 1:259),[6] originated in *My Genealogy* as "eternity and instantaneousness command" ("povelevaiut vechnost' i mgnovennost' "; *Dreams of Georgia*, 272), has led her to reflections on death and eternity. It is resumed in the pilot theme of the previous chapter that evokes Pasternak. Having looked into Pushkin's declaration on where he would like to be buried and under what circumstances, Akhmadulina goes out to seek the place of burial in Tarusa that Tsvetaeva coveted from abroad.

In the poem "A Finger to the Lips" ("Palets na gubakh") the speaker steals along the street wondering who Alferov, the man in whose honor it was named, could have been.[7] Humor does not slacken. Someone, possibly space, admonishes her to be silent and to understand that she, stealing along in the night to the property of others and involving herself in their affairs, is no match for this upright citizen:

> I steal along the street. Who was poor Alferov,
> in whose honor it has been named? Silence!
> He is not like others who are involved in shady deals,
> stealing along in the night to the property of others.

> По улице крадусь. Кто бедный был Алферов,
> чьим именем она наречена? Молчи!
> Он не чета другим, замешанным в аферах,
> к владениям чужим крадущимся в ночи.

Up the slope she marches. Although it ("kosogor") figured previously in the poem "The Village of Bekhovo's Peasant" ("Derevni Bekhovo krest'ianin") as the place to survey the Oka River and Tarusa—"From the slope / a view on Tarusa and the Oka" ("S kosogora / vid na Tarusu i Oku"), only now does its import grow clear—it is a former cemetery: "This entire slope was once a cemetery. / Here SHE wanted to sleep" ("Ves' etot kosogor byl nekogda kladbishchem. / Zdes' Ta khotela spat' "). Indeed, it is the same Khlystian cemetery site where Tsvetaeva, at least in her prose piece "The Kirillovnas," wanted in Romantic fashion to be laid to her final rest.

6. Marina Tsvetaeva, *Sochineniia v dvukh tomakh*, compiled by Anna Saakiants (Moscow: Khudozhestvennaia literatura, 1980), 1:259.

7. Akhmadulina informed me in 1983 that she deliberately changed the street's name to Alferov from a similar sounding name to avoid what to many would seem inaccurate references to a current writer coincidentally bearing the street's real name. The writer was under criticism at the time.

Akhmadulina, then, herself locates the literary source for a writer seeking his own burial site, as Pushkin did.[8] Curious here in spite of the distance of emigration in 1934 are Tsvetaeva's doubts concerning the cemetery's survival. A capitalized pronoun alerts the reader to the topic of Tsvetaeva in Akhmadulina's poem as well as to her spiritual presence. The theme of Tsvetaeva, it will be recalled, reemerges in the collection as soon as greenery and bloom appear in nature; it continues into this poem and in "The Three-Day Bird Cherry" ("Cheremukha trekhdnevnaia"). As summer wanes into autumn and the collection draws to a close, Pushkin's presence intensifies during his favorite season of "golden autumn." Tsvetaeva's name will not be spelled out in "A Finger to the Lips," but the appropriate section from her prose testifies to her unfulfilled wish of being buried in the Khlystian cemetery. Even the cemetery no longer exists, as if Tsvetaeva's doubts were partly instrumental in turning the absence of the cemetery into a reality. Linguistically, in "A Finger to the Lips" Akhmadulina imitates Tsvetaeva's childhood by employing the obsolete stress for cemetery, "kladbi´shche," rendered patent through the rhyme: kladbi`shchem—liubiv´shem.

Currently, the persona stops lest the readership, who adore the dead poet, attempt to take revenge on the places that loved her. This could be the speaker's explanation for the destruction of the cemetery, which was possibly an attempt by the authorities to stamp out a religious sect. Quickly, she changes the subject to signal her return to places familiar from the summer. The persona returns, as she puts it, to visit her own shade in the Tarusa region where most of the poems were hitherto crafted. Already feeling confined, the house strives to leave its imprisonment in a situation where its soul, the garden, is free, and the poet prepares the vision of light versus darkness in the garden as a cape ("nakidka"). There is reason to believe that the house within the garden on Alferov Street is the dacha rented by the Tsvetaevs "so that SHE would return here / whose house and garden it is"

8. Among the writers who likewise sought burial sites either for themselves or for their speakers are Lermontov, Robert Louis Stevenson, A. A. Fet, the brilliant Armenian poet Avetik Isahakian (1875–1957), and Akhmatova in "Khoroni, khoroni menia, veter" ("Bury, bury me, wind," no. 27 in *Stikhotvoreniia i poemy*). See my "Anna Akhmatova's Translations from the Armenian: Two Poems by Avetik' Isahakian," *Journal of the Society for Armenian Studies* 2 (1985–86): 163, 166 n. 17. Tiutchev, on the other hand, in "Spring Calm" ("Vesennee uspokoenie") wants to be laid out in the thick grass rather than in the damp earth (1:48) with the same intentions as Pushkin: to feel eternal nature and to hear the shepherd's pipe. Also, A. A. Fet's poem "To Turgenev" ("Turgenevu") details finding a coveted vacant corner to build a house and a garden where the speaker can later die a natural painless death. A. A. Fet, *Sochineniia v dvukh tomakh*, compiled by A. E. Tarkhov (Moscow: Khudozhestvennaia literatura, 1982), 1:308–9.

("chtob Ta siuda vernulas' / ch'i eti dom i sad). Above all, the garden is full of apple trees bearing apples—"So the labors of the apple tree are concluded" ("Vot iabloni trudy zaversheny")—that were lacking in the berry-filled garden of the Kirillovnas: "There was never anything said about the Kirillovnas' house, only about the garden. The garden had gobbled up the house. If I had been asked at that time what the Khlystian women did, I would have replied without pause: They stroll in the garden and eat berries" (2:78). Tsvetaeva pointedly stresses the absence of apples in the garden of the Kirillovnas:

> But I don't recall apples. I remember only berries. However strange it may be in a town like Tarusa where in a fruitful year—and every year was fruitful—apples were brought to the market in baskets for linen and even the pigs would not eat them—there were no apples at the Kirilovnas because they used to come to us for them, to our "old garden," that is, made old and unkept by us, where there were very valuable kinds that had grown wild—semi-edible ones that were used only for drying. (2:79)

Now in a poem imbued with Tsvetaeva's presence the apple tree of the poem "I have the secret of wondrous blooming" ("and the apple tree has left / the blossoming for tomorrow") reappears, but its blossom suddenly emerges at the end of her verse line, ostensibly to connote that verse anticipates nature's renewal that is preserved within its lines: "Ours is always play, the apple tree's is work" ("U nas—vsegda igra, u iabloni—rabota"; 76). The poet's work as a game explains the phrase "games and mischief." The comparison evokes the Russian adage "Give time to your business, and an hour to amusement" ("Delu vremia, potekhe chas"). So the apples maintain the Tsvetaeva theme in a circuitous way through connection with the Kirillovna piece, much like the lives of the women in the sect, which flowed outdoors in full view while their full import remained an enigma to the young Marina. Also evocative of Tsvetaeva is mention of the speaker's table: "and this night were diligent and carefree / my bosom table and the lamp on the table" ("I byli v etu noch' prilezhny i bespechny / moi zakadychnyi stol i lampa na stole"). Tsvetaeva's cycle of six poems to her writing table "Table" ("Stol"; 1:312–17), actually the kitchen table, tenders a wry eulogy to the table and to art that differentiates her from the smug Philistines surrounding her.

The poet interpolates a hauntingly beautiful image of the Bekhovo church floating, as if in the legendary town of Kitezh, across the Oka River to make the sign of the cross over them, as the house, garden, and the speaker "fly" across the fields through the medium of the "homeless" house's attic toward the church.[9] The imaginary Kitezh with its church bells audible only to the righteous corresponds to the intact church of Bekhovo. Furthermore, in obsolete colloquial parlance "perekrestit' " (to make the sign of the cross over) also means "to baptize" and possible reasons for this baptismal image could be that Akhmadulina is half Tatar and her Tatar ancestors were probably not baptized, or this is to ward off evil spirits and the devil who will figure in the following poem "The Rider Garden." Above all, a preserved church is a strong tie to the past, to which the persona manages to cling, as well as a powerful connection with the speaker's spirituality.

House and garden become personified through metaphors; rather, the house was personified earlier and now the condition extends to the garden. The process is a take-off on Tsvetaeva's poem "A Path Runs down the Hill" ("Bezhit tropinka s bugorka") from her cycle of four poems "Oka," which feature the languid movement of the Oka River and the church bells ringing in the shade:

> A path runs down the hill
> As if (it were) under children's feet,
> Still in the same way through sleepy meadows
> Lazily moves the Oka;
>
> Bells peal in the distance,
> One peal rushes after the other,
> And they all sing of the good old
> Children's [childhood] time.
>
> Бежит тропинка с бугорка,
> Как бы под детскими ногами,
> Все так же сонными лугами
> Лениво движется Ока;

9. According to legend, Kitezh was saved from the invading Tatar hordes of Batu in the thirteenth century through submersion in Lake Svetloiar near the city of Nizhnii-Novgorod. The attic as a theme in Pasternak connoting the place of his "poetic invention" and even his double is mentioned in Jerzy Faryno's "Whose Messenger Is Akhmatova's *Poema bez geroia?*" in *The Speech of Unknown Eyes: Akhmatova's Readers on Her Poetry*, ed. Wendy Rosslyn, 2 vols. (Nottingham: Astra, 1990), 1:108.

Колокола звонят в тени,
Спешат удары за ударом,
И всё поют о добром, старом,
О детском времени они.

(1:33)

Although some flying is done in the poem "A Finger to the Lips" through the medium of the house's attic, the actual flying and swift movement is left for the poem "The Rider Garden" with its cover of night and its magical possibilities. In "A Finger to the Lips" the movement is presumably mental and visual from the heights of the attic:

Also there was an attic there. Until it was totally dark,
the house, garden, and I had flown on it into the
      distance, to the fields.
And a white sail sailed: that's the Bekhovo church
that sailed across the Oka to baptize us.

Еще там был чердак. Пока не вовсе смерклось,
дом, сад и я—на нем летали вдаль, в поля.
И белый парус плыл: то бёховская церковь,
чтоб нас перекрестить, через Оку плыла.

The realization strikes the reader that the church is on the opposite bank. In Akhmadulina's "The Rider Garden" with its epigraph from Tsvetaeva's piece "The Garden" ("Sad") and an alliterative title, the movement, unlike in Tsvetaeva, is not the flying of a path but of a garden that is clothed in a black cloak changed from the earlier cape created by "zaria" (here: sunset). The poet presents an obvious poetic image for night that so totally envelops the garden in darkness that it transforms the preceding poem's light mantle created by the sunset:

The Rider Garden flies along the steep slope.
What glitter and what a storm!
I'll hide my face in its black cloak,
nestling up to the protection of its seniority.

Сад-всадник летит по отвесному склону.
Какое сверканье и буря какая!
В плаще его черном лицо мое скрою,
к защите его старшинства приникая.

The subtext to this poem is Tsvetaeva's literal prose rendition of Goethe's ballad "Der Erlkönig" and a comparison to the Romantic poet and translator Vasilii Zhukovskii's (1783–1852) free verse translation "The Forest King" ("Lesnoi tsar' ").[10] Tsvetaeva shows that in Goethe "mist" (in Russian "tuman") equals "devil," in the father's words.

Trying to break loose of the walls' tight confines mentioned in "A Finger to the Lips," the house makes a movement toward the speaker as toward an old friend. The fence, the lock, and winter do not let her into the house, notwithstanding that all three—the house, garden, and the persona—are privy to an important secret. A "matreshka" effect, that of nesting dolls, was achieved during their common summer labor, which the persona manages to bring to full cycle back to herself by inhaling the dampness in stanza 6 of "A Finger to the Lips." In Goethe the father's reply to his son's vision is, "Father, don't you see the Forest King? The Forest King in a crown and with a tail?"—"My son, that is a patch of fog" ("Otets, ty ne vidish' Lesnogo Tsaria? Lesnogo Tsaria v korone i s khvostom?"—"Moi syn, eto polosa tumana!"). In Akhmadulina it all sounds innocuous at this stage and redolent of the succession of her surrogate muses:

> The three of us—the house, garden, and I—are privy
>   to an important secret.
> Our combined summer labor was quiet and solitary.
> I [was] in the house, the house [was] in the garden, the
>   garden [was] in the ravine's dampness,
> I inhaled the dampness, and the circle closed.
>
> Дом, сад и я—втроем причастны тайне важной.
> Был тих и одинок наш общий летний труд.
> Я—в доме, дом—в саду, сад—в сырости
>   овражной,
> вдыхала сырость я—и замыкался круг.

The secret is probably the artistic legacy of her antecedent, of Tsvetaeva here as it refers to Pushkin. A paraphrase of Tsvetaeva opened an earlier poem, not included in *The Secret*, "Two Cheetahs" ("Dva geparda"):

10. Vasilii Zhukovskii, *Stikhotvoreniia*, 9th ed., corrected and enlarged, ed. P. A. Efremov (St. Petersburg: Glazunov, 1895), 2:18–19.

This hell, this garden, this zoo—
There where swans and the zoopark are,
in the focus [gun sight] of universal gaze
two cheetahs lie in embrace.

Этот ад, этот сад, этот зоо—
там, где лебеди и зоосад,
на прицеле всеобщего взора
два гепарда, обнявшись, лежат.

(*Dreams of Georgia*, 176)

There are three layers as well to the secret of secrets: a case, a medallion, and the secret that encloses the sacred sacrosanct secret ("the secret of secrets, forbidden to the lips"—"taina tain, zapretnaia dlia ust"). Enclosure within three levels faintly reverberates Akhmatova's capacious image in *Poem without a Hero*: "but the box has three bottoms" ("u skatulki zhe troinoe dno"; 373),[11] particularly with "taina tain" as the innermost layer, which further recalls Akhmatova's line "or is this the secret of secrets again within me?" ("il' eto taina tain opiat' vo mne?") in the poem "Although the land is not native" ("Zemlia khotia i ne rodnaia"; no. 484). Obviously, in these poems of Akhmadulina the levels of Pushkin and Tsvetaeva evoke Akhmatova's use of double subtexts or allusions.

Stanza 7 finds the speaker either actually returned to her summer shade or reverting to a time-altered childhood simultaneous with Tsvetaeva in this house. In opening the gate, regardless of the fears harbored by the house and the garden of the netherworld inhabited by the shade from the depths of the ravine, she plays on the ambiguity to the hilt:

The house and garden were afraid. I went and opened
the gate to the lower [nether?] world where the shade
    resides,
in order to see the house and garden from the depths
    of the ravine
and to see or want nothing else.

11. Anna Akhmatova, *Stikhotvoreniia i poemy*, compiled by V. M. Zhirmunskii (Leningrad: Sovetskii pisatel', 1976), 373.

Пугались дом и сад. Я шла и отворяла
калитку в нижний мир, где обитает тень,—
чтоб видеть дом и сад из глубины оврага
и больше ничего не видеть, не хотеть.

And thus the stage is set for the events in "The Rider Garden." The shade of summer past seems to transform the house and garden to their former appearance, even the orange lampshade is there. Shades ("teni"), of course, are evocative of Akhmatova and Annenskii.[12] The transformation's objective, however, is to create verse on this basis:

> The abandoned garden knew and the homeless house
>   knew
> that the house was not for living, that the garden was
>   not for quit-rent,
> that the house and garden were for tears, for righteous
>   labor.

> Знал беспризорный сад и знал бездомный дом,
> что дом—не для житья, что сад—не для оброка,
> что дом и сад—для слез, для праведных трудов.

Ostensibly, the house is "bezprizornyi" (abandoned, unwanted) because of the absences of Tsvetaeva and, less so, of the present tenants. It enlarges on the pervasive image of the orphan, which recalls Tsvetaeva's cycle "Poems to an Orphan" ("Stikhi sirote"; 1:333–37).

An intricate play on roots and semantics coheres several of the notions in the collection. Through the root -zor (sight, see) of "besprizornyi" (abandoned, orphaned, homeless—used for children) the absence of Tsvetaeva becomes patent. The orphaned state of the world is expressed through the concluding lines to the poem "Return to Tarusa": "Oh, how orphaned is this paradise and how empty if it is true that Marina is not in it." But Tsvetaeva figures not only through her cycle "Poems to an Orphan" but also through her green eyes in the verdure and the water of Tarusa. Folk etymology probably grips the speaker's consciousness and links the root of the Oka

12. For an interesting assessment of the topic, see O. Ia. Obukhova, "Obraz teni v poezii Anny Akhmatovoi," in *Anna Akhmatova i russkaia kul'tura nachala XX veka. Tezisy konferentsii*, ed. Viach. V. Ivanov et al. (Moscow: AN SSSR, 1989), 29–32.

River (*ok*) with the obsolete poetic Russian word for eye—"oko." More connections can be found because historically the Russian word for window "okno" derives from "oko" and thus justifies the already considered play on words, roots, meanings in "zaokonnost' " as denoting not only "beyond the window" but also "beyond the Oka." Ostensibly, Akhmadulina is gazing into and through Tsvetaeva's eyes, and her eyes are looking back, surveying the present state and creation of poetry.

Its abandonment notwithstanding, the house tried to show visitors that its concerns were ordinary, to produce fruit—which it did:

> We didn't expect guests but if they came,
> the house lied that it was a simpleton, the garden
>   would grow sad
> and would pretend to be looking after the family
> and had to go bear fruit.

> Не ждали мы гостей, а наезжали если—
> дом лгал, что он—простак, сад начинал грустить
> и делал вид, что он печется о семействе
> и надобно ему идти плодоносить.

Space and objects commingle, moving about to their hearts' content—all because the speaker inhaled the dampness from the ravine evocative of the great dampness of space and of the shade lingering there.

The persona's main objective is to return to this house its true and important occupant, Tsvetaeva:

> While the ravine is absorbed in concerns about
>   mushrooms,
> I'll request a book so that SHE returns here
> whose house and garden these are . . . sh: a finger to
>   the lips.

> Пока овраг погряз в заботах о грибах,
> я книгу попрошу, чтоб Та сюда вернулась,
> чьи эти дом и сад . . . тсс: палец на губах.

Almost a shade or chimera themselves because Tsvetaeva's house and garden have been reconstructed as they were in her time only in the poetic speaker's imagination, the house and garden do not care about other gardens, and, empty, they only await with trepidation their current owner's return in September. It would seem that Akhmadulina's personification of the house is grounded in Akhmatova's "Northern Elegies," for, according to Vilenkin in *In the One Hundred and First Mirror,* it furnishes a frank treatment of "pro domo mea," albeit as he affirms:

> The author's biography does not unfold here either in chronological sequence or in any detail, and of course in no way in terms of a "plot," rather, it develops as spurts, visions or, conversely, as conscious efforts, by opening wide now one, now another closed door to this very *domus* which in other poems is not for nothing continually called "damned," "alien," "vacated forever," and here in one of the elegies, it is even ominously personified: the house // ". . . watched me // With its squinted ill-disposed eye."[13]

Of further interest is the mention in *Dreams of Georgia:* "It's someone else's house" ("on chuzhoi dom"; 113) and in Vilenkin that Akhmatova's house was alien to her (159).

Although the poem concludes with the speaker's statement that she will probably not return to the house and garden ("I leave the house and the garden. / It's doubtful that I will return. Sh, a finger to the lips"—"Ia ukhozhu ot doma i ot sada. / Navriad li ia vernus'. Tss: palets na gubakh . . ."), the next poem finds the persona as a "passenger" with the Rider Garden on an unnamed horse, probably Pegasus—the mythological steed of poets. The rest transpires on the wings of art, as it were. Clinging to the defense of the garden's seniority, she recalls from somewhere in the past that something is amiss and that even time has strayed beyond normal lateness; the lines display a fine mounting of balladic tension through sound texture and rhythm in the amphibrachic tetrameter employed also by Zhukovskii for his "Forest King": "I remember, I know, that the business is magical. / There has never been such a late hour" ("Ia pomniu, ia znaiu, chto delo nechisto. / Vovek ne byvalo stol' pozdnego chasa"). In this "postlate period" the Rider Garden speeds through the storm that one rider has already passed, presumably the horse in Goethe. The intimation of such a "transtemporal" hour can be found in Tsvetaeva's triptych "The Hour of the Soul" ("Chas dushi"; 1:253–55), which prefigures and validates the

13. V. Ia. Vilenkin, *V sto pervom zerkale: Anna Akhmatova* (Moscow: Sovetskii pisatel', 1987), 159. He is discussing "The Second" ("Vtoraia," no. 635).

existence of this hour and state: "In the deep hour of the soul and the night / that is not marked on clocks" ("V glubokii chas dushi i nochi, / Ne chisliashchiiisia na chasakh"). Obviously, events unlikely at other hours can occur during this one. Furthermore, the notion of a certain unusual hour could derive from Tiutchev's poem "A Vision" ("There is a certain hour"— "Est' nekii chas"). At this hour, Tiutchev opines, only the Muse dreams prophetic dreams: "Only the virginal soul of the Muse / Do the gods alarm in prophetic dreams!" ("Lish' Muzy devstvennuiu dushu / V prorocheskikh trevozhat bogi snakh!"; 1:17). Finally, Tsvetaeva takes Tiutchev's three opening words as an epigraph to the second poem, which she begins with the same words: "There is a certain hour—like a cast-off load" ("Est' nekii chas—kak sbroshennaia klazha") in the cycle "Pupil" ("Uchenik"; 1:151– 52). Tsvetaeva construes this certain lofty hour as "the hour of apprentice- ship" ("chas uchenichestva") and "the supreme hour of solitariness" ("odinochestva verkhovnyi chas").

The poem "The Rider Garden," bearing the only epigraph in the collec- tion, proclaims Tsvetaeva's presence. Taken from her poem "The Garden" in which Tsvetaeva wishes for a garden in her old age, a solace for suffering throughout her life, it is ostensibly a wish for a garden full of muses, as in antiquity. It is almost as if the Rider Garden were now trying to reach the mortal remains of Tsvetaeva since it dashes up the slope to the former site of the Khlystian cemetery where she wanted to be buried. The time being beyond nighttime—an hour so late that it rarely occurs—the rider, wrapped in a black cloak, speeds through the storm and its sparkle. Already one rider (probably from Zhukovskii's translation of Goethe's ballad, if not Goethe's rider) has sped by. Hiding her face in the black cloak of the present Rider Garden, the speaker nonetheless questions his identity as well as how the horse was obtained. The Rider Garden and the steed, mane flying, leave this domain. Reins in one hand, the rider gathers ("upasaet") her fear (i.e., the speaker—metonymically) to his chest with the other. Consequently, the persona addresses the garden as her protector from the sorcery rife in the air at this unorthodox hour. Images from Tsvetaeva, reworked for the pres- ent situation, are rampant here.

Stanza 6, then, commences the overt theme of Goethe's German ballad "Der Erlkönig," freely translated into Russian by Zhukovskii as "The Forest King. A Ballad," which Tsvetaeva took as the theme of a literary essay "Two 'Forest Kings' " ("Dva 'Lesnykh Tsaria' "). In it she furnishes a literal Russian translation and a close comparison of the ballads by Goethe and by Zhukovskii. Also pertinent is the rider image in Tsvetaeva's poetry, and in her narrative poem *On the Red Steed* (*Na krasnom kone*) in particular.[14] In Akhmadulina the speaker huddled under the black cloak of the rider parallels the child riding with his father in Goethe. Unlike the folkloric three questions and answers posed by the child to his father in Zhukovskii and Goethe, Akhmadulina's persona asks three questions in stanza 3 without any reply, and in stanza 5 she addresses the Garden-Guardian before asking two more questions (which happen to be the familiar ones about the Forest King's tail and crown). Finally, in a departure from the poem's two predecessors, the speaker questions the very necessity of their flight from the Forest King. Presumably, the fear is the result of literary tradition hailing back to Goethe. The fearlessness, on the other hand, is predicated on the older tradition of the steed as poetry and the meaning of steeds in Tsvetaeva. The arising conflict finds no resolution. To be sure, the voice laughing at her earlier and disparaging her now is the devil: "with a tail and a crown" ("s khvostom i s koronoi"), as in Goethe. It maintains derisively:

> But I hear the voice of the all-powerful sneer:
> Despicable infant at your father's bosom!
> Brief death under the tsar's caresses
> is more eternal than day and night's destruction.

> Но слышу я голос насмешки всевластной:
> —Презренный младенец за пазухой отчей!
> Короткая гибель под царскою лаской—
> навечнее пагубы денной и нощной.

(79)

It would seem that the devil in Akhmadulina's verse considers this a repeat performance of Goethe's ballad. In Goethe the devil ("Father, don't you see the Forest King? The Forest King in a crown and with a tail?") perniciously cajoles the child by appealing to the latter's desire for motherly attention by his daughters. The father's reply to the son's vision of the Forest King in Tsvetaeva is "My son, that is a patch of fog!" (2:458). Similarly, Zhukovskii has "Oh no, that is the fog showing white over the water" ("O net, to beleet tuman nad vodoi").

On flying out of its appointed cultivated boundaries—possible only because the house and garden no longer stand or at least not in their previous

---

14. See Marina Tsvetaeva, *Stikhotvoreniia i poemy,* compiled by A. A. Saakiants, Biblioteka poeta, Malaia seriia (Leningrad: Sovetskii pisatel', 1979), 359–76.

form and have been reconstructed only in the speaker's imagination—the garden leaves the speaker open to assault from the lord of the nighttime forest. In Akhmadulina too, the Rider Garden tries to allay her fear:

> O Garden-Guardian! Whose unseen leonine
> tail is so angered? Whose crown glitters?
> "Fear not! That is the long (patch of) fog over the
>   plain,
> that is the yellow principal fire of Orion.

> О сад-охранитель! Невиданно львиный
> чей хвост так разгневан? Чья блещет корона?
> —Не бойся! То—длинный туман над равниной,
> то—желтый заглавный огонь Ориона.

Orion figures "legitimately" in the poem since Tsvetaeva explains that the word in German denotes a tail for both the devil and a comet in contrast to a dog's tail (2:459). In some myths Pegasus became a constellation.

The reassurance of the lord of the nighttime forest, however, fails to allay the persona's fear. Just as in Goethe where the Forest King wants to love the child to death, and does so, here too he extols the more eternal quality of an early demise under his caresses as opposed to the slow deterioration of life by day and night that occurs over time. It seems to be a mode of speeding up the inevitable in this transtemporal period. There is here a Romantic sense of life leading implacably toward death and of there being little reason to lament a pleasant and early end instead of a slow and inevitable decline.[15] Since the Forest King is shrouded in the fire of Orion (visually it could be his tail), the persona begs for the protection of darkness: "O Rider-Parent, give darkness and warmth! / let's return to our fatherland of the secluded precipice" ("O vsadnik-roditel', dai t'my i teplyni! / vernemsia v otchiznu obryva-otshiba!").[16] Mocking her as his poor choice, the Forest King demands to know if this is her own speech or that of the crowd:

---

15. The Romantic hero's emphasis on time over place renders more credible the ability to fly. As F. D. Reeve so aptly puts it, "The romantic hero . . . imposed himself on eternity without concern for place. F. D. Reeve, *The White Monk. An Essay on Dostoevsky and Melville* (Nashville: Vanderbilt University Press, 1989), 17.

16. The garden is a parent because it gives birth to plants, hence to verse in the understanding of the speaker in this period. The garden is literally playing the role of father here for the speaker. "Na otshibe" means "v storone ot seleniia" (at the edge of, at a distance from a settlement).

(He) with the tail and in a crown laughs: "Are these the
    crowd's
or are these your words, mischosen one?"

For others there is no hour so late.
It's just right for you. It will never be so late again.
I feel disdain for you. Don't bid me farewell!
The Rider Garden whispers to me: "Don't listen, have
    no fear."

С хвостом и в короне смеется: —Толпы ли,
твои ли то речи, избранник-ошибка?

Другим не бывает столь позднего часа.
Он впору тебе. Уж не будет так поздно.
Гнушаюсь тобою! Со мной не прощайся!
Сад-всадник мне шепчет:—Не слушай, не бойся.

In Goethe it was the father who tried to calm the child's fears. Unlike in
Goethe's poem, in which the child arrives home dead, here the Rider
Garden returns the speaker alive to his isolated domicile on the slope. Even
so, the speaker shows dissatisfaction, possibly an ambivalent longing for the
experience of an illustrious Romantic demise, and chides the garden: "O my
garden, my concerned destroyer! / Why did we flee from the Forest King?"
("O sad moi, zabotlivyi moi pogubitel'! / Zachem ot Tsaria my bezhali
Lesnogo?"). An unexpected reaction to her earlier fear—fearlessness—
surfaces in the name of "pogubitel' " for the garden that brought her home
safely and in her belated wish to have submitted to the Forest King, presenting peripety, as it were. The persona now feels that all the factors were
present, but fate was not quite right. But for what? She is most likely not
actually wishing for an early demise, but rather for acquiring the ability to
create inspired poetry. Having assumed its usual state, the garden pretends
not to hear or to understand her lament:

The garden pretended that it was a garden, and not a
    rider,
that the word of the Forest King is reversible
And there is no one, but I bow to anyone:
everything was given but fate did not suffice.

Сад делает вид, что он—сад, а не всадник,[17]
что слово Лесного Царя отвратимо.[18]
И нет никого, но склоняюсь пред всяким:
все было дано, а судьбы не хватило.

The persona's attitude is that of men regretting the lost opportunity and wishing they could have responded to a siren's lure to plunge willingly to their death for the tenuous promise of love. In other words, hers is regret for the promise of inspired verse. Her wish is that the child fated to the Forest King not be afraid in the future nor even preserved from this difficult lot:

We are both pretenders. At black midnight
in late transtemporality, the Rider Garden gallops.
May the child fated to the Forest King
not be afraid and not be saved.

Мы оба притворщики. Полночью черной,
в завременье позднем, сад-всадник несется.
Ребенок, Лесному Царю обреченный,
да не убоится, да не упасется.[19]

17. Not only does the word "vsadnik" replicate "sad" but its frame—*vsadnik*—encircles "sad" with the sounds "vnik"; cf. "On vnik v delo" meaning "to get to the heart of matters." Compare also Akhmadulina's "the plants leaned toward me" ("rasten'ia *nik*nuli ko mne" (*Dreams of Georgia*, 20).

18. The word "otvratimo" is not found in standard modern Russian without the negative particle *ne-*. "Neotvratimyi" (inevitable) and "neotvratimo" (inevitably) exist, but not the form without the negation.

19. "Zavremen'e" evokes Akhmatova's "zazerkal'e" (beyond the looking glass) and "gost' zazerkal'nyi" (guest from beyond the looking glass) in *Poem without a Hero* (Part One) here in the meaning of being very late, with time not following the usual rhythm. Vilenkin construes "zazerkal'e" as the inner depths or layers of the poem. Compare his usage: "In order not to let it [confusion] burst into public hearing, in order to deprive it of unbearable straightforwardness the author hurries to cover it partly, to tone it down a little, to lead it away to the indecernible depths of the *poema* into 'beyond the looking glass' " (*V sto pervom zerkale*, 265). Also relevant is Akhmadulina's notion of *zaokonnost'* in the poem "I am merely a volume inhabited by something" ("Ia lish' ob"em, gde obitaet chto-to"), possibly in the Annenskiian sense of the beyond or of creativity in nature—hence of becoming part of nature in death. Bella Akhmadulina, *Izbrannoe. Stikhi* (Moscow: Sovetskii pisatel', 1988), 317. Akhmatova has "zaokonnaia sineva" (transwindow dark-blueness) in *Poem without a Hero*. Moreover, it recalls Tsvetaeva's "In the innermost hour of the soul and of the night, / Not recorded on clocks" ("V glubokii chas dushi i nochi, / Ne chisliashchiisia na chasakh"), which is a time for creating worlds ("Chas dushi"; 1:253–55).

Already in the preceding poem the garden had adorned in gold this particular house with the exemplary golden ball blooming there.[20] The golden sunset can be imagined here:

> The garden was not curious about the affairs of other
>   gardens.
> It clothed that house in gold inside with me
> so securely as an epithet clings to an object.
> (An example blossomed in the garden: here's a balloon,
>   it's golden.)

> К делам других садов был сад не любопытен.
> Он в золото облек тот дом внутри со мной
> так прочно, как в предмет вцепляется эпитет.
> (В саду расцвел пример: вот шар, он—золотой.)

In part, the golden ball here could be the golden-colored apples from the apple trees whose labors had just concluded. Apples in late August and in September in Akhmadulina reverberate with Tsvetaeva's poem "August is asters" ("Avgust—astry"), which draws on the imperial origin of the month's name and evokes Akhmadulina's preoccupation with the days of particular months; the first two of the poem's three stanzas read:

> August is asters,
> August is stars,
> August is bunches
> Of grapes and of rusty
> Ashberry—is August!

> With your full-weight, favorable
> Imperial apple(s)
> You play like a child, August.
> As if with your palm, you stroke the heart
> With your imperial name:
> August!—Heart!

---

20. The word used by Akhmadulina "shar" can also denote a balloon. In contemporary parlance, the usual word for ball is "miach."

Август—астры,
Август—звезды,
Август—грозди
Винограда и рябины
Ржавой—август!

Полновесным, благосклонным
Яблоком своим имперским,
Как дитя, играешь, август.
Как ладонью, гладишь сердце
Именем своим имперским:
Август!—Сердце!

(1:98)

The golden ball has been pivotal to Akhmadulina since childhood, as mentioned in her interview to the journal *Ogonek* cited in Chapter 4. Here Akhmadulina, in rejecting possessiveness and possession (also a fact of Akhmatova's biography),[21] seems to be replying to Goethe's devil whose attempt at possessing the child culminated in the latter's death.

Akhmadulina's image of a cloak in connection with a garden probably stems from Tsvetaeva's poem "The House" ("Dom"), in which the house conceals its forehead under the hood of a cloak of ivy:

From under frowning brows
The house—as if a day
of my youth, as if my youth
Greets me: "Hello, it's me!"

So intrinsically familiar is the brow
That, embarrassed to be big,
Is hiding under
The cloak of ivy which has entwined it.

21. See Kornei Chukovskii, *Sobranie sochinenii*, 6 vols. (Moscow: Khudozhestvennaia literatura, 1965–69): "She [Anna Akhmatova] totally lacked the sense of property. She did not like and did not keep belongings, she parted with them with remarkable ease. Like Gogol', Coleridge and her friend Mandel'shtam, she was a homeless nomad and she did not value property to the degree that she willingly freed herself of it as of a burden. Even in her youth, in the years of her brief "blossoming," she lived without cumbersome closets and bureaux, often even without a desk" (5:726).

Из-под нахмуренных бровей
Дом—будто юности моей
День, будто молодость моя
Меня встречает:—Здравствуй, я!

Так самочувственно-знаком
Лоб, прячущийся под плащом
Плюща, срастающийся с ним,
Смущающийся быть большим.

(1:304)

Curiously, Tsvetaeva also has a triptych "The Cloak" ("Plashch"; 112–14), which may well have suggested the idea of the cloak to Akhmadulina.

Throughout the collection, the speaker animates objects, much like Tsvetaeva, whose poem "The House" is a prime example. Reality does not return at once to the speaker following the transtemporal ride on the horse with the Rider Garden after midnight.[22] Objects play tricks on her. Already the opening stanza of the piece "Insubordination of Objects" ("Neposlushanie veshchei") establishes the animation of objects:

> What is there to say about the free spirit of the
>   candles—
> We are all susceptible to their sorcery and evil eye.
> Or there are no inanimate objects,
> or I have not come across them even once.

22. Ostensibly, the reason that the garden can fly in the night is that at this point in time it is an imaginary garden with an imaginary version of the house that the Tsvetaevs rented in the summer. If this line of reasoning is correct, then perhaps an earlier reflection of the house and garden is found in the second poem in the "Tarusa" cycle:

> Here stood the house. A century ago
> there was a day: the grand piano was installed in the living room,
> the children were brought in, the windows to the garden were opened,
> where presently fierce is the quiz enthusiast ["viktorina" is a quizzing
>   game].

> Здесь дом стоял. Столетие назад
> был день: рояль в гостиной водворили,
> ввели детей, открыли окна в сад,
> где ныне лют ревнитель викторины.

(11)

However, one hundred years before Akhmadulina wrote the poem Tsvetaeva had not been born; she could be referring to Tsvetaeva's mother or to Lermontov as well, as indicated by its proximity in the collection to the poem on Lermontov "A deep gentle garden sloping to the Oka."

> Что говорить про вольный дух свечей—
> все подлежим их ворожбе и сглазу.
> Иль неодушевленных нет вещей,
> иль мне они не встретились ни разу.

(81)

With mention of a water sprite in the water pipe, the imposing devil of "The Rider Garden" following the garden's return to its habitual form and domain, appears diminished in stature, importance, and power to a less awesome sprite. It too laughs. Laughter, it would seem, is a concomitant feature revealing a devil's presence:

> Right now they made fun of me:
> The object clicked not for, but in lieu of light
> and the water sprite imprisoned in the pipes
> did not give water [allow water to pour] and began to
>   shake with laughter.

> Сейчас вот потешались надо мной:
> В е щ ь—щелкала не для, а вместо света
> и заточённый в трубы водяной
> не дал воды и задрожал от смеха.

Obviously, the rattling of water pipes is interpreted in the light of folklore and literary tradition. Laughter in a devil evokes the first line of the Symbolist writer Fedor Sologub's (1863–1927) poem "Evil" ("Likho"): "Who is it that laughed so quietly near me? / My Evil, one-eyed, wild Evil!" ("Kto eto vozle menia zasmeialsia tak tikho? / Likho moe, odnoglazoe, dikoe Likho!").[23] Sologub's poem "Gray Nedotykomka" ("Nedotykomka seraia") clarifies the connection between Likho and Nedotykomka, also a kind of petty demon (234).

Everything seems to be in constant motion and striving to get away, even the shawl that was a gift to her "toward evening yesterday"—conceivably a remnant of the nighttime cloak or of what the black cloak turned into. So the speaker understandingly urges the objects on, knowing that they will be caught temporarily by another for brief service. Metonymically, the steed

---

23. Fedor Sologub, *Stikhotvoreniia*, Biblioteka poeta, Bol'shaia seriia (Leningrad: Sovetskii pisatel', 1975), 112.

image lingers, with remnants of allusion to a horse through "ponukat' " ("to giddap") and "beg" ("running"):

> I giddap their free run—
> let it be caught with someone's hand,
> like this free, fleeting snow,
> convoked from all the hills by the Oka.
>
> Я понукаю их свободный бег—
> пусть будет пойман чьей-нибудь рукою,
> как этот вольный быстротечный снег,
> со всех холмов сзываемый Окою.

The thawing snow little comprehends its own lack of freedom as it breaks loose from immobility on the surface of the earth to acquire motion and speed only for a time, as captured in the movement of the Oka. The uncontrollable movement of objects is orchestrated by him whom she does not mention. Rather, she removes her hand from the line she is writing to make the sign of the cross. The result is an angry devil who opened the door of the cupboard loudly and then quickly shut it tightly behind him at the sign of the cross, a mundane repetition of the Bekhovo church's function. Something dangerous has been averted. It echoes Fedor Sologub's novel *The Petty Demon* (*Melkii bes*), in which the devil hides under the cupboard. And the potent formidable balladic devil has been diminished, like the cloak of night that became a shawl, and the mighty steed that has now been reduced and trivialized to the flight of objects.

The next poem, "Return to Tarusa" ("Vozvrashchenie v Tarusu"), treats the persona's return to the town, which makes the reader wonder when she had left, other than with the Rider Garden. The theme of return to Tarusa following an absence during which the two beloved sisters and caretakers have died will be taken up in the later poems, currently outside any collection, namely in "Ladyzhino," "Happiness in Tarusa" ("Radost' v Taruse"), "Sorrows and Jokes" ("Pechali i shutochki"), and "Saturday in Tarusa" ("Subbota v Taruse").[24] Whether the absence in "Return to Tarusa" was occasioned by delirium, by a trip South, by a return home to Moscow and Peredelkino, or even to Pesochnoe, Tsvetaeva's summer home in the Tarusa

---

24. Bella Akhmadulina, *Stikhotvoreniia* (Moscow: Khudozhestvennaia literatura, 1988), 289–99, 308.

district, the speaker now returns to Tarusa in May. No mention is made of the two sisters here. Because the last reference to a month was to late September in the poem "A Finger to the Lips," it can be argued that the speaker has been away for some time. Even if time has elapsed, the speaker can also be returning to Tarusa from one of the nearby venues. On the road from their summer place Pesochnoe to the Kirilovna place in Tarusa Tsvetaeva writes with emphasis on the word "exit" ("vykhod"), which Akhmadulina also utilizes, as shown in Chapter 6:

> That was an entrance to a different kingdom. . . . And suddenly enlightenment: but after all, [it's] not an entrance ["vkhod"], not a crossing ["perekhod"], [but]—an *exit!* (After all, the first house is always the last house!) And not only an exit from the town of Tarusa, [but] from all towns! An exit from all Tarusas, walls, shackles, from one's own name, from one's own skin! From one's own flesh into spaciousness.
>
> From all of Tarusa, to be exact, from all "visiting," that is, from all sweets, other people's children . . . above all I like this second of going downhill, of entrance, of descending—into the green, cold, stream's darkness, of passing—the endless gray ivy-and-elder wattle behind which—this is how it has remained in me—all the berries ripen at the same time. (2:78)

Stanza 1 probably describes the hill on which the former Khlystian cemetery near the Kirillovnas was located: "In front of the Oka is an incline of earth / and toward Tarusa a wearisome approach." ("Pred Okoi preklonnost' zemli / i k Taruse tomitel'nyi podstup"; 2:83). Because it was a cemetery for a religious sect, the locus could also have been sacred to the Khlystians on pilgrimage, whose walking staff (metonymy) slowed down in climbing the dusty slope.[25]

Nature, garbed in yellow, flaunts the youthful Tsvetaeva's golden hair. All too soon it will turn white under a covering of snow, again like the premature graying of Tsvetaeva's hair of which she made artistic use in her poems "The Gold of My Hair" ("Zoloto moikh volos"; 1:211) and "Gray Hair" ("Sedye

25. Of relevance here is Mandel'shtam's poem "My Staff, My Freedom" ("Posokh moi, moia svoboda"; 1:99), which mentions going to distant Rome ("i v dal'nii Rim poshel"), and thus echoes Akhmadulina's poem "Raphael's Day." Osip Mandel'shtam, *Stikhotvoreniia*, compiled by N. I. Khardzhiev (Leningrad: Sovetskii pisatel', 1974), 1:99.

volosy"; 1:211, 214–15). Stanza 2 of Akhmadulina's poem sadly and begrudgingly accepts the perfection of this moment. The speaker's eye takes in the church at Bekhovo, possibly formerly serving the sect. She parallels an early poem in which all there was left for her in her already full and fulfilled life was old age, namely the poem "Sluggishness" ("Medlitel'nost' "), where the concluding stanza reads:

> This moment or year will come of its own accord:
> unexpected meaning, languor, acme...
> Only old age is missing.
> Everything else has already occurred.
>
> Сам придет этот миг или год:
> смысл нечаянный, нега, вершинность...
> Только старости недостает.
> Остальное уже совершилось.
>
> (*Dreams of Georgia*, 145–46)

Here the lyrical ego expresses satisfaction with her life: "I would say that life has been successful, / everything has been realized, and it's not in the least painful" ("Ia b skazala, chto zhizn'—udalas', / vse sbylos', i niskol'ko ne bol'no"). The state of making no requests of life—here probably due to fulfillment—could be Akhmadulina's reply to Lermontov's reflective poem on life "I walk out alone onto the road" ("Vykhozhu odin ia na dorogu") in which, unlike her response "it's not at all painful," his speaker is in pain "Why is it so painful and difficult for me?" ("Chto zhe mne tak bol'no i tak trudno?")[26] But he too expects nothing further from life, other than freedom and quietude: "I no longer expect anything from life" ("Uzh ne zhdu ot zhizni nichego ia"). In the perorating lines Lermontov's poetic speaker expresses the wish that in death he could still experience the pleasures of life and nature, which evokes an earlier theme of Akhmadulina. Her satiated lips make no request of splendor in the blooming plain. Still, use of the root "tsvet" (bloom, blossom, flower) in "the beauty of the flowering plain" ("blagolep'e *tsvet*ushchei ravniny")[27] prepares for the reason for sadness— the absence of Tsvetaeva: "Oh, how orphaned is this paradise and how empty,

---

26. See M. Iu. Lermontov, *Sobranie sochinenii v chetyrekh tomakh* (Moscow: AN SSSR, 1958–59), 1:543–44.

27. Note that "blagolep'e" is an obsolete lofty synonym for beauty ("krasa"), and "ravnina" is close to "field."

/ if it's true that Marina is not in it" ("O, kak sir etot rai i kak pust, / esli pravda, chto net v nem Mariny"). Having cleverly prepared the reader and paid homage to the water in the Oka River (compare the name Marina, images of water in several of Tsvetaeva's poems, and the "green cold stream's darkness" in Tsvetaeva's prose passage on the word "vykhod") and the fact of burgeoning yellowness and bloom, the persona cannot believe that Marina is not contained within this blooming paradise. Unless Marina is present everywhere, this splendid place is orphaned and empty.[28] Poetry, naturally, should be continued by poets and appreciated by the populace; and who better suited to appreciate and enhance the blooming of nature and poetry inaugurated by Tsvetaeva than Bella Akhmadulina, whose very first name harbors the meaning of beauty in Latin, French, and Italian. In the speaker's opinion, the abundant water in various natural states of rain, snow, flowing water, green growth, and the magnificent blooming in nature, particularly of a golden or yellow hue is all due to Tsvetaeva. Imbibing her artistic legacy and taking it beyond the flowering stage in Tarusa becomes the work of Akhmadulina the poet. With the onset of autumn, blooming ceases.

With the poem "It grows dark after four, and by five" ("Smerkaetsia v piatom chasu, a k piati") the speaker furnishes the final piece on Tarusa through confused perception or imagination. Now it is she, the persona, who, accompanied by her dog, takes up the staff introduced in the previous poem:

> It grows dark after four and by five
> it has already grown dark. What is sweeter than late-
>   night
> roamings, vigils, wanderings on the road,
> isn't it so, my hound and my staff?

> Смеркается в пятом часу, а к пяти
> уж смерклось, Что сладостней поздних
> шатаний, стояний, скитаний в пути,
> не так ли, мой пес и мой посох?

                                                            (84)

Although the grass in proximity to snowdrifts would seem like October or late March, the month, we are told, is February. Suddenly there is a free and wild

---

28. See Sofiia Liubenskaia's "O poeticheskom iazyke Belly Akhmadulinoi," *Russian Literature* 17 (1985): 164–65, on the theme of the orphan in Akhmadulina.

lantern that, having chosen darkness as its medium, refuses to light the way (periphrastically, "to serve Edison's cause"—"sluzhit' Edisonovu delu"). Still, the lyrical ego is devoted to these lightless places and to their lack of people as well as to their moonlessness, which, displeased with her intrusion, has set fast upon her heels, like a pack of borzois, the pozemka wind that, blowing close to the ground, can, like a dog with its nose to the ground, catch scents easily. The road slopes gently, but there is a pass between the modest incline and the descent. From this vantage point the speaker perceives how free and scarlet is the fire in its narrow dwelling. Pondering the meaning of the window and the fire, any wayfarer, including herself, will slow his gait, and a nocturnal rider (the garden?) would slow his horse. Her hound and staff (metonymy for herself) take pause as well. Stanza 6 elucidates the reason that her hound and staff linger—they are her faithful guides ("povodyri"); she, however, sees the fire in the castle, albeit the word "povodyr' " implies blindness in the one being led. Beginning in stanza 6 the poem wafts of the historic Prince Oleg (d. 912) addressing the sorcerer in Pushkin's ballad "Song of Oleg the Seer" ("Pesn' o veshchem Olege"; 2:106–9). The speaker queries her entourage—the hound and the staff—using the obsolete high-style word "otvetstvuite" for "answer" in lieu of the current "otvet'te" or "otvechaite":

> Answer, trusty guides:
> beyond the slope and beyond the bend
> what is that shining castle in the distance
> and if it is not a castle, then what is there?

> Ответствуйте, верные поводыри:
> за склоном и за поворотом
> что там за сияющий замок вдали,
> и если не замок, то что там?

The effect is almost that of the lamp conjuring up the images of the distant past. Like the large moth,[29] the persona is drawn in her thoughts to the flame thereby returning the reader to the image of thoughts like "motyl'ki" (butterflies or large moths) in Chapter 7.[30] No one is making magic or

---

29. "Motylek," which usually means "butterfly," can, according to the *Seventeen-Volume Dictionary of Russian*, denote "moth," as it does here. (see Chap. 7, nn. 6 and 8)

30. Cf. the frequent use of the images of "motyl'ki" and "babochki" in the works of the Armenian bard Saiat-Nova (1712–95), whose use is closer to nature but turns symbolic when

drinking at a feast there; the poetic speaker determines that all this is partly
of the lamp's fabrication. She includes herself and the two guides as part of
the invention. For here is a settlement without settlers, possibly because it is
in the past and all have died:

> So no one is practicing witchcraft there or drinking?
> But here's what is more terrible and funnier:
> in part all of us, my staff and hound,
> are the fabrication of my lamp.
>
> And this in the settlement where there are no peasants,
> is salvation, my hound and my staff.

> Там, значит, никто не колдует, не пьет?
> Но вот что страшней и смешнее:
> отчасти мы все, мои посох и пес,
> той лампы моей измышленье.
>
> И это в селенье, где нет поселян,—
> спасенье, мой пес и мой посох.

With her hound and staff as her salvation, she thanks whoever sent them the
lifesaving light: "And it's not important / who sent us the redeeming light.
We're grateful that it's been sent" ("A kto nam spasitel'nyi svet posylal— /
nevazhno. Spasibo, chto poslan").

---

referring to love. In the poem "What goal did you pursue" ("Kakuiu ty presledovala tsel' "; no. 118),
the concluding stanza in A. Tarkovskii's translation reads:

> Saiat-Nova said, "I to the candle,
> Like an enamoured butterfly, fly,
> In the blaze of love I want to burn in such a way
> That the sparks do not singe my beloved!"

> Саят-Нова сказал: «Я на свечу,
> Как бабочка влюбленная, лечу,
> В огне любви я так сгореть хочу,
> Чтоб искры яр мою не обжигали!»

(151–52)

Other examples are found on pages 136, 137, 141, 150 of Saiat-Nova, *Stikhotvoreniia*, compiled by
G. A. Tatosian, Biblioteka poeta, Bol'shaia seriia (Leningrad: Sovetskii pisatel', 1982). Compare
Mandel'shtam's use of the butterfly as a symbol of a life without a trace, of fleeting, funereal beauty.
See Nadezhda Mandel'shtam, *Tret'ia kniga* (Paris: YMCA Press, 1987), 190.

As if in response to the earlier symbolism of old age and to Tsvetaeva's current absence, dusk approaches in the poem. The image of the staff of any pilgrim from the earlier poem individualizes into the speaker's own here. The lantern's caprice chooses darkness—that is, it becomes extinguished. With darkness closing in, the persona's preference for lightless places encompasses the state of moonlessness and, metaphorically, the absence of people, also a form of emptiness ("pustota"). The darkness includes the persona's strange lack of sight here, possibly only due to the darkness or to the difficulty in peering into the past, which equals darkness for the blind one and "pustota," requiring the hound and the staff as guides. The absence of people and her emptiness are ostensibly the result of Tsvetaeva's absence, as indicated in "Return to Tarusa" (83). Somehow the persona doubts Tsvetaeva's total absence. As for herself, what she actually sees proves not to be the enchanted castle with the burning light, but the lamp under her red kerchief (her mind under her red hair?), and so all—she, the lamp, the hound, the staff—but not Tsvetaeva—are figments of her imagination. The speaker still questions "who sent the redeeming light?"—meaning inspiration and creative talent; it is a variation of the concept "the guiding sound." Old age, among other things, is implied in the blindness and the darkness. Whereas Tsvetaeva's poems on Tarusa, "The Ferry" ("Parom") and "Autumn in Tarusa" ("Osen' v Taruse"), could conceivably be antisymbols of spring and youth versus old age, her pieces are light-spirited, unlike Akhmadulina's ponderous intonations. Although Akhmadulina's speaker tries to convince the reader of the contrary, the time in the poem is most probably October and not February. She could be putting it all down in poetry in February. Sightlessness and the road evoke Akhmatova's poem "It's hot under the awning of the dark threshing barn" ("Pod navesom temnoi rigi zharko"; no. 26), in which the beggar—"the old friend"—is blind ("nezriachii") either literally or figuratively, and the road of life as well as the walking stick are prominent.

In the poem "The Forgotten Ball" ("Zabytyi miach"), the large orange lampshade from stanza 10 of "A Finger to the Lips" that the persona calls magical and that shone with all its might (76) turns into a forgotten orange ball which caused annoyance in summer. It recalls the loss of the balloon in *Chills* ("How the balloon slips from a child's hands"). She is possibly utilizing a tacit simile between the real orange ball and her orange lampshade with the orange autumn sun. The light and the color spread to the plant calendula, which *Webster's Dictionary* defines as "any of a small genus of yellow-rayed composite herbs of temperate regions." Viewed from above, the flower, orange-yellow, not only resembles a ball but looks like a rayed sun. The plant grows from June to the October frosts in Russia.[31] The light and color in the verse spread to the calendula, and the ball and plants become accomplices in gilding nature. Indeed, day establishes its zenith in the calendulas, a reflective source of gold color, echoing or rippling many times over the glowing forgotten ball. Autumn appears to have taken the orange ball as the absolute achievement toward which it must strive in painting nature, under its jurisdiction for the duration:

> Here's the reason for autumn, here's the catch,
> to teach in a bonfire from dusk to dusk
> the disobeyers, the apostates of color,
> whose absolute has been forgotten in the garden by the
>   children.

> Вот осени причина, вот зацепка,
> чтоб на костре учить от тьмы до тьмы
> ослушников, отступников от цвета,
> чей абсолют забыт в саду детьми.

The third line ostensibly refers to those who abandon Tsvetaeva, and the fourth under children implies her poetic heirs. With some help from the shining sun the garden becomes engulfed in orange flames:

> But this garden! Whose retrial
> called it green? It's an incendiary of dachas.
> They're all gorgeous. But the first place goes to the
>   maple,
> it waited (for the time) when they would forget the ball.

---

31. In the Brokgaus and Efron Encyclopedia the name of the flower reverberates etymologically with "kalendy," which is defined as: "for the ancient Romans it was the name of the first day of every month. When the pontifex's assistant glimpsed the crescent of the moon for the first time" (14:21). The association connects with the themes of the moon and of day.

Но этот сад! Чей пересуд зеленым[32]
его назвал? Он—поджигатель дач.
Все хороши. Но первенство—за кленом,
уж он-то ждал: когда забудут мяч.

The absolute perfection toward which autumn must strive in forming its palette is lying in the garden as a paragon, much like a tuning fork furnishing the standard pitch. Once it has surpassed the brilliant color, the maple, however, hopes that the ball will be forgotten. Yet the ball, suspiciously like the dimmer (hence orange) autumn sun, is the reason for autumn's existence. Akhmadulina furnishes her own "defamiliarized" coinage "from dark to dark" ("ot t'my do t'my") instead of the usual "from dusk to dawn" ("ot zari do zari"). During daylight the ball metaphorically tortures into compliance with her color requirements all disobeyers and apostates from the absolute color dictated accidentally, as it were, by innocent children who left the ball by chance or by neglect. The poem exemplifies a magnificent, wry picture of the flaming glory of this autumnal garden. With this resplendent color dominating, the persona questions the correctness of calling the garden green when anyone can see it is a blaze of oranges.

The plants vie with one another and with the maddeningly absolute ball for supremacy and consistency in color. Indeed, all earthly fire has accepted the challenge of emulating the ball and possibly the autumnal sun. The forgotten ball consistently dominates the persona's consciousness and imagination, a fact documented in the poem inasmuch as the word "ball" figures in the title and in every stanza (twice in stanza 6) other than stanza 3, in which it is referred to only obliquely. The word "forget" in various morphological forms figures in the title and in every stanza. Its degree of forgetting comes under question. The children may have abandoned the ball but they have not forgotten it to the extent that the speaker and all of nature are plagued with its presence through imitative multiplication until the first snowfall when the word "zabyt" leaves its subject, "miach," to be placed in final position in the poem. Now the ball and its induced nature have indeed been forgotten, save for this poem. Yet until the snowfall the so-called forgotten (or abandoned) ball played games with her when she strolled along

32. The colloquial "peresud" denotes a retrial, the plural ("peresudy") means leisure discussions, empty conversation, gossip. The best definition in this context is probably "reevaluation" or "new decision."

the aspens, gazing at the ball and finding "candle-ends," i.e., the remains of the blazing yellow-orange flowers of the calendulas. And she even finds one while composing stanza 6: "And here's one more" ("A vot eshche odin"). An important literary source for the forgotten ball is Vladimir Nabokov's (1899–1977) novel *The Gift* (*Dar*). In it Fedor Godunov-Cherdyntsev's book of verse begins with the poem "The Lost Ball" ("Propavshii miach"); it involves a ball which has rolled under the nurse's bureau and is found later in the concluding poem, "About the Ball that Was Found" ("O miache naidennom").[33]

In the poem "Butterfly" ("Babochka") the exact date, October 16, reveals the short duration of the snowfall. Golden autumn, so reminiscent of Pushkin's glorified "golden autumn," and currently of Tsvetaeva, has returned to induce a hibernating butterfly—in all likelihood, since it is indoors, a huge moth, which Russians often call "motylek"—to activity.[34] Its brief awakening is compared to resurrection from death. Using a phonetic spelling— "skushno"—in lieu of the correct "skuchno," like Tsvetaeva in her usage of the phonetic spelling "shto" (this pronunciation is characteristic of Muscovites) for the correct "chto," Akhmadulina's speaker scrutinizes the compelling hunger for fleeting life and reality that has made the moth awaken alone. Its lust for a temporary return to life, expressed through the attempt to break through the double windows incarcerating it, is likened to a battle with the grave. The rapid beating of its wings and the ensuing buzzing evoke the airport image. Akhmadulina removes several steps between the image of the fluttering wings and that of an airplane taking off, a simile through conditional metonymy:

> From the mortal grip, from the sleep of the grave
> you are breaking away so that if hearing were sharper,
> I'd have to, as at an airport,
> cover my eyes and bend my head.

33. Vladimir Nabokov, *Dar* (New York: Izdatel'stvo imeni Chekhova, 1952), 35. An admirer of Nabokov, Akhmadulina met him a few months before his death. Moreover, Richard C. Borden in "H. G. Wells' 'Door in the Wall' in Russian Literature," discusses a "child's ball, irretrievably lost when it had . . . rolled into a gutter" in Iurii Olesha's (1899–1960) novel *Envy*. Borden finds that this "irretrievably lost" object from childhood encapsulates the character Kavaterov's fears that his own metaphorical "childhood" may be irretrievably lost (*Slavic and East European Journal* 36, no. 3 [1992]).

34. Cf. in connection with "motyl'ki" Pushkin's poem "The Monk" ("Monakh"; 1:21), in which the devil turns into a fly and makes the monk think of sin, i.e., anything undesirable forced upon an unwilling person, with flies and moths symbolizing the thoughts.

Из мертвой хватки, из загробной дремы
ты рвешься так, что, слух острее будь,
пришлось бы мне, как на аэродроме,
глаза прикрыть и голову пригнуть.

The butterfly ("babochka"), harkening back to her image of thoughts like butterflies ("mysli kak motyl'ki"), now clarifies the comparison between the reawakening of the butterfly (although usually large moths, not butterflies, are trapped between double windows) inside the panes with herself:

Whether I die or not, I will first exhaust
the candle and my brow: let them devise how
I will bless the predatoriness of love of life
with the spoils of life in dimming pupils.

Умру иль нет, но прежде изнурю я
свечу и лоб: пусть выдумают—как
благословлю я хищность жизнелюбья
с добычей жизни в меркнущих зрачках.

Enlisting all her mental and intellectual resources, the persona resurrects her thoughts and poem-writing in the final stanza:

It's time! In the window burns the recluse fire.
The line between my brows has deepened.
I write: October the sixteenth, Tuesday—
And the Resurrection of my butterfly.

Пора! В окне горит огонь-затворник.
Усугубилась складка меж бровей.
Пишу: октябрь, шестнадцатое, вторник—
и Воскресенье бабочки моей.

Capitalizing "Voskresen'e" (Resurrection) specifies the importance of the reawakening of creative thoughts in the persona; however, the word's spelling introduces semantic ambiguity, if not confusion: as every student of Russian learns soon enough, in modern Russian the spelling with the soft sign (-'e) denotes "Sunday" and the days of the week are not capitalized in Russian. Even so, such an interpretation of Akhmadulina's line does nothing toward advancing the ideas here. The other definition of the word, with

a different spelling in modern Russian—"Voskresenie" (Resurrection)—
fits in very well. Still, given Akhmadulina's preoccupation with old writing
and times, it is easy to discern here the nineteenth-century practice of not
clearly distinguishing the two alternate endings. Indeed, she habitually uses
the contracted ending form for words in -*ie* throughout the current collection, a practice still accepted in poetry. In other words, the meaning here is
"resurrection."

The awakening of the moth seems to signal the speaker's travels. Having
exhausted the garden theme with this poem, the speaker now writes "occasional," less thematically integrated pieces that highlight her circuitous return home to Peredelkino via mention of Moscow, Gagra in the Caucasus
on the Black Sea coast, Riga, Leningrad, and Moscow again. Now the
dominant factors that earlier became the themes of the moon, day, and the
garden are no longer in charge of her creative process; their exclusive
guiding force ends once the speaker has left behind the uniquely inspira-
tional artistic locus of Tsvetaeva's Tarusa to explore subject matter other
than the creative process, or less fully dominated by it.

The fun and games unfold as an evolving and revolving process essential
to the poetry. As an evolving process in Akhmadulina's verse it has changed
over the years through development and intensification, even crystallization,
as it were; as a revolving process, it intermittently reveals the obverse side of
the coin, the black to the white, the sorrow to the fun, or even the fun in
sorrow and the sorrow in fun, for one changes into the other continually in
the ongoing process of life and art, and life into art, and art into life.

9

Revered Writers—2

Вдохновения не сыщешь; оно само
должно найти поэта.

—Pushkin

As the collection *The Secret* commences the process of closure made patent through the poetic speaker's distance from Tarusa, Pushkin advances to the foreground, and he and Tsvetaeva share the limelight in the final poems. Contemporaries of Akhmadulina, engaged in the arts, receive attention alongside the writers.[1]

In the poem "Moscow: The House on Begovaia Street" ("Moskva: dom na Begovoi ulitse") dedicated to the actor and balladeer Vladimir Vysotskii (1938–80), the opening line addresses him as the frequenter of all Moscow social gatherings and parties, which probably lasted until the first rays of dawn. During an interview in the journal *Ogonek* Akhmadulina recalls her friend: "It's painful to recall Vysotskii. I had the good fortune to be considered his friend. Oh, if only you knew how I wished at that time that he would be published. In his lifetime only once did he manage to publish a poem in *Den' poezii*. However, it brought nothing but grief. Today it's apparent how much the fact that his poems were not published harmed him. He would pull out with his voice up to three versions of a line without a single solution."[2]

The Moscow Hippodrome is located at 22 Begovaia Street, the street being Vysotskii's home neighborhood. With parties ending at dawn and guests leaving only then, the transmuted image of the goddess Aurora becomes understandable. It harkens back to the earlier five-fingered glove of dawn in "Following the 27th Day of March" (*The Secret*, 49). Here,

---

1. Bella Akhmadulina, *Taina. Novye stikhi* (Moscow: Sovetskii pisatel', 1983).
2. Interview with Bella Akhmadulina, in *Ogonek*, no. 15 (1987).

conversely, the rays do not radiate, or branch out, in exactly five, but they certainly spread out evoking the calendula image as shown by Akhmadulina's metaphoric epithet: "branched dawn" ("rassvet sokhatyi").[3] This transformed image of dawn, then, still hails back to Homer. The dawn once again suggests human form here, as in Homer, but now the evocation is carried out through reference to dawn's breast:

> Habituès of Moscow gatherings,
> the heavenly vault barely awakens,
> I love when the branched dawn
> tears with its breast the thicket of haze.

> Московских сборищ завсегдатай,
> едва очнется небосвод,
> люблю, когда рассвет сохатый
> чащобу дыма грудью рвет.

With the hippodrome, or racetrack, located on Begovaia Street and with the historically convenient presence of the root *beg-* ("run") in the word, the image of horses grows explicit through the word's first root—*ipp*odrom for the Greek word for "horse."[4] By connecting through the root *sokh* in "sokhatyi" with the agricultural wooden plow ("sokha"), the twin images acquired by roots—the horse and dawn, branched like a plow—retain rustic ties and prepare the ground for various other artistic and literary references. They are not slow in coming. The horse motif, expressed in convoluted periphrastic and metonymic terms, already assumes a new face in the lines of an earlier poem:

> Thus confusion enters the feet of the steed
> and his reckless eye strains to get away.

3. The Seventeen-Volume Dictionary lists "sokhatyi" as "razvetvlennyi, razvilistyi" (branched, forked).

4. The nucleus for races and horses, which will develop into the classic Pegasus, symbolic of the poet, occurs as early as in *Chills:*

> Am I ill—for the third day I am trembling
> like a horse awaiting the race.

> Хвораю, что ли,—третий день дрожу,
> как лошадь, ожидающая бега.
>
> (*Dreams of Georgia*, 223)

Так оторопь коню вступает в ноги
и рвется прочь безумный глаз его.

("A Stroll"; 73)

A characteristic description of a living room, possibly in an old home, merely serves as an outlet or opening onto the inextinguishable racing horse:

On Begovaia Street—there is the plush
and captivity and turn of window of one living room,
where an inextinguishable steed gallops
to outrun the heavenly fire.

На Беговой—одной гостиной
есть плюш, и плен, и крен окна,
где мчится конь неугасимый
в обгон небесного огня.

(90)

This is an obvious reference to Vysotskii's independent-minded poem on racing, "The Ambler's Race" ("Beg inokhodtsa").[5]

Thus outside one of the windows stretches the Hippodrome with a statue of a racing horse (if this is not a picture in the apartment). What one sees on returning to or leaving this apartment in the early hours of dawn are the empty stands as expressed through metonymic oxymoron by Akhmadulina: "And the cataracts of the pale early hour see / the dawn delirium of the empty stands" ("I vidiat bel'ma rani blekloi / pustykh tribun rassvetnyi bred"). The quatrain sounds absurd if taken literally, for "bel'mo" is the cause of blindness in the eye, but it echoes the blindness image in the preceding poems while still remaining but a hint. Naturally, its use is as a metaphoric simile; literally, the pale earliness (dawn) peers with pallid colorless eyes before the sun's appearance when visibility is lower. This could be an allusion to Pushkin's "transparent twilight" ("prozrachnyi sumrak") in the introduction to *The Bronze Horseman*. The "bel'mo" adds yet another human (or divine) feature to the dawn, along with breast and gloves for hands.

The rapid succession of words with comparable sounds—alliteration—

5. See Vladimir Vysotskii, *Poeziia i proza*, compiled by A. Krylov and Vladimir Novikov (Moscow: Knizhnaia palata, 1989), 145–46.

and contiguous ideas and meaning is evocative of Tsvetaeva, namely the words "bel'ma," "bleklyi," "bred," "bleshchut," "bystroletnyi," "beg." Pale dawn changing into morning assumes the mien of a race horse, as if one horse were chasing away the horse of the previous day (which conjures up the earlier image of day-diety). Indeed, the classical divinity of the dawn, Eos, rides in a chariot drawn by horses or else rides a horse. Another allusion in the poem possibly comes from *The Bronze Horseman*, in which Pushkin says, "One dawn rushes to relieve the other, / Giving night one half hour" ("Odna zaria smenit' druguiu / Speshit, dav nochi polchasa"). Akhmadulina paints the horse's image metonymically in the race between dawn and dusk: "Snorts and shines the swift-flying / race which transforms into morning" ("Fyrchit i bleshchet bystroletnyi, / perekhodiashchii v utro beg"). The delirium of the persona from the previous poems now reverberates with that of dawn. The horse image of the hippodrome pursues its metonymical development with the mane of the hippodrome curling as the mist rises with the trot (more equine imagery for the day) of the young day strengthening. The remainder of the night is drunk to the dregs by "the hot-tempered drowziness at the party table" ("vspyl'chivaia drema zastol'ia").

The twofold intertwined development of partying until dawn on Begovaia Street and the night giving way to morning continues in the image of an awakened guest:

> Already somebody is asking for cabbage soup in the
>   kitchen,
> and the face of the nighttime beauty
> has faded. The (cigarette) stubs of morning. Autumn.
> Everyone straggles home.

> Уж кто-то щей на кухне просит,
> и лик красавицы ночной
> померк. Окурки утра. Осень.
> Все разбредаются домой.

Stanzas 7 through 9 develop the theme of the lingering, now unwelcome, guest after all others have left. The image recalls Pushkin who in canto 8, stanza 51, of *Eugene Onegin* alludes to friends departing from life or languishing in Siberia:

But those to whom in friendly meeting
I read my first stanzas . . .
Some are no longer with us, and others are far away,
As Saadi[6] once said.

Но те, которым в дружной встрече
Я строфы первые читал . . .
Иных уж нет, а те далече,
Как Сади некогда сказал.

Returning to the theme of death in his poem "Whether I wander along noisy streets,"[7] Pushkin goes on here in his concluding lines to extol an early demise so favored by the Romantics and which Akhmadulina intimates in "The Rider Garden":

Blessed is he who early leaves the festival of life
Without having drunk to the dregs
The goblet full of wine,
Who has not finished reading its [life's] novel
And suddenly was able to part with it [life],
As I was able to with my Onegin.

Блажен, кто праздник жизни рано
Оставил, не допив до дна
Бокала полного вина,
Кто не дочел ее романа
И вдруг умел расстаться с ним,
Как я с Онегиным моим.

Like Pushkin, Akhmadulina's persona suddenly questions whether she too is not all alone when her soulmates have departed:

Do I not likewise in the lunar desert
stand? Accomplices of the soul,
who colored the populous feast,
Departed headlong or unwillingly.

6. Saadi is a famous Persian poet of the thirteenth century whose favorite topics are love and the garden.
7. A. S. Pushkin, *Polnoe sobranie sochinenii v desiati tomakh*, ed. B. V. Tomashevskii (Moscow: AN SSSR, 1962–66), 3:135.

Не так ли я в пустыне лунной
стою? Сообщники души,
кем пир был красен многолюдный,
стремглав иль нехотя ушли.

This evokes Pushkin's poems of abandonment by Decembrist friends and
the death of friends.

The reference in Akhmadulina appears to be to loss by death, sudden as
in Vysotskii's case, as well as possibly to emigration, examples for her being
the writers Vasilii Aksenov and Vladimir Voinovich (b. 1932):

Some to the absence of southern countries,
some to the distance without name in which
the universalness of fate is salutory
and terrifying if you are a renegade.

Кто в стран полуденных заочность,[8]
кто—в даль без имени, в какой
спасительна судьбы всеобщность
и страшно, если ты изгой.[9]

With Akmadulina's persona as the single remaining guest, the hostess
seems to have tested her forehead for fever through a light touch of her
lips ("prigubila") to make certain that the cause for the fever is here.
Unexpectedly, the persona's forehead is cold: "She put her lips—it was as
if she had destroyed me— / an incomprehensible coldness of my forehead" ("Prigubila—kak pogubila— / nepostizhimyi khlad chela"). It reverberates with the earlier "dushepogubnyi" and "A Finger to the Lips."
Reminiscent of Tsvetaeva are the tone and syntax as well as the play on
roots to meld meaning. The speaker then waxes philosophical on the

8. In terms of morphological parts this word "zaochnost'," deriving from "za okom" (beyond the
eyes, away from the eyes), could acoustically be construed as being connected with "za Okoi"
(beyond the Oka). Akhmadulina's play on the meaning of "beyond" and "very far away" inherent in
the prefix "za-" continues in the poem "I walk along the environs" with "beyond the heavens or
transheavenly": "Sufler v zanebesnom ukryt'e shepnul." Bella Akhmadulina, *Sad. Novye stikhi*
(Moscow: Sovetskii pisatel', 1987), 151.

9. In the first line there is a fine periphrastic image of leaving for the proxy of "noon(day)"
countries (meridional; southern), fashioned on Pushkin's image of the midnight lands (septen-
trional; northern; i.e. St. Petersburg). In the fourth line the word "izgoi" (outcast or maverick) is
from old Russian.

cyclicity of life, in which nothing really repeats but merely renews itself. Concerning forgetfulness and the creation of legends she reiterates her assertion on not being able to enter the same river twice by playing on the forms of the verb "to be"; "The entire future has happened before, / and there'll be a story that I was [i.e. existed]" ("Vse budushchee—prezhde bylo, / a budet—byl', chto ia byla"). This is reminiscent of Akhmatova's use of the epigraph from T. S. Eliot in part 2 of *Poem without a Hero*—"In my beginning is my end"—and she also uses as an epigraph the line from Pushkin's *Eugene Onegin* from the lines quoted above: "Some are no longer (with us), and others are far away." It also faintly echoes Tsvetaeva's opening line "Dying, I won't say: I was" ("Umiraia, ne skazhu: *byla*").[10] The lingering guest eventuates as the double of Akhmadulina's speaker; she too is lingering in life, but the good-natured laughter sounds from the gaping abyss. An otherwise frightening coda is abated by the word "good-natured." It could imply the devil or else Pushkin whom she earlier credited with being preoccupied with an abyss. Oddly, the last two stanzas dwindle to two lines each from the favored four to a stanza.

In the poem "Travel" ("Puteshestvie") the speaker philosophizes on man and on his complaints to what he considers his personal star (94). This quoted man speaks using flowery periphrasis and stands out through lexical tautology as in the verse of Pushkin.[11] The cart of life evokes Pushkin's poem "The Wagon of Life" ("Telega zhizni"; 2:164) and serves to underpin its philosophical reflections on life. Akhmadulina deliberates as follows:

> "I drive the cart of life onto a cliff.
> The exhalation of my lungs is such that it was rejected
>   by a hungry (reed) pipe.
>
> I gave away your gift, and my book does not know
> that it won't find a reviewer more fastidious than I.
> Let me celebrate inactivity. Send me to the resort of
>   oblivion.
> Let me open my mouth not for singing but for gaping
>   about."

10. Marina Tsvetaeva, *Sochineniia v dvukh tomakh*, compiled by Anna Saakiants (Moscow: Khudozhestvennaia literatura, 1980), 1:113; my emphasis.
11. Cf. chapter 10 on Annenskii's poem "Teacher," in Sonia Ketchian, *The Poetry of Anna Akhmatova*, which shows that Annenskii called attention to this device in Pushkin.

«*Воз* житья я на кручу *везу.*
Выдох легких таков, что отвергнут голодной
свирелью.

Я твой *дар* раз*дар*ил, и не ведает книга моя,
что брезгливей, чем я, не подыщет себе
рецензента.
Дай от*праз*дновать *праз*дность. Сошли на курорт
забытья.
Дай уста отомкнуть не для *пенья,* а для
ротозейства».

Here the words "rot" (mouth—used as a root here) and "usta" (mouth, lips) and "otomknut' " (to open—unusual in this usage) and "zeistva" (used as the second in a compound word from "ziiat' "—to gape) are anachronistic synonyms. The words "dar" (gift, talent) and "pen'e" (singing) can be construed as contextual synonyms for poetry. Beginning with stanza 6, alliteration links this poem with the preceding one: "breg," "bred," "bravada" (bank, delirium, bravado). The wisteria ("glitsiniia") that is growing out of the grave is one of the new plants that the poet consistently introduces, some with ambivalent function: namely, here thistle ("chertopolokh"), with "chert" as one of its roots reminds us of the devil, and rosebrier ("shipovnik") evokes Pushkin's *Eugene Onegin* and the promised rose mentioned earlier. Admittedly, Akhmatova's poem "Here began Pushkin's exile" ("Zdes' Pushkina izgnan'e nachalos' "; no. 303) could have reinforced the devil image in Akhmadulina seeing that it conjures up the Caucasus, Pushkin, Lermontov, and the devil metonymically thereby serving as a close step to the past writers. The collection *The Garden* introduces a new vivid array of plants.

The poem "The Rose" ("Roza"; 97) enters the mentality of the South in olden times as later refracted in classical Russian literature: Pushkin, Lermontov, Bestuzhev-Marlinskii,[12] and Lev Tolstoi. The lyric speaker, on the one hand, is presently in Gagra on the Black Sea selecting roses at a market, and she assumes the role of an old khan, on the other. Spiritedly interweaving the two strands (evocative of the two temporal planes in the poem "My Pachevskii"), she selects fresh roses at Gagra's open market as if

---

12. Aleksandr Bestuzhev (1797–1837) was a Decembrist, exiled to Siberia and later to the Caucasus, who wrote Romantic prose under the penname of Marlinskii. He is now known as Bestuzhev-Marlinskii.

she were a muslim khan choosing slave girls at a market with the help of a vizier. The tone is loud and expansive. The humor becomes evident when the speaker shows to what advantage she employs her elbows in public transportation to protect the roses from injury. It could be her individual development of Pushkin's poem "O rose maiden" ("O deva-roza") with its identification of the beautiful maiden with a rose (2:204). The general ambience of the past evokes Pushkin's long Romantic poem *The Fountain of Bakhchisarai* (*Bakhchisaraiskii fontan*; 4:175–95).

The slave imagery and the suggestion of a harem in this poem recall the imagery in Akhmadulina's poem on the young Akhmatova in whose poetry roses proliferate, "I envy her—young" ("Ia zaviduiu ei—molodoi"; *Dreams of Georgia*, 164), with references to Persian lilac, the similarities of their surnames, and on her own audacity in retaining her inherited name, much like Tsvetaeva, in lieu of a pseudonym.

The rose image acquires specific humanization through connection with a variety of rose named the Luxemburg, the city bearing the name Luxembourg, and the Polish-born German revolutionary Rosa Luxemburg (1871–1919) in whose honor two streets and a side street seem to be named in the poem "A Suburb: The Names of Streets" ("Prigorod: nazvan'ia ulits"). Merrily juggling the words, sounds, and unexpected meaning, the speaker points out that the inhabitants distinguish in their own way between these streets:

> Not by registration, but in order to distinguish,
> in order not to get lost in different huts [or: "rose
>   thickets"],
> there is Rosa-Prima (and) Rosa-Second.
>
> Не по прописке—для разбора,
> чтоб в розных кущах не пропасть,
> есть Роза-прима, Роза-втора.
>
> (*The Garden*, 153)

The play on Rosa conjures up the English word primrose (literally, the first rose) and its Russian counterpart "pervotsvet" of the poem "I have the secret of wondrous blooming." In light of the fact that "vtora" means "second" in Polish, namely, "the second Rosa"—"Roza-vtora"—it is most likely a reference to the Polish-born revolutionary Rosa Luxemburg. Furthermore, the "smart botanist" ("botanik-pereumok") with whom the poetic speaker is apparently drinking tea sweetened with rose-petal jam evokes the gardener of the same poem. As the bird-cherry honey did earlier, the fragrant flowery brew seems to have somehow affected her senses to the extent that she snaps, "let them send for a psychiatrist" ("puskai poshliut za psikhvrachom").

Another street, named after the hussar poet Denis Davydov (1784–1839), further corroborates Rosa Luxemburg as the name of a street. Yet where for the heroic poet-soldier this area must be lonely, the speaker appears to be intimating that the other, unnamed street is best remembered for the botanical Luxemburg Rose. One expects that Akhmadulina is aware of such a rose:[13]

> In the night
> for you, a singer, for you, a hero,
> isn't it sad in these parts?

> Ночной порою
> тебе, певцу, тебе, герою,
> не грустно в этой стороне?
>   (155)

In the poem "Gagra: The Cafe Ritsa" ("Gagra: kafe 'Ritsa' "), the lyric persona's sojourn in the resort town of Gagra in Georgia continues through a curious opening simile: the day wreathes (like smoke), huge and sticky, as if it were a dream, viscid and huge. The unusual quality here is that both the tenor and the vehicle of the simile are qualified by the same two adjectives in reverse order: "As if a dream, viscid and huge, / wreathes day, huge and viscid" ("Kak budto son tiaguchii i ogromnyi, / klubitsia den' ogromnyi i tiaguchii"; 100). One envisions the two images side by side in an orderly mirror image symmetry provided by the smokelike quality, the wreathing. By singling out the same two qualities for the tenor and the vehicle and by not curtailing the reader's imagination through the tandem adjectives, the poet in effect equates the properties of the two. Accordingly, if day wreathes, so too can dream ("son") in this simile of equivalence.

Lines 3 and 4 of stanza 1 appear to paraphrase a song on magnolias by the poet and singer Aleksandr Vertinskii (1889–1957), "The Magnolia Tango"

---

13. In 1912 a yellow rose was named in honor of Marie Adelaide, grand duchess of Luxembourg. See J. H. Nicolas, *A Rose Odessey* (Garden City, N.Y.: Doubleday, 1937), chap. 16.

("Tango magnoliia").[14] The tone is humorous, but then the speaker feels that these healthy athletic types—the average people for whom she writes—have not read a single book. Although their carefree attitude during vacation appalls the speaker, she will spare them her sadness. The atmosphere of abandon while vacationing recaptures the story "Change of Lifestyle" ("Peremena obraza zhizni") by Akhmadulina's friend, the prosewriter Vasilii Aksenov. She appeals to a higher force, personified as Sea-Sky (More-Nebo)[15] to send misfortune to her (this brings to mind Akhmatova's poetic speaker who found a state of grief the only way to create verse) and good and miracles to the suntanned catchers of glasses and plates. It is not clear whether these are customers.[16] The heaviness of the day, viscid and huge, now overcomes the speaker and is possibly threatening the reader as well.

In the poem "It's not the same as twenty years ago" ("Vot ne takoi, kak dvadtsat' let nazad"; 102), the lyrical ego's strange perception of day and her own state as well as the possible residue of bird-cherry delirium in the previous poems probably put her in a kind of stupor, or daze, for a mental return to the past. The poetic persona encounters herself from twenty years ago. The sultry stickiness of the day, as if conducive to retention of the past, the sun and the water outside Russia coupled with the sensation of return as the same, yet not quite the same, person, evokes Akhmatova's poem on Tashkent from the cycle "The Moon in Zenith" ("Luna v zenite"), in which nothing has changed in the sultry land throughout that long time period: "I have not been here for about seven hundred years" ("Ia ne byla zdes' let sem'sot"; no. 373).[17] In Akhmadulina the present day is further along toward evening. Otherwise everything appears the same for her in stanzas 3 and 4. At this point the footprints in the sand remind the speaker of the girl, the speaker's personal sacrifice, just as in nature where one object or ele-

14. Aleksandr Vertinskii, *Pesni i stikhi 1916–1937* [San Francisco]: Globus, [1970?], no pagination.

15. There is here a primordial approach to the sky akin to that shown in Moses of Khorene's *History of the Armenians*, trans. Robert W. Thomson (Cambridge: Harvard University Press, 1978), 123.

16. In March 1987, Akhmadulina explained to me that this higher force is meant to be close to God, if not God. The poetic speaker's search for a higher force is analogous to the contemporary Czech writer and former president of Czechoslovakia, Vaclav Havel's concepts as expounded by Michael Henry Heim in his review of *Letters to Olga* ("Havel's Singular Vision," *The Boston Globe*, 13 March 1988). The third of Havel's "layers of life" is that which many experience as God. Although he rejects the notion of God, Havel's "commitment to the third, absolute horizon or 'being,' . . . is as zealous as many believers' commitment to their God."

17. Anna Akhmatova, *Stikhotvoreniia i poemy*, compiled by V. M. Zhirmunskii (Leningrad: Sovetskii pisatel', 1976), 218.

ment unites with the other through sacrifice in stanza 5.[18] The persona, now philosophical, shows in an earlier stanza that the swimmer possibly became part of the sea (evoking Marina Tsvetaeva), that the sea gull devoured the gray mullet, a fish ("kefal' "), and that the wasp fed insatiably on the flavorful pear ("diushes"):

> They have merged, the sea and the swimmer,
> the gray mullet and the sea gull, the rusty honey and
>   the sting.

> Соединились море и пловец,
> кефаль и чайка, ржавый мед и жало.

> *(The Garden,* 102)

The current persona approaches her former self sarcastically, if not with some envy for her earlier enthusiasm, her youth, and her fresh beauty: in stanza 6 an older and wiser persona finds this younger self unfledged and insecure; in stanza 8 the pronouncement is made that in time all this younger persona's fervent wishes will be realized, therefore she would be wise to enjoy her youth more fully than she does (always the advice of a sagacious older person); in stanza 9 an almost religious image creeps in for expressing the need to be humble: "verigi nemoty" ("chains of muteness"). In turn, the image echoes the speaker's own dumbness in her early works during writer's block as well as her image of a fish's muteness ("ryb'ia nemota")

---

18. Cf. Akhmatova's poem "It's nice here: both rustling and crunch" ("Khorosho zdes': i shelest, i khrust"; no. 265):

> And on the luxurious festive snows
> A ski track as a remembrance of the fact
> That in some distant ages
> You and I passed by here together.

> И на пышных парадных снегах
> Лыжный след, словно память о том,
> Что в каких-то далеких веках
> Здесь с тобою прошли мы вдвоем.

Also relevant are Akhmatova's poems "My shade remained there and is pining" ("Tam ten' moia ostalas' i toskuet"; no. 185) and "Having been resurrected from the past, silently / Toward me comes my shade" ("Iz proshlogo vosstavshi, molchalivo / Ko mne navstrechu ten' moia idet"; no. 405). A further connection may be found in Tiutchev's poem "And so I again saw you" ("Itak, opiat' uvidelsia ia s vami"), in which the speaker returns to unloved native sites. There at the brink of day and evening he articulates, "My childhood age looks at me" ("Moi detskii vozrast smotrit na menia"). His childhood self is visualized as a long-dead younger brother. F. I. Tiutchev, *Lirika,* 2 vols., compiled by K. V. Pigarev (Moscow: Nauka, 1966), 1:107.

and Akhmatova's words "And my wonderful muteness" ("I nemoty moei chudesnoi") in the poem "I prayed so much: 'Quench' " ("Ia tak molilas': 'Utoli' "; no. 126). In the perorating stanza in true religious vein she advises the young persona to court difficulties and misfortune in order to develop into a better writer, thereby sounding like Pushkin in his pronouncements on the poet as prophet, but without the element of advice, and like Akhmatova in particular where the holy fool ("iurodivyi") advises Akhmatova's persona in the early poems. Ironically, neither the present persona nor the past one can hear each other due to obstruction of sound images by the barrier of time which permits only visual images and evokes the earlier double window panes: "You are saying something importantly in reply, / but I cannot hear you, nor you, me" ("Ty chto-to vazhno govorish' v otvet, / no mne—tebia, tebe—menia ne slyshno"). A most useful mode of distancing time.

Thus the speaker should keep in tune with her present self and understand herself well at any given moment, for the future may hold introspection but not live communication. In other words, the speaker overcomes diachronic visual barriers but not diachronic sound barriers, hence the need for a poem. Apparently, the notion of crossing the border between reality and artistic singing in a strophe becomes Akhmadulina's solution to Akhmatova's approach to time and space in verse, and its relation to reality.

If the great Russian satirist Nikolai Gogol' (1809–52) had a vision in Rome and the philosopher and poet Vladimir Solov'ev (1853–1900), who influenced the Russian Symbolists, had three visions of Sophia—the symbol of wisdom, Akhmadulina's speaker in the poem "Riga" follows their lead in having her own vision in the Latvian capital of Riga. It is probably caused by the spikes on Riga's historic churches whose sharp outlines pierce, as it were, the sunrise and contribute toward heightening her own perception and memory. This strange piece unfolds with the pain inflicted on the ears by poems coming into being (as if they come out ready to scream like a newborn child) to the blood that reddens the mouth as the poems leave her throat. Addressing the spike-judge of her work and bringing to mind the reverse fish image of a fish's muteness, the speaker complains about the cathedral's demands on her. As perhaps a takeoff on Akhmatova, for whom prayer to the Muse turns into song before eventuating as verse, Akhmadulina's persona likes to sing her poems wordlessly without delighting either her own hearing or that of others. Rationalizing that auditory senses receptive to poems acknowledge no designated time off, she nonetheless demonstrates that creation is not possible every moment and that the creating apparatus must rest and heal in the interim between the crafting of poems. The reader realizes that the lyrical ego has reached a special state, saturated with verse before producing her own in response.

In stanza 5 the speaker compares herself as poet to Roland of the medieval ballads. Uncertain how to explain the change in her creative process, she has forgotten, or forsaken, the letters for trills and roulades. This could possibly be an indication of a more advanced stage of poetic creation. As an expansion of the poem "I have the secret of wondrous blooming," the speaker appears to have acquired a unique sensitivity to catch the sounds and strains of poems, leaving them in her stead. Through the poems the persona continues to live for further poems, if not also for her readership. Somehow the spike seems to be extracting the poems from her throat. The speaker employs a common image—that of the moment of poetic creation as death, albeit an ecstatic one as in love. From the city spires she requests sorrow ("gorest' ") in return for her voice, love, and life, as a remembrance of her:

> Flee not misfortune—but preservation from
>   misfortune.
> Fear the vanity of mortal excess.
> You are saying something importantly in reply,
> but I cannot hear you, nor you, me.
>
> Беги не бед—сохранности от бед.
> Страшись тщеты смертельного излишка.
> Ты что-то важно говоришь в ответ,
> но мне—тебя, тебе—меня не слышно.
>   (*The Garden*, 103)

The remaining poems, other than "While with blue vein" ("Pokuda zhilkoi goluboi") and "We began together" ("My nachali vmeste"), have all been published in *Dreams of Georgia*. In the evasive poem "Not white-hot" ("Ne dobela raskalena") the speaker describes the city of Leningrad without naming it; presented are its inimitable white nights, the Neva River, and the Summer Garden. Instead of the city's name, the sounds in the word Leningrad are evoked through the sounds in the words of places portrayed, beginning with the first line, subsequently gaining in disorder and intensifying in the following lines to a true alliterative portrait: "*le*to," "*Let*nii s*ad*," "*nagrad*," "us*lad*." The "disorder" and clustering of words evoke Pushkin's poem "Luxurious city" ("Gorod pyshnyi"; 3:79). In the poem "Dedication" ("Posviashchenie") the speaker playfully refers to the city in a way that now evokes its former name as if in anticipation of the return to the name Saint Petersburg in October of 1991:

> . . . in the city of Saint-White Nights
> and on the corner of Nevskii Boulevard

> в Санкт-белонощном граде
> и Невского проспекта на углу.
> (*The Garden*, 50)

Implicit throughout the collection is the notion of travel, be it in time, space or the mind (culturally). The poem prepares for the longer one that will bear the title as a name.

The felicitous alliteration of sounds from the city's name is resumed in the first line of the poem: "Again to my eyes is given the reward of Leningrad" ("Opiat' dana glazam nagrada Leningrada"; 107). It serves to connect the spires of Riga with the one by the Neva in Leningrad immortalized by Pushkin in *Eugene Onegin:* "admiralteiskaia igla" ("the spike of the Admiralty"). Now the pain from the spike is directed to the eyes, almost as if the ephemeral beauty of Leningrad blinds while dazzling, ostensibly more so during the white nights. The image recalls the earlier notion of a hound and staff as a guide for the blind. Indeed, the pain, the wound, and the spike are inseparable from the city. Although the pupil of her eye has been pierced through, her vision has not been impaired owing to the healing qualities in the round dome, which is salutarily simple and modestly gold, possibly in contrast to the ornate designs on St. Basil's various cupolas. The earlier image of "bel'mo" reverberates here. While the speaker admires Peter the Great's audacity and foresight in predetermining the existence of the bard of this city's columns and spikes, she has no use for tsars. This one, however, must be begrudgingly lauded not only for the harmonious perfection of the city, but for providing the city of his name with its own singer by bringing a moor from Africa to be "tamed" and Russified. Yet who will bring the fire of foreign places to ordinary Russian locations such as Opochka and Tver'?

> To take out of Africa and to tame a moor,
> to graft the burning of foreign lands to Opochka and to
> Tver'—

the meaning is concealed for the time being, it's dark
    and early in the mind,
but the nascent iamb is maturing in the illiterate
    blood . . .

Из Африки изъять и приручить арапа,
привить ожог чужбин Опочке и Твери—

смысл до поры сокрыт, в уме—темно и рано,
но зреет близкий ямб в неграмотной крови . . .

The lyrical ego advances the notion that Leningrad (currently named St. Petersburg as in Pushkin's time) deserves to be sung by Pushkin because it is as harmonious and exacting as his working notebook where nothing can or should be changed. A tacit parallel can be discerned here with Akhmadulina's own genealogy: the Italian who settled in Russia, the Tartar on her father's side of the family as expounded in her humorous poem bearing an identical title with Pushkin: "My Genealogy."

The poem "Return from Leningrad" ("Vozvrashchenie iz Leningrada") finds the speaker returning home to a loft from the living, vibrant art of Peter's city, so vibrant that it breathes like nature—obviously to have the artist produce:

Only not to tear one's eyes from Peter's city,
only to read the harmony in all its features
and to think: here's granite, yet it breathes like
    nature . . .
But it's necessary to go home. Platform. Entrance.
    Loft.

Все б глаз не отрывать от города Петрова,
гармонию читать во всех его чертах
и думать: вот гранит, а дышит, как природа . . .
Да надобно домой. Перрон. Подъезд. Чердак.

Its location is an ancient street in the heart of Moscow, once the residence of cooks. In comparison, the one-hundred-year-old comely house she enters is youthful and overly familiar with its elders. In this and the following poem, previously published in *Dreams of Georgia,* a circumspect portrayal of Akhmadulina's unique museum-like home with the artist and set designer

Boris Messerer unfolds, without, however, mention of him by name, other than as the "we" who reside there. The description of the building is accurate, as she ascends the stairs from the final sixth floor of the elevator to the seventh. The elevator goes no higher because the attic was not originally designed for habitation. Her simile probably denotes the quickly passing motion of her previous life while now she climbs to new exhilarating heights: "My former life is the foothills to these steps" ("Bylaia zhizn' moia—predgor'e sikh stupenei"). At this dizzying altitude the inspiring moon is closer to her window and to her; moreover, the depths of the heavens are closer: "How huge is the moon near the window. We ourselves / devised a dwelling near the heavenly depths" ("Kak velika luna vblizi okna. My sami / zateiali zhil'e vblizi nebesnykh nedr"). From this great height one can discern the "boundaries of existence":

> The splash of eternity in the night undermines the
>   walls
> and covets the instant that you and I are side by side.
> What a distance can be seen! And if one looks more
>   carefully,
> It's possible to distinguish the boundary of being.

> Плеск вечности в ночи подтачивает стены
> и зарится на миг, где рядом ты и я.
> Какая даль видна! И коль взглянуть острее,
> возможно различить границу бытия.

Indeed, the universe outside the window is a primer for the would-be learned person, the know-all of the poem "I have the secret of wondrous blooming," discussed in Chapter 3. The speaker spells it out for reading but does not want to read it. Rather, she hopes to savor the moment as it grows light, whereas on the Tverskoi Boulevard stretches a string of street lights still lit. There is a display of jubilation at being in her Moscow residence once more, but the persona is no longer communing with living, growing nature for its innermost secrets. Her period of physical and mental rest is at hand. Thus from living floral nature as the primer for her art the poetic speaker graduates to a venue with nature as the heavens and the supreme being.

In the poem "Features of the Studio" ("Primety masterskoi"; 111), dedicated to the designer of the volume, Boris Messerer, the speaker invites a guest, probably the reader, to the studio-apartment to which she returned in the previous poem. Again, no mention is made that Messerer is Bella Akhmadulina's husband. The guest is a "future guest," but Akhmadulina creates a double play on the word's semantics seeing that literally the archaic high-style word "griadushchii" means "coming" as in "griadushchii god" (the coming year). The description of the place reiterates the previous poem's imagery; namely, the lines here "Under this subheavenly roof, / which has been surpassed only by the abyss / of the almighty gloom" ("Pod etoi kryshei podnebesnoi, / kotoraia odnoi lish' bezdnoi / vsevyshnei mgly prevzoidena") rephrase, or intimate, analogous ones in "Return from Leningrad"; similarly, the phrases "near the sky's depths," "how huge is the moon near the window," "higher there is only a backwood," "an attic" ("vblizi nebesnykh nedr," "kak velika luna vblizi okna," "vyshe—tol'ko glush'," "cherdak") in "Return from Leningrad" equal here "under this subheavenly roof" or "where everyday life neighbors with the universe" ("gde byt—v sosediakh so vselennoi"). The piece is an emotional ode, or "light ode" with an address—"O guest" ("o gost' ")—plus humor and exhortations for the guest to partake of food and drink, as in an anacreontic ode. Akhmadulina apparently prefers this humorous type of ode in the rare instances when family is mentioned. Compare also the emotional ode to her daughters "Expecting the Christmas Tree" ("Ozhidanie elki").[19] This ode could be Akhmadulina's modern answer to the Roman poet Virgil (70–19 B.C.), mentioned in the poem, who is famous for his eclogues.

To the reader unfamiliar with Boris Messerer's studio crammed with paintings and antiques, the poem represents an enigmatic challenge. Its playful attitude with elegiac overtones mirrors jovial teasing in order to hide deep sentiments for a deeply loved one. The humor in the piece is underpinned by elements of the anacreontic ode, a genre that propagates epicurean motifs of love, wine, and song, based on the verses of the Greek poet Anacreon (570–478 B.C.). It will be recalled that anacreontic poems were particularly popular in Europe during the Renaissance and the Enlightenment. In Russian literature the poets Konstantin Batiushkov (1787–1855) and Pushkin were famous for such poems.[20] Anacreontic poems have a rather formal organization, often with an address, to offset the earthly in-

19. Bella Akhmadulina, *Sny o Gruzii* (Tbilisi: Merani, 1979), 147–48.

20. For a discussion of the place of the anacreontic ode in these poets see the first part of K. N. Grigor'ian, *Pushkinskaia elegiia. Natsional'nye istoki, predshestvenniki, evoliutsiia* (Leningrad: Nauka, 1990).

ducements of carefree merriment. The poems tend to glorify the enjoyment of life and of the moment at hand in true Bacchanalian spirit due to the transience of everything in life. Accordingly, this piece blends a certain irreverence, even mischief, with sadness at the fleeting quality of life and of joy, conveyed through the address to the future visitor and through mention of personal passing as well as of ghosts.

The poem continues Akhmadulina's penchant for moving with ease from one time boundary to another. Here it projects her speaker, certain that the studio will still be in existence, into the future. She herself will be a negative presence by then, an antipresence, as it were. For clarity, she addresses the guest as "future guest," which slightly undermines the future time plane of the poem unless the meaning of "coming guest" is recalled to bring it closer to the speaker's present. Shifting time levels as well as a speaker existing as a thinking nonbeing are no novelty for Akhmadulina. Indeed, in the humorous narrative poem *My Genealogy* her unborn self urged on to marriage various preceding generations of her ancestors to set the stage for her own later appearance. For example, the persona "helped" one young Italian female ancestor to elope with her lover rather than enter a monastery in accordance with her greedy father's wishes. The yet nonexistent persona likewise in spirit accompanied her Tartar ancestors up to the moment of her birth. In "Features of the Studio" one can observe an opposite pole of nonexistence—that following existence and life—if one were to compare it to the "negative" presence of her yet unborn persona in *My Genealogy*. Another poem on Boris Messerer's loft studio and on Akhmadulina's love for Boris, "Later I'll recall that I was alive" ("Potom ia vspomniu, chto byla zhiva"; *Dreams of Georgia,* 171) advances the notion of the future with the same striking word "s toskoi griadushcheiu" ("with future yearning"); it also pronounces the speaker's belief in recollecting after death.

Overt humor and the lightheartedness of friendship enter the poem "A Song for Bulat" ("Pesenka dlia Bulata"). In speaking of the current year she seems to be referring to the time in the collection, although this poem was also published previously in *Dreams of Georgia* (237). The years that the poems were written are never indicated at the poem's end, making it impossible to determine the precise year of writing unless the poem is included in the only dated volume to date, *Poems,* 1988. Placement in *The Secret,* however, displaces the time to the present. The speaker mentions their ability to enter another time period, and in the poem "Humorous Epistle to a Friend" ("Shutochnoe poslanie k drugu") ends with a sagacious image "What a long road it is / from Petersburg to Leningrad" ("Kakaia dolgaia doroga / iz Peterburga v Leningrad"; 118). In the poem "A Song for Bulat" the reproach can be of the sun, of space, or of "edinstvennost' " (uniqueness) in the opening six lines. The golden key to magic, presented to the speaker by her good friend the poet and bard Bulat Okudzhava, will be conveyed to others. Akhmadulina employs the allusions here to Bulat having a key to connote the Russian title to Pinnoccio, *The Adventures of Buratino, or the Golden Key* (*Prikliucheniia Buratino, ili Zolotoi kliuchik*). The key reverberates in a biographical mode with the gold key to the secret and with the plant "kliuchik," an alternate name for the primrose in the poem "I have the secret of wondrous blooming," in which it was the source for art and its mysteries. Some of the artistic themes expounded throughout the collection now assume a personal aspect through the lasting friendship of the two poets. Themes come to light of the longevity of poetry and the pain, even blood, in producing it: "Words from the lips are as if blood onto the handkerchief. / But they are for an age, not for an instant" ("Slova iz gub—kak krov' v platok. / Zato na vek, a ne na mig"). So although writing is difficult, and blood is spewed as the wordless verse is uttered, the consolation remains that the result of her painful labors will last an age, or an entire life long (note that she spells "na vek" ["for an age"] as two words as opposed to "navek" ["forever"]). Bulat's golden key will ensure that all will go well henceforth. In the image of her tears creating rhymes Akhmadulina evokes Akhmatova's combative lines, "To warm their satiated body, / They need my tears" ("Chtob gret' presyshchennoe telo, / Im nadobny slezy moi"; no. 118). The speaker prays for muteness here, unlike in other poems. Thus Akhmadulina moves closer to Akhmatova. In connection with poetic inspiration the persona no longer depends on rain, unless its role in the collection is fulfilled by the flow of the Oka River. At this period in her creative life nature dictates poetry to her.

The untitled poem with a heading in parentheses, perhaps in lieu of a subtitle: ("A Humorous Epistle to a Friend"), continues the jocular mood of the previous poem (117). Enclosure of the subtitle in parentheses, its smaller lettering, and the three asterisks on the line above it, which are characteristic of untitled poems, signify that the heading is not the title. What is more, the table of contents lists the poem's first line ("While with blue vein") and not the subtitle.

The speaker requests that Bulat take her back in time with him; he is, after all, adept at switching time levels because he has been writing historic prose, such as the piece on the Decembrists—*A Swallow of Freedom. A Word on Pavel Pestel'* (*Glotok svobody. Slovo o Pavle Pestele*).[21] As they head backward in time, the theme of Pushkin amplifies. This return to the past is as comfortable for her as a return home: "It's time to go home / to the past" ("Pora domoi / v byloe"). At a nineteenth-century ball, the uninvited pair catch sight of Pushkin—dusky and wan; perceiving, however, the intensity of his love for his beautiful wife Natal'ia Nikolaevna, they dare not stare:

> . . . There, by the column . . .
> so dusky and pale . . . This love
> cannot be borne! That is he. But is it he?
> No need to know, and don't look.
>
> Там, у колонны . . .
> так смугл и бледен . . . Сей любви
> не перенесть! То—он. Да он ли?
> Не надо знать, и не гляди.
>
> (117)

This poem probably reflects Tsvetaeva's "Poems to Pushkin" ("Stikhi k Pushkinu").[22] The pain of intruding on Pushkin's helplessness and passion for his wife and of glimpsing his human vulnerability prompts the lyric persona to leave abruptly this time period:

> Why is it given? Why do we have admittance
> into the beauty of foreign parts, into the days of others?
> Bulat, it's the same everywhere.
> Bulat, get in! Coachman, hurry!
>
> Зачем дано? Зачем мы вхожи
> в красу чужбин, в чужие дни?
> Булат, везде одно и то же.
> Булат, садись! Ямщик, гони!

And before returning to her own time, life, and then principal residence of the writer's town of Peredelkino outside Moscow, the speaker expresses splendidly the long arduous return journey:

---

21. Bulat Okudzhava, *Glotok svobody. Slovo o Pavle Pestele* (Moscow: Politizdat, 1971).

22. Marina Tsvetaeva, *Stikhotvoreniia i poemy*, compiled by A. A. Saakiants, Biblioteka poeta, Malaia seriia (Leningrad: Sovetskii pisatel', 1979), 135, 287–98. The first in this group of poems to Pushkin is omitted in the two-volume edition of 1980.

> How the snow flies! How much snow there is!
> How you are loved by me, my brother!
> How long the road
> from Petersburg to Leningrad.
>
> Как снег летит! Как снегу много!
> Как мною ты любим, мой брат!
> Какая долгая дорога
> из Петербурга в Ленинград.

The next poem places the speaker at home in Peredelkino, contemplating the church. To be sure, the church at Bekhovo, the one in Riga (the spires), and others mentioned in the collection seem to consolidate now in the golden cupola of the church in Peredelkino in the poem "Peredelkino after a Separation" ("Peredelkino posle razluki"), dedicated to the noted pianist Stanislav Neigaus, the son of the famous pianist and teacher Genrikh Neigaus (1888–1964) and Zinaida Nikolaevna who became the poet Pasternak's second wife. This is an avenue toward retaining her memory of them. The position of the church and the sunset seem to open up the sky to answers raised in the speaker's travels and to others to come:

> The long riddle was growing dark,
> and now the answer will flash.
> I look at the cupola at the hour of sunset,
> and the clear entrance to the sky is open.
>
> Темнела долгая загадка,
> и вот сейчас блеснет ответ.
> Смотрю на купол в час заката,
> и в небо ясный вход отверст.

The poem ushers in religious notes and philosophical questions on the soul's immortality. Indeed, in the collection with its unique concepts, and the concept of "uniqueness" ("edinstvennost' ") in particular, the speaker moves consistently toward presenting a supreme higher being.

In the next poem, titled "In Memory of Genrikh Neigauz" ("Pamiati Genrikha Neigauza"), an attempt is made to speak of two kinds of music, one created by traditional musicians, the other, by poets.[23] She herself is not

---

23. There is ostensibly some reason for juxtaposing poems to a son and a father with a German name that means "new house" and the speaker's return to her house. Of further interest is the

a seeker of torment, having found everything necessary and having over-come all obstacles. Yet the superfluous sound remains, and to be alive is beyond one's power, for music is "the torment of my torments" ("muka muk moikh"). While there are two kinds of music, the speaker will prefer to make do with one. Apparently, after communing with nature and the universe, the persona now utilizes traditional music for fleshing out the intricate dimensions in the poems. Her friend's music is instrumental in this, for she is his pupil.

Humor echoes through the concluding untitled poem "We began to-gether: the workers, winter, and I" ("My nachali vmeste: rabochie, ia i zima"; 123) in the comparison of herself with the workers and with winter. The movements of the workers through coordination or through anonymity of their majority are likened to a *corps de ballet*: "Of them I know Matvei and Kuz'ma / and Pavel Junior, surrounded by a *corps de ballet*" ("Iz nikh mne znakomy Matvei i Kuz'ma / i Pavel-men'shoi, okruzhennye kordebale-tom"). Implicit are acquired similarity with precision, assurance, grace, and experience. The metaphor, the locus, and the home environment at Peredelkino bring the speaker closer to the poet and person Bella Akhmadu-lina by evoking Boris Messerer's father Asaf Mikhailovich Messerer, a former dancer and longtime balletmaster at the Bolshoi Theater, as well as Boris's first cousin Maya Plisetskaia, the former prima ballerina of the Bolshoi Theater.

The collection has gone through a complete growing cycle, with the opening poem focusing on spring and the appearance of the first flowers, "pervotsvet," followed by the flowers after it until the blossoming of the apple tree when the flowers and poetic words commingle through the prox-imity of the window where the speaker sits gazing out and at the end of growing with the arrival of winter in the final poem. Indeed, throughout the collection she can frequently be found by the window or windows observing nature and the universe in her quest for poetic inspiration and material. The window locale evolves into *zaokonnost'* in the poem "Ladyzhino" (*Poems*, 1988, 289). In the concluding poem, she sits not by a window but beneath one, without specifying whether she is inside or outside, but the change of locus to her home in Peredelkino brings in the reality of everyday life: the

---

musician Genrikh Neigaus's friendships with Akhmatova and with Pasternak. See V. Ia. Vilenkin, *V sto pervom zerkale: Anna Akhmatova* (Moscow: Sovetskii pisatel', 1987), 66–67, and Boris Kats and Roman Timenchik, *Anna Akhmatova i muzyka. Issledovatel'skie ocherki* (Leningrad: Sov. kompozitor, 1989), 149, and *Muzykal'naia zhizn'*, no. 13 (1987):15.

workers and the structures to be built. It also recalls the worn-out balcony of an early poem in the collection, as if to say that something is being done about the matter, now that she is definitely ensconced in the present. The words employed to paint the arrival of winter evoke the opening line to Evtushenko's poem "The window looks out onto the white trees" ("Okno vykhodit v belye derev'ia"): "The window I sit under for my undertaking, / looks out onto their noise" ("Okno, pod kakim ia sizhu dlia zatei moei, / vykhodit v ikh shum"). In both instances, but more so in Akhmadulina, the window faces something not usually referred to in this grammatical construction. Her window overlooks the noise of the workers deploring the force of the mortar, i.e. metonymy for argument. As if anything can prevent the impending autumnal "fading of groves and fields" ("uviadanie roshch i polei"), the speaker states there was no hindrance to the withering of grove and field. It brings to mind the earlier concept of the beauty of fields and woods as the principal source for poetry. Her creative activity is obviously winding down in this collection. Yet use of the word "zateia" (humorous for "work" or "venture") for the occupation that eludes her, just as the lack of materials delays the workers, poses ironic contrast to the dancer image above. The reference as "zateia" belittles her work in contrast to the construction carried out by the workers. Another comparison of poetic creation comes to mind here, that of Maiakovskii and the sun shining, or writing as the act of mining for precious ore.[24] Furthermore, the speaker's emphasis and communion with nature advances from nature mostly in the form of growing plants to the far reaches of nature in the universe, a path probably inaugurated by the artistic gravitation toward the moon. From this exalted distance, which facilitates communion with the supreme being, the speaker has no compunctions in returning to mundane life and pursuits. In fact, the touching comaraderie with the workers seems to keep the speaker sufficiently level-headed to prepare for the next stage in her art.

September accedes to a warm October, which thwarts winter's venture ("zateia") and further depreciates her use of the word as "work," paraphrased with famous words by the bard of autumn, Pushkin: "October has arrived" ("Oktiabr' nastupil"—Pushkin has "already"—"uzh"—in second place). Naturally, as his presence grows pervasive at this time, it reveals the

---

24. The poems in question are "Neobychainoe prikliuchenie, byvshee s Vladimirom Maiakovskim letom na dache" and "Razgovor s fininspektorom o poezii" ("Poeziia—ta zhe dobycha radiia / V gramm dobycha, v god trudy"), in V. V. Maiakovskii, *Sochineniia v dvukh tomakh* (Moscow: Pravda, 1987), 1:120–23; 1:60.

concluding bent of the collection: "There is more of Pushkin all around, /
to be exact, only he remains in my mind and in nature" ("Stalo Pushkina
bol'she vokrug, / vernei, tol'ko on i ostalsia v ume i prirode"). A circumspect
means of bidding farewell for the time being to Tarusa and to Tsvetaeva who
entered the collection early on with the theme of blooming and of Tarusa,
and whose abiding source is also Pushkin.[25]

While warmth in October enables workers to build, it causes commotion
among plants that are personified as though they were animals by dint of *kto*
("who" refers to animals in Russian): "in the garden there is a crush, some
have bloomed, some have been resurrected, some are born" ("v sadu
tolcheia: kto rastsvel, kto voskres, kto rodilsia"). Only dusk setting in early
indicates the true season with shorter days.

Restlessness overcomes the persona on October 19, the special day for
Pushkin immortalized in his verse, the day in 1811 that the Lyceum of
Tsarskoe Selo opened its doors for the first time to furnish an intellectual
and emotional family to the budding poet. The speaker seems to crave a
reply of Pushkin's time: "And where are my friends, where are the rap-
tures?" ("A gde zhe druz'ia, gde vostorgi?"). If these circumstances were to
be duplicated, perhaps the persona's own talents could approach those of
Pushkin: "And my age is more cruel, and my gift is completely negligible"
("I vek moi zhestoche, i dar moi sovsem nikakoi"). Compare with Pushkin's
poem "The Monument" ("Pamiatnik"—"in my cruel age I glorified freedom," "v moi zhestokii vek vosslavil ia svobodu"; 3:373) and with his poem
"Unnecessary gift, chance gift" ("Dar naprasnyi, dar sluchainyi"; 3:62). A
tear appears for an unspecified reason (probably for Pushkin's early demise
and less likely for the impossibility to soar to his poetic heights), which, as
she confides to Pushkin, is to be dedicated to Kiukhlia, that is to his friend,
the poet and critic Vil'gel'm Kiukhel'beker (1797–1846).

Winter, however, gains ascendency once more, and albeit it began with
the speaker and the workers, it has concluded its labors. Additionally, having
erected their structure (a tacit analogy is achieved of winter's structure of
snow and ice and that of the workers), the workers come to take leave of the

25. In March 1988, Bella Akhmadulina informed me that she has not returned to the modest
Dom arkhitektora in Tarusa since the death of the two sisters who served as custodians. "And I do
not plan to go back," she insisted. The locus is orphaned without the kind and competent women.
In the meanwhile, due to her poems, the House of the Architect has been "discovered" by numerous other non-architects. In 1988 Akhmadulina worked at *Dom kompozitora* in Repino where her
closest friends were seventeen visiting cats and a goat who, preferring to sit on Akhmadulina's
porch, refused to return to its owners to be milked.

speaker. Similarly, she is taking leave of the reader. Unlike the vacationers at Gagra who, she felt, never read her works and were oblivious to her, these three with simple, ordinary names—Pavel, Matvei, and Kuz'ma—stress their firsthand acquaintance with her as a person, and not through her books. They wish she would, just for the fun of it, write a poem about them. Surprisingly, she likes them for not being readers, either critical or gushing, of her books. She ostensibly relishes a friendship just for herself. Interestingly, the collection *The Garden* also concludes with a poem on the theme of the worker and the poet "All the darkness is absent and in disfavor" ("Vsia t'ma—v otsutstvii, v opale").

November arrives in a Pushkinian manner, like an epilog, as it were. Where Akhmadulina has "November is outside [in the yard]" ("Noiabr' na dvore"), Pushkin is known for "November stood by the yard" ("Stoial noiabr' uzh u dvora"). In November the speaker questions herself about her endeavor and its mysterious connection with the window that overlooked the construction. Without replying to this question, in the final lines she admires the moon on this night, attributing it to Pushkin: "How successful Pushkin has been with today's moon! / Wonderfully turbid and huge, obviously, before a frost!" ("Kak Pushkinu nynche luna udalas'! / Na slavu mutna i ogromna, k morozu, dolzhno byt'!").

The persona's leave-taking of the reader and of her topic is precipitous, as if unwanted but necessary. She returns to the moon and to her inspiration, created by Pushkin. Her perception of this heavenly body, after all, is colored by his verse and perception. One senses that no Russian poet can ever view the moon objectively, without Pushkin's vision accenting the later poet's vision. With the Tsvetaeva and Tarusa themes already phased out in this poem, the persona is ready with the advent of winter and the presence of the moon to commence further poetic creation of a different order. Having begun with early spring and the first bloom of "pervotsvet": "This spring I" ("Ia etoiu vesnoi"), she stops before winter—formerly her private time for crafting some of her best verse—settles in totally. Moreover, even after *The Secret* the poetic speaker continues through her verse to seek and to define her place in society, nature, and the universe. In the poem "I am merely the foothills to my mountain and a quantity of being" ("Ia—lish' gory moei podnozh'e i bytiia velichina"; *The Garden*, 117), she perceives herself as a directing particle of nature, a veritable dried flower in the writer Henrik Ibsen's book to point out a page to the reader. The pinnacle arrives in the poem "I am merely a volume inhabited by something" ("Ia lish' ob"em, gde obitaet chto-to"), in which the speaker is merely a vessel for the habitation of something great, the stranger-meaning ("smysl-neznakomets"), which she does not know.[26] It echoes in loftier form her earlier concept of being an instrument for the creation of verse. Above all, the window to nature, life, and the universe becomes transwindow, or transfenesterism ("zaokonnost' ") here, and in freeing herself from the confines of this great force, the speaker will merge with the universe through the poetic word:

> I disperse. I become the universe,
> we are in collusion, we are one.

> Я растекаюсь, становлюсь вселенной,
> мы с нею заодно, мы с ней—одно.

When the "word"—art, poetry, philosophy, and religion—arrives, it renders all people brothers and sisters and enables men and women to become part of the greatness and infinity in the universe:

> Only the word vanquishes delirium and chaos
> and speaks to mortals of immortality.

> Лишь слово попирает бред и хаос
> и смертным о бессмертье говорит.

If this speaker has furnished crucial aspects of the poetic word, she is worthy of being remembered and of becoming part of the universe. And she can be content with a mission well performed.

In conclusion, it can be asserted that in *The Secret* the use of several names for the first flower "pervotsvet" and its relation to the poetic word in the poem "I have the secret of wondrous blooming" is an indication of a device to be utilized throughout the collection, namely, of the several objects that in their respective sequence of poems will alternately serve as surrogate muses for the verse-creating process and as surrogate ephemeral loves: the moon, day, space, and the bird cherry. On the other hand, the poem "I have the secret of wondrous blooming" anticipates through the meaning of blooming in the root of the key word "pervotsvet" the appearance of Tsvetaeva, who will then be followed by other poets until Pushkin's presence and verse reign supreme. From the early verse to the present the speaker serves as an eager instrument for successively changing higher forces in the ongoing creation of verse.

26. Bella Akhmadulina, *Izbrannoe. Stikhi* (Moscow: Sovetskii pisatel', 1988), 317.

Conclusion

Прости, за то прости, читатель,
что я не смыслов поставщик,
а вымыслов приобретатель
черемухов и моих.
—Bella Akhmadulina

The poetry of Bella Akhmadulina, observed as one body of artistic output with a particularly felicitous sequence of placement within her cohesive collection of verse *The Secret* and ripples carrying over to its sequel collection *The Garden*, presents an elaborate and varied canvas. While each poem can be appreciated on its individual merit, its richness of meaning, language, and form reaches full potential and best captures the sensibilities of the audience only within the broad framework of the whole, and specifically within the author's thoughtful groupings, in which each poem enlarges on its predecessor, or predecessors, and prefigures the next piece as well as others to come. The secret is unveiled gradually in several stages that highlight its various aspects. As Helen Vendler writes of Keats, here too, we see Akhmadulina "growing in power" until she "learns to orchestrate the relations of theme, symbol, trope, syntax, and register of diction in ever more powerful ways."[1]

In *The Secret*, as was seen, Akhmadulina takes her engagingly executed early theme of poetic creation and poetic craft as the crux of her artistic scrutiny to the point of utter concentration, augmented by dazzling verbal virtuosity and brilliant imagery. Having attained this pure crystallization, as it were, she then fleshes out her work with fresh vistas on nature and the cultural wealth of Russia and the world. The poet's metapoetic art originates in and of nature which in *The Secret* undergoes a complete growing

---

1. Helen Vendler, *The Odes of John Keats* (Cambridge: Harvard University Press, Belknap Press, 1983), 292.

cycle from the first to the last poem and continues into the first part of *The Garden*. To this end, Akhmadulina employs the link between the meaning of beautiful contained in her first name in her ancestral language of Italian and that of blooming in nature and the significance of bloom in Marina Tsvetaeva's surname and in her imprinted presence in her beloved summer residence of Tarusa. The image of Tsvetaeva as the artistic distillation and embodiment of nature serves as a touchstone for enlarging on the poetry in her own original and inimitable way. As the theme of Tsvetaeva reaches its apogee midway in *The Secret*, the theme of Pushkin from the early poetry and prose percolates here to the point of the two themes' coexistence until it prevails alone in the concluding poem.

Without the classic Muse for inspiration in her verse-creating process, Akhmadulina's persona finds surrogates in her esteemed writers, especially Pushkin and Tsvetaeva on the one hand, and aspects of nature in a broad sense—the moon, day, space, the blooming bird cherry, and the "guiding sound"—on the other. Her speaker gives herself what Helen Vendler calls for Keats in his odes "the dramatic role not of creator but of audience" to her surrogate muses. Only after fulfilling this designated role can she compose verse for her own reading audience. Her search and aspirations in this endeavor constitute the majority of poems in *The Secret*. What is more, where Keats substitutes the poetic imagination for religion as a means of arriving at the truth, Akhmadulina moves from poetic imagination immersed in nature to arrive at a sensibility akin to religion and the worship of a supreme being as observed in nature. Indeed, the surrogates for the Muse from nature lead the creating persona to a higher, spiritual being, a "uniqueness," for which she becomes a sort of instrument in the power of art. In fact, as seen from the epigraph above, the speaker continues to separate the product of her surrogate muses (here, the bird cherry) from her own. Through the generative powers of art the sensation of oneness with nature expands after *The Secret* into a merging with the universe where the spiritual tones give way to overtly religious notes.

For all the apparent solemnity of the metapoetic theme so ardently espoused by Akhmadulina, from the outset her oeuvre has been marked by humor and a predilection for the risible of which salient examples were her long poems *Chills, A Tale of Rain,* and *My Genealogy*. In *The Secret* the irony and good-natured humor find augmentation in the form of the persona's squabblings with nature to preserve Tsvetaeva's presence in Tarusa; they also give way to her hallucinations under the influence of the pungent flowering bird cherry and of the honey made from the blossoms which eventuate as riding gardens and flying attics and excursions into the past and the future. That games are to be played out with the reader in the collection is duly noted in *The Secret*'s fourth poem, "A deep gentle garden sloping to the Oka," in which the speaker postulates the "rules of the game." Yet all the while it was Pushkin's example that generated these permutations on humor and it was his eternal presence that incited the fun and games. Indeed, it was his presence that was playing the games on the speaker as an example that the creation of art is not only a solemn act but also one of fun and mischief, bringing to mind Pushkin's attitude toward his Muse and the considerable games he played, light-hearted for his reading audience and satiric on his detractors, of which his *Tales of Belkin* (*Povesti Belkina*) are but one example. Where some critics blamed Akhmadulina for "no sense" in her poetry and her overt reply in the verse was noted, her tacit reply was not. For she has playfully construed their criticism as "nonsense" and has brought it to the level of "fun and games" as yet another aspect of the key to her poetics in the promised secret that unfolds before the reader in addition to the presence of nature and her revered writers. Even the "return" of objects and themes in a new light mimics in *The Secret* in a lighter vein the inherent cyclicity of nature that is such a pivotal notion in the collection that her device is bared in the poem "The Morning after the Moon." What is more, Akhmadulina has had fun with and by means of layers and nuances of language and sound, with literal and figurative meaning in presenting the poems. And the spellbound reader follows the speaker's disclosures, while an ingenious part of his mind makes independent discoveries not made obvious by the poet. Thus the fun and games involve the reader's active thought processes. Most readers of this study will no doubt finish reading and wonder if part of the undisclosed secret is not the fact that through these two seminal collections of poetry Bella Akhmadulina has joined the esteemed ranks of her adored poets.

Spectacular in thought and execution, riveting in sound and meaning, intricately intertwining her entire oeuvre with Russian and world literature and culture, the poetry of Bella Akhmadulina stands as a pinnacle of the postmodernist period in Russian literature, and still more is to come. Without being prescriptive, one can expect that this extraordinary poet, who is at the peak of her creative ability, will chart new directions with possibly less emphasis on metapoetry than in *The Secret* and more emphasis on philosophic, spiritual, and existential topics with an admixture of bubbling humor for good measure.

Belmont, Mass.
March 1992

Index of Names

Index of Works Cited in English

Index of Works Cited
(Russian Titles)